D1593041

The
Garland Library
of
War and Peace

The
Garland Library
of
War and Peace

Under the General Editorship of
Blanche Wiesen Cook, *John Jay College, C.U.N.Y.*
Sandi E. Cooper, *Richmond College, C.U.N.Y.*
Charles Chatfield, *Wittenberg University*

The Political Theories of Modern Pacifism

an Analysis and Criticism

by

Mulford Q. Sibley

and

Introduction to Non-violence

by

Theodore Paullin

and

Pacifist Living— Today and Tomorrow

by

**The Peace Section,
American Friends Service Committee**

with a new introduction
for the Garland Edition by

Mulford Q. Sibley

Garland Publishing, Inc., New York & London
1972

The new introduction for this
Garland Library Edition is Copyright © 1972, by
Garland Publishing Inc.
24 West 45 St., New York, N.Y. 10036

———

All Rights Reserved

———

Library of Congress Cataloging in Publication Data

Sibley, Mulford Quickert.
    The political theories of modern pacifism.

    (The Garland library of war and peace)
    Reprints of Pacifism and government, ser. 5, no. 1,
July 1944, Non-violent action in tension areas, ser. 3,
no. 1, July 1944, and of the 1941 ed. of Pacifist
living--today and tomorrow.
    Includes bibliographical references.
    1. Pacifism. 2. Nonviolence. I. Paullin,
Theodore. Introduction to non-violence. 1972.
II. Pacifist living--today and tomorrow. 1972.
III. Title. IV. Title: Introduction to non-violence.
V. Series.

JX1953.S54   327'.172   70-147612
ISBN 0-8240-0371-3

Printed in the United States of America

Editor's Preface

This volume is representative of absolute pacifists who not only wanted peace but would not sanction any given war effort – who wrestled with the political implications of their position in the context of World War II. It reflects the experience of that generation of pacifists which was active in the interwar years; but it represents, too, an attempt to treat nonviolent forms of social action in the spectrum of political options, and it thus forms a transition to modern systematic analysis.[1]

The refusal to participate in war, the tradition of nonresistance, has its sources in the life of the early Christian Church, in oriental religions, and in the continuous witness of members of the traditional peace churches – the Mennonites, Quakers, and Brethren. They took their position in obedience to their understanding of religious truth, and they interpreted it as a calling upon the individual. In the nineteenth century a few peace advocates outside the peace churches adopted this position, and some even interpreted it as a measure with which to oppose war

[1] *See especially A. Paul Hare and Herbert H. Blumberg, eds.,* Nonviolent Direct Action – American Cases: Social-Psychological Analyses *(Washington, D.C.: Corpus Publications, 1968), noting particularly "Types of Principled Nonviolence" by Gene Sharp, pp. 273-313.*

itself. For the most part, however, their position was essentially religious and individualistic. Absolute pacifism was fused with the progressive impulse for social reform under the pressure of World War I.

For two decades thereafter liberal pacifists found themselves involved in political questions and social ethics. They participated in what Donald B. Meyer aptly described as the Protestant search for political realism.[2] *By the time European nations became committed to a second mass war numerous churchmen had concluded that nonviolent alternatives to conflict were not always available and, following the lead of Reinhold Niebuhr, they sought to distinguish situations warranting the use of military force from those where violence would be counter-productive.*

Among those pacifists who remained consistent to their total renunciation of warfare some argued from essentially religious grounds; but even they acknowledged their responsibility to deal with the political consequences of nonviolence.[3] Pacifist Living, *a pamphlet produced by a study committee of the Peace Section of the American Friends Service Committee, was designed to help pacifists relate their lives to wartime circumstances. It illustrates the governing assumption of liberal pacifists after more*

[2]*Donald B. Meyer,* The Protestant Search for Political Realism, 1914-1941 *(Berkeley: University of California Press, 1960).*

[3]*See Lawrence S. Wittner,* Rebels Against War: The American Peace Movement, 1941-1960 *(New York: Columbia University Press, 1969), chapters 1-5.*

than two decades of political involvement that the individual who resists military conscription even on religious grounds still has an inescapable political responsibility. This is all the more striking because to a large extent American provisions for conscientious objection to war were firmly predicated on the opposite assumption that obedience to religious tenets could be separated from political judgments. Whether or not the pacifist position is valid, therefore, this little pamphlet is worth reconsidering in order to appraise that position fairly and historically.

World War II threatened more than individual lives; it threatened the pacifist position itself, and a few individuals tried to establish valid social and political principles upon which it could be based. A principal instrument of this effort was the Pacifist Research Bureau which produced a series of concise studies of national and international problems and of non-violence itself.[4] In most of them pacifists applied their principles in an analysis of public issues, hoping to work out the basis for postwar reforms. In the studies reprinted in this volume, The Political

[4] The subjects of the Pacifist Research Bureau's studies included in addition to those here reprinted: The Balance of Power; Coercion of States: In Federal Unions; Coercion of States in International Organizations; Comparative Peace Plans; Pacifist Diplomacy in Conflict Situations; The New Economics and World Peace; The Constitutionality of Peacetime Conscription; Principles and Practice from Delaware to Dumbarton Oaks; The Genesis of Pearl Harbor; Conscientious Objectors in Prison; The United Nations and International Law; Coercion in Penal Treatment, Past and Present; and The Road to Peace.

PREFACE

Theories of Modern Pacifism *and* Introduction to
Nonviolence, *the authors sought to systematize and
clarify the pacifist principles themselves.*[5] *By this
time there was the beginning of a literature
interpreting pacifist ethics in political terms: Clarence
Marsh Case,* Non-Violent Coercion: a Study in
Methods of Social Pressure* *(1923); Richard B.
Gregg,* The Psychology and Strategy of Gandhi's
Nonviolent Resistance* *(1929) and* The Power of
Nonviolence *(1934); Aldous Huxley,* Ends and
Means* *(1937); Krishnalal Shridharani,* War Without
Violence: the Sociology of Gandhi's Satyagraha*

[5] *Born in Missouri in 1912, Mulford Q. Sibley graduated from Central
State College, Oklahoma, in 1933, earned his M.A. at the
University of Oklahoma the following year, and his Ph.D. at the
University of Minnesota in 1938. For the next decade he taught at
the University of Illinois, but he returned to the University of
Minnesota where since 1957 he has been a professor of political
science and a distinguished teacher. His writings include the
prize-winning history of conscientious objection in World War II,*
Conscription of Conscience, *which he wrote with Philip E. Jacob
(1952),* Introduction to Social Science *(1953, 1957, 1961),* The
Quiet Battle *(1963), and numerous articles in addition to the study
reprinted in this volume,* The Political Theories of Modern Pacifism
(1944).

*Theodore Paullin was born in Colorado in 1910. He graduated from
the University of Wisconsin in 1931, where he earned his M.A. the
following year and his Ph.D. in 1935. Subsequently, he taught history
at Park College, the University of Kansas, Swarthmore College, and
since 1947 at Central Connecticut State College. He interrupted his
teaching career to be the assistant director of the Pacifist Research
Bureau from 1942 to 1945, and for it he wrote:* Comparative Peace
Plans *(1943),* Coercion of States: In Federal Unions *(1943), and*
Introduction to Nonviolence *(1944).*

*Both Sibley's and Paullin's studies are cited as important early
analyses by contemporary students of nonviolent action theory such as
A. Paul Hare and Gene Sharp.*

PREFACE

(1939); and Mohandas K. Gandhi, Nonviolence in Peace and War* *(1942).*[6] *Case's work was important as the earliest study by a trained political scientist interested in the social dynamics of conflict resolution. Gregg popularized the notion of non-violent action and related it to western ideas about psychology, military training, and social organization. Huxley developed the relationship of ends and means which was implicit in much of Gandhi's thought.*

In the midst of World War II pacifists both gained respite from their intense political activity and came under social pressure from the fact that military violence was widely held to be legitimate. It was time to reevaluate not only peace programs but also pacifist principles. The Pacifist Research Bureau became the vehicle for this task, and thus it was the antecedent of modern programs of peace research and current studies of conflict resolution.

Charles Chatfield
Wittenberg University

[6] *The titles marked with asterisks in the text are reprinted with new introductions in the* Garland Library of War and Peace.

Introduction

The Political Theories of Modern Pacifism: An Analysis and Criticism *was originally published more than twenty-five years ago, during World War II. Since then much political history has been made, including the last years of that war, the outbreak and continuation of the Cold War, the Korean War (or "police action"), McCarthyism, escalation of violence in the Middle East, and war in Indochina.*

But while the details of political relations shift from year to year, many of the patterns remain essentially the same. When this essay was written, important and basic questions included: the relation of ends and means in politics; the legitimacy of violence as strategy and tactics; the efficacy of violence for good ends; and the technical and ethical problems created by the existence of weapons of mass destruction. These questions remain central in the politics of 1971. Indeed, they are, if anything, more vital than before; for weapons have become still more awesome in their power to annihilate and the difficulty of defending violence as a political method is far greater.

Meanwhile, since the forties, experiments in non-violent resistance have proliferated, partly as expressions of deeply-held principles and partly because

11

they were the only methods available in some situations. During World War II the Danes and Norwegians were amazingly successful in resisting Nazi rule through non-violent means. Thus, virtually all the Jews of Denmark were rescued in the face of Nazi decrees and an occupying army which threatened their very existence.[1] After World War II, too, there were significant ventures in non-violent resistance in Hungary against Russian occupation forces, in Poland during and after 1953, and in the United States during the great civil rights movement of the sixties.[2] We might mention also the non-violent resistance and civil disobedience carried on against the waging of the war in Vietnam.

[1] *See Bjarne Hoye and Trygve M. Ager,* The Fight of the Norwegian Church Against Nazism *(New York: Macmillan, 1943); A.K. Jameson,* New Way in Norway *(London: Peace News, 1948); and Børge Outze,* Denmark During the German Occupation *(Copenhagen: Scandinavian Publishing Co., 1946). See also Hannah Arendt,* On Revolution *(New York: Viking, 1963).*

[2] *On the theory and practice of non-violent resistance in general, with specific case histories, see Mulford Q. Sibley,* The Quiet Battle *(New York: Doubleday Anchor, 1963; Boston: Beacon Press, 1969). The theory and practice of Gandhi's strategies are developed in Joan V. Bondurant,* Conquest of Violence *(Princeton: Princeton University Press, 1958). On non-violent resistance in Hungary, before the Hungarians turned to violence, see Paul Willen, "Communist Hungary: The Locusts and the Briefcases,"* The Reporter, *Oct. 21, 1954. On non-violent strategies in the American Civil Rights struggle, see Martin Luther King,* Stride Toward Freedom: The Montgomery Story *(New York: Harper, 1958) and* Why We Can't Wait *(New York: Signet, 1964). See also, for example, Mulford Q. Sibley, "Direct Action and the Struggle for Integration,"* Hastings Law Journal, *February, 1965, pp. 351-400. Staughton Lynd,* Nonviolence in America *(New York: Liberal Arts Press, 1965) provides a documentary history.*

INTRODUCTION

The Political Theories of Modern Pacifism *should be read in the light of the political events and experiments in non-violence which have occurred since it was written, and against the background of the monumental failures of violence in the same period.*

The failures of violence include World War II itself. Although the war led to the collapse of Nazi Germany, it also contributed greatly to the expansion of the "closed" society of the Soviet Union and to the enormous enhancement of military power in the United States. The Cold War of the late forties and the fifties was rooted in the uneasy alliance and continuing competition of the United States and the Soviet Union during World War II. That conflict is still with us − in a divided Germany, in the problem of Berlin, in the stresses and strains of an increasingly militarized United States, and in the deprivations and death suffered by all participants in the war.

When World War II began there was much talk of "pin-point" bombing and of methods which would discriminate between combatants and non-combatants. By the end of the war − such is the inherent "logic" of military violence − both sides had forgotten their promises: indiscriminate destruction was the rule, as shown in the wiping out of Dresden, Hiroshima, and Nagasaki. Both sides killed prisoners of war; both obliterated whole populations; both ultimately were more concerned about winning than about justice or a new social order.

And yet men did not seem to learn the lesson, for

the notion that a "balance of terror" would deter war and defend human lives in the course of a war was a central theme in international relations after 1947. There had not been a nuclear war by 1971, to be sure; but it would be unfair to ascribe that grace to the balance of terror — instead, the so-called peace of the past generation is more plausibly explained as a bit of good fortune. And it really was not peace in any even half-genuine sense. The Korean War, the Vietnamese War, civil war in Indonesia, Israeli-Arab wars, American and Soviet imperialism, and the governance of most human beings by essentially tyrannical regimes showed how far from peace mankind remained. Violent regimes often were challenged by violent rebels, and when the rebels won power they usually emulated the regimes which they had overthrown in the name of "democracy" or "communism."

Even generals recognize that war as a method of defense is utterly counter-productive in today's world. Consider, for instance, the words of the late General Douglas MacArthur: "The Second World War even with its now antiquated armaments clearly demonstrated that the victor had to bear in large part the very injuries inflicted on his foe. . . . War has become a Frankenstein to destroy both sides. . . . If you lose, you are annihilated. If you win, you stand only to lose. No longer does it possess the chance of

14

INTRODUCTION

the winner of a duel — it contains rather the germs of double suicide."[3]

Still, we continue to support the mythology that war and preparation for war will somehow preserve human life. Vast billions are appropriated for the military machine every year (currently some $200,000,000,000 a year for the whole world) on the assumption that an organized military force can give assurance of protection from "invasion" and from devastating blows by an "enemy." But no proof is adduced for these assertions — for there is no proof. The assertions are beliefs or myths which we keep repeating despite their dubious foundations. Poland was heavily armed in 1939 and had a system of conscription for defense; yet it was invaded by both Russia and Germany. France was thoroughly armed in 1939; and yet it was physically conquered by Germany. Czechoslovakia had a huge army in 1968; and yet when invaded by the Soviet Union it either would not or could not defend itself from attack. As far as one can see, military forces in Vietnam on both sides have contributed primarily to the destruction *of human life rather than to its preservation. Despite all this, we continue to buy increasing numbers of missiles and to train for more and more killing on the ground, presumably, that the missiles and the training to kill will somehow protect human beings. What a*

---

[3] *"Seventy-Fifth Birthday Address,"* Los Angeles, Jan. 26, 1955, reprinted in The Congressional Record, *101: Appendix, 682-683, Feb. 7, 1955 (daily edition).*

15

hoax! Yet this hoax constitutes the foundation for the foreign policies of the so-called Great Powers.

One reason disarmament efforts have been so unsuccessful is that most human beings still believe — despite overwhelming evidence to the contrary — that military weapons can somehow defend them in war or deter others from making war. Thus, when Nation A makes a disarmament proposal, Nation B will usually find that the scheme gives an advantage in weapons to Nation A; and because of the belief system that weapons constitute "protection," Nation B will reject the proposal. When Nation B offers a disarmament plan, Nation A will usually be able to see in it a military "advantage" for Nation B; and since Nation A still holds to the myth that we protect through destruction or threatened destruction, B's offer will be spurned. All this has happened several times since World War II in negotiations between the Soviet Union and the United States. So long as the myth persists that surrender of weapons weakens a nation, while possession of weapons "strengthens" the other side, so long will multilateral disarmament probably be doomed. Only when men are thoroughly convinced of the pacifist contention that armaments do not strengthen anything worth-while (protection of human life, for example) will a government cease to care whether the opposing side has a few more missiles than it possesses. Only when this attitude prevails will multilateral disarmament be possible on a large scale.

INTRODUCTION

This transformation in attitude would naturally involve a commitment to adopt unilateral *disarmament — a willingness to disarm whether any other nation does so or not. Once one becomes convinced that armaments neither defend human life in war nor deter from war — a pacifist position — then one will not care if the so-called opponent possesses arms. Unilateral disarmament based on these premises would entail phased reduction and elimination of all military weapons over a period of, perhaps, five years. Other nations would be invited to inspect the process, for the whole program would exclude that large degree of secrecy which is the hall-mark of contemporary international relations.*

But unilateral disarmament would not take place in a vacuum. It would be accompanied by a whole series of measures designed to substitute justice for force and to reduce the possibility that men might be so frustrated that they would turn to violence. For example, the newly-found pacifist policy would share a substantial part of the savings on arms with the rest of the world; provide for full adherence to the International Court of Justice; expand international co-operation in health, welfare, and other areas of human concern; renounce all special and exploitative economic privileges; and greatly reconstruct domestic society, particularly the cities. If, despite these non-violent constructive measures, a military invasion

17

*from abroad should occur, organized non-violent
resistance would be employed.*[4] *If defense of human
life is the objective, policies of this kind would be far
more realistic and effective than reliance on military
violence. What is more, they probably would lead to
competitive* disarmament, *for every Great Power
groans under the burden of its arms and citizens of
each nation would exert enormous pressure to emu-
late that state which had unilaterally disarmed.*

*But, it might fairly be asked, what does the pacifist
mean by violence? This is a question which sometimes is not put by exponents of pacifism or, of it is
propounded, is not faced in all its dimensions.*

*We do not mean by violence all forms of coercion —
restraining a child as well as bombing a city — but
we do mean all harsh forms of coercion, those*

[4] *See Mulford Q. Sibley,* Unilateral Initiatives and Disarmament
*(Philadelphia: American Friends Service Committee, 1962) and
"Unilateral Disarmament," in Robert A. Goldwin,* America Armed
(Chicago: Rand McNally, 1963), pp. 112-140.
*In 1958, the former naval officer Stephen King-Hall advocated what
was essentially a scheme of non-violent defense, on the ground that in
the modern world defense by military violence was virtually impossible.
See Stephen King-Hall,* Defense in the Nuclear Age *(London: Gollancz,
1958). On non-violent resistance to invasion, see also the Working Party
of the American Friends Service Committee,* In Place of War: An
Enquiry Into Nonviolent National Defense *(New York: Grossman,
1967); Gene Sharp,* The Political Equivalent of War — Civilian Defense,
*International Conciliation pamphlet 555 (New York: Carnegie
Endowment for International Peace, 1965); and Adam Roberts,* Civilian
Resistance as A National Defense *(New York: Peligan, Penguin, 1969).*

INTRODUCTION

which by their very nature kill or seriously injure human beings in body or spirit. All war is violence, although violence will surely be reflected in many acts besides warfare.

Perhaps we can think of violence as tending toward one pole of a line which has persuasion as its other end. Whether or not a given act is violent will depend somewhat on its context and the intention behind it. Thus, the use of police force to prevent two potential killers from attacking one another could hardly be called violence; whereas the unrestrained attack would have been. The quick chastisement of a child by his mother is not violence, whereas the deliberate bombing of a city is. Detention of a drunken person overnight in preparation for curative treatment is not violence, as contrasted with the administration of the "third degree" by police.

It is sometimes difficult to determine where the line should be drawn in given instances. But some types of actions are always performed in contexts which give them a violent cast — war, organized physical revolt, police torture, capital punishment, assassinations. The pacifist will generally be at least suspicious of all physical force, particularly of its indiscriminate use, even though he admits that on occasion it may be used non-violently.

The pacifist affirms five fundamental positions, as he did twenty-five years ago: (1) violence always hinders the development of a peaceful democratic order; (2) the nature of most existing socio-political

19

orders is such that only fundamental change, or "revolution," can make them just; (3) revolution can take place only through non-violent means; (4) increasing the threshold at which violence occurs will require a decentralized world order; and (5) pacifism is directly relevant for politics.

Violence encourages irrationality and is itself often the product of thoughtlessness. It breeds more violence and makes it difficult to establish either a peaceful or a democratic order. Wars waged in the name of democracy are contradictions in terms, for the means of violence tends always to lead to the ends of tyranny, dictatorship, and arrogance in rulers. "We had to destroy this village in order to save it," said an officer in Vietnam; and his statement typifies the kinds of justifications offerred for violence.

However, the nature of many existing socio-political orders is such that only revolution, or fundamental change, can make them just. In the Soviet Union, of course, the secret police have little respect for human personality; and distortion, suppression, and the rewriting of news and history are essential elements of the system. In the United States social controls are often more subtle; but here, too, the system encourages only limited political choices, officially-sponsored mythology exalts the military and the patriotic resort to violence, and semi-sacred institutions such as the CIA and FBI are virtually beyond criticism, perhaps beyond control. Nor is the distribution of income calculated to promote free-

dom and equality here where the upper 10% of income recipients receive about 28% of the income and the lower 10% get only 1% of the wealth. In Brazil and Greece, to cite two other examples in the so-called free world, there is thoroughgoing tyranny.

It had become evident to many by the sixties that a very high percentage of all the political systems in the world required fundamental changes if they were to become measurably just.

But how can revolution take place? This question elicits the third political proposition of pacifism. Although we usually associate revolution with violence, our experience with modern violent revolutions should make us seriously doubt that the systematic killing of human beings can bring about fundamental changes. This applies to revolutions of the masses and elites alike. Employment of means which show disrespect for human life and personality will almost certainly tend to result in ends that denigrate human beings and humanitarian values.

Propositions of this kind can be illustrated in the history of violent revolutions. When French revolutionists turned to violence, they were forced to submit to that dictator and master of violence, Napoleon. When the Bolsheviki began to disregard the principles of non-violence on a large scale, they helped distort their revolutionary objectives and created agencies of repression fully as obnoxious as those which had existed under the Czars. It can be persuasively argued that had the "Loyalists" won in

*the Spanish Civil war, the character of the ensuing
regime would not have differed sharply from the
actual government of Franco, except in terms of the
specific persons shot, jailed, or exiled.*

*It is an illusion to believe that in our day violence
can assist us in achieving the goals of brotherhood,
democracy, equality, and freedom. This has been
fully recognized by such a modern apostle of revolution as Dom Helder Camara of Brazil, who has
characterized violence as ineffective in combatting
injustice and tyranny: "His personal observation in
Brazil of the enormous advantage enjoyed in a
technological age by those who control the weaponry
and techniques of violence," together with considerations of morality, led him to become a
pacifist.* [5]

*With Dom Helder Camara the contemporary
pacifist argues that the challenge of our day is to
discover methods for achieving fundamental social
change which do not frustrate the ends of liberty,
equality, and fraternity, as violence always tends to
do.*

*The ethic of non-violence—what Gandhi called
ahimsa—imposes basic limits on all actions for social
change. On one hand, it forbids acquiesance in
tyranny and injustice. On the other hand, it com-*

[5] Gary MacEoin, "Dom Helder: His Thought, His Personal Life, His
Pastoral Style," National Catholic Reporter, *November 20, 1970, Book
Review Supplement, p. 9-A. See also Jose De Broucker,* Dom Helder
Camara: The Violence of a Peacemaker *(New York: Orbis Books,
1970).*

INTRODUCTION

mands us to seek fundamental change only through non-violent means—persuasion, parliamentary action, political organization, non-cooperation in injustice, and, under certain circumstances, mass civil disobedience. Tyrannies exist because slaves exist. Eliminate slavishness, or willingness to obey the tyrant, and tyrannical power collapses. However slowly change appears to take place in our time, developments in the United States, eastern Europe, India, even the Soviet Union suggest that non-violent actions have begun to undercut tyranny since World War II, despite the punishment of individuals and the turbulence of societies which we have known.[6]

Pacifism is not merely a doctrine of negations, however. It seeks to discover the basis for a society in which violence is less likely to break out — whether it be the violence of the rulers (overtly or through severe exploitation) or the violence of ordinary citizens. There are many facets of this quest, of course: some involve problems of personality development, others entail an analysis of economic power, while yet others seek to plumb the circumstances under which irrationality is likely to develop in human affairs. Of all the issues demanding constructive thought by pacifists, one of the most important is the development of community.

When men lose a sense of community, they

[6]*For further discussion, see Mulford Q. Sibley,* The Quiet Battle, *particularly Reading 15, pp. 187-204, and "Concluding Reflections," pp. 359-377.*

INTRODUCTION

become alienated, as we say, from others as well as themselves. They tend to become apathetic, or, in certain circumstances, to express themselves through violence. How can we so structure social life that men and women feel themselves wanted and needed by others? How can men maintain their own individualities while yet fully recognizing themselves as part of a larger whole? There are, of course, no easy answers to these questions: they are perennial in the history of political ideas and particularly in modern political thought. Pacifism, in raising issues of this kind, is implicitly putting queries raised by such men as J.-J. Rousseau in the eighteenth century, William Morris in the nineteenth, and Paul Goodman in the twentieth.[7]

Modern industrialism tends to destroy old community life and the imperatives of complex technology, unchecked and uncontrolled by political deliberation, seem to entail greater and greater centralization of economic and political power. But centralization usually carries with it bureaucratization

[7]Although Rousseau is not always clear about details, it seems evident that a genuine general will — which becomes the basis for legitimacy in his conception of government — cannot truly arise except in a relatively small community which is virtually classless and without economic luxuries. Men can be themselves and yet belong to others only in such a community, argues Rousseau in The Social Contract. A confederation of these small societies would constitute the world order. In William Morris' News From Nowhere, the non-apathetic non-violent individual arises in the kind of society which repudiates many of the values characteristic of modern industrialism and the nation-State. In the works of Paul Goodman (Growing Up Absurd, for example), the supposed meaninglessness of modern life is related to loss of community and the absence of significant work challenges. Generally speaking, Goodman might be characterized as an "anarchist."

24

(of the State and the giant corporation) and impersonalism, which, when pushed to extremes, heighten alienation and weaken community. Specialization of labor, moreover, by multiplying occupations, encourages a diversity of professionalized outlooks and languages, which weaken the ties of everyday language that help hold men together. While the development of complex technology has the potentiality for creating material abundance, it may also, if uncontrolled by political deliberation relating it to social and other ends, tend to become an end in itself and to make men seem simply servants of the machine. Moreover, new class structures arise that reinforce feelings of helplessness and frustration. The material benefits of technology so hypnotize men that at first they fail to see the enormous social costs they are paying in the form of destructive exploitation of natural resources, ungovernable cities, steady but unplanned depopulation of the countryside, rapid disruption of family life, general alienation, and the tendency to subordinate needs of men to the demands of the machine.

How, under conditions of this kind, can we revive community, make men and not things the goals of organization, and keep technology a mere instrument rather than allowing it to become a master? If we could find answers to questions of this kind, the pacifist contends, we could at least contribute to raising the threshold at which violence is likely to break out. We could then deal with such phenomena as violent crime, civil wars, and international conflict at their roots.

Although pacifists are by no means united in their answers, there is a strong tendency to find solutions along lines of a world decentralized structure which will attempt to control the rate of technological change and even, under certain circumstances, limit the degree of industrialization. To be sure, we "can't go home again," in the sense that we cannot restore an imaginary ideal primitive community. We can, moreover, surely develop devices to plan technological growth in light of all human values — aesthetic, social, and religious, as well as economic — and place boundaries on industrialism. In light of the ecological problem, we can also discover methods for encouraging the decline of population and of demand for material things. For many of its exponents, pacifism implies a kind of world decentralized socialism.

When we say "world," we suggest of course the need for some kind of overall coordination at the world level. A few fundamental decisions — for example, those involving allocation of economic resources, establishment of food reserves for famine relief, administration of world water-ways — would be made by the world organization. In this respect pacifism runs counter to conventional notions of national sovereignty. And yet, it does not believe that a world organization for the military coercion of states can avoid large-scale war and violence. Instead, it sees organization as basically concerned with questions of economic and social justice, with peace as a kind of by-product.

A few basic decisions must be made at the center, for the world has become so interdependent economically that only deliberate decisions about primary questions can keep technologies and economic imperatives subordinate to the complex values of humanity as a whole. But most actual policy formulation and administration could be greatly decentralized in units smaller than the national state. Neighborhoods of 300 to 500 souls within moderately populated cities of perhaps no more than 250,000 could conceivably become the fundamental units of decision-making; and their physical basis could encourage local face-to-face endeavors. Decisions might increasingly be made by consensus rather than majority rule; the vital factor would be discussion between and among men and women who know one another not only intellectually but emotionally.

The full implications of such a structure cannot, of course, be developed here. It has much in common with certain versions of anarchist pacifism and it is in accord with Gandhi's teaching, at least in some measure. Underlying it would have to be a radical change in outlook or attitude; a heightened consciousness of man's relations to nature and to man; a serious doubt about whether technological progress necessarily means moral, social, and political progress;

27

and an awareness that the means of political ordering cannot be sharply divorced from its goals.

The world has yet to learn that the principles of pacifism are both morally desirable and prudentially sound. In moral terms, the pacifist believes that it is not legitimate to take human life even at the command of the State. Killing people is wrong, whether the order comes from myself, from a group of men calling themselves the "government," or from the leader of an alleged revolution. We must adjust our actions to this moral belief and not adjust our moral belief in non-violence to the supposed necessities of war and revolution. All our actions must be within these limits, whatever our long-run objectives may be. An ultimate moral principle is not to be trifled with. For the pacifist, violence to human personality, even in political struggle, is ruled out because it is ethically unrighteous — period.

At times, this principle may mean that the pacifist is confronted with the alternative of whether to commit acts of violence or to submit to them. When this choice does indeed arise — and it is not nearly as common as is generally thought, for non-violent resistance alternatives of an active kind usually exist — he says that one should submit to death rather than kill. It is better to be the victim than the executioner, if these are indeed the only alternatives. This is an ultimate judgment of right and wrong very much like Socrates' "It is better to suffer injustice than to commit it."

INTRODUCTION

But pacifism is also sound prudentially. It is "practical" because its principles are right; it is not right because it is "practical." Politically, this implies that we cannot gain such ends as liberty, equality, fraternity, and justice by means which do violence to human personality and by their very nature undermine desirable objectives. To say that one can help build "democracy" by bombing a city and destroying half its inhabitants is to assert what even to a child must seem ridiculous. To argue that we can construct a co-operative commonwealth by taking up arms and "conquering power" is to make the same child wonder at our obvious dichotomy between means and ends. The pacifist adheres to the Scriptural statement that one cannot gather figs from thistle trees. Sow violence and, whatever one's professed objectives may be, he reaps violence. If one's goals be inequality, exploitation, and alienation, in other words, then violence is an appropriate means.

The non-pacifist expects the impossible: that through war one will obtain peace and through violent revolution one may somehow attain a non-violent democratic society. The non-pacifist flies in the face of all political realism.

The perspective of the pacifist, of course, would make the American Civil War, if its goal was emancipation of the slave, a gigantic failure. World War II itself would be seen as a conflict which, while it eliminated a tyrant, helped spawn more tyranny. The quiet battles carried on by exponents of non-

INTRODUCTION

violence in colonial Pennsylvania, by non-violent resisters in Czarist and Soviet Russia, by blacks in South Africa and the United States, and by opponents of war in every land would be understood as vastly more significant for a co-operative, democratic order than any war or violent revolution. Such heroes of violence as Caesar, Napoleon, Eisenhower, Lenin, Mao, and Che Guevara would be supplanted by heroes of the spirit and non-violence like St. Francis, Gandhi, Bishop Grundtvig (great founder of the Danish folk school and co-operative movements), and Martin Luther King. Sharing the view of Robert Southey's The Battle of Blenheim, *all the alleged victories of violence, whether in war or revolution, would be seen as spurious:*

"And everybody praised the Duke,
 Who this great fight did win."
"But what good came of it at last?"
 Quoth little Peterkin.
"Why, that I cannot tell," said he,
"But 'twas a famous victory."

The challenge to human beings in the remaining years of the twentieth century is whether they will choose the politics of pacifism or the politics of death.

Mulford Q. Sibley
Department of Political Science
University of Minnesota

PACIFISM and
GOVERNMENT
Series V: Number 1
July 1944.

THE POLITICAL THEORIES OF MODERN PACIFISM

AN ANALYSIS AND CRITICISM

By
MULFORD SIBLEY

THE PACIFIST RESEARCH BUREAU
1201 CHESTNUT STREET
PHILADELPHIA 7, PENNSYLVANIA

Distributed by
THE FELLOWSHIP OF RECONCILIATION
2929 Broadway
New York 25, New York

FINANCIAL SUPPORT

The Pacifist Research Bureau is financed entirely by the contributions of organizations and individuals who are interested in seeing this type of research carried on. We trust that you may desire to have a part in this positive pacifist endeavor to aid in the formulation of plans for the world order of the future. Please make contributions payable to The Pacifist Research Bureau, 1201 Chestnut Street, Philadelphia 7, Pennsylvania. Contributions are deductible for income tax purposes.

DIRECTOR'S FOREWORD

It is hoped that this critical study of the political theories of pacifism may aid those who seek to formulate theories for politics and government keyed to the needs of our times. The non-pacifist may embrace as much of pacifist thought as he believes is relevant to present conditions. The study may also aid pacifists in reformulating those portions of pacifist theory most open to criticism, and thus aid them in contributing more fundamentally to political thought.

Dr. Mulford Sibley, of the Department of Political Science, at the University of Illinois, is the author of this booklet. As Dr. Sibley correctly points out, the word "pacifist" is used with varying shades of meaning. The word is used in the name, The Pacifist Research Bureau, to refer to the philosophy that man should exercise such respect for human personality that he will employ only love and sacrificial good will in overcoming evil and that the purpose of all human endeavor will be the creation of a world brotherhood in which cooperative effort contributes to the good of all.

This pamphlet is the first in a new series by the Bureau: *Pacifism and Government,* which will be distinguished by its orange cover. A list of pamphlets published or in preparation appears on the back cover.

HARROP A. FREEMAN,

Executive Director

June, 1944.

Any organization ordering 500 or more copies of any pamphlet published by the Pacifist Research Bureau may have its imprint appear on the title page along with that of the Bureau. The prepublication price for such orders is $75.00 for each 500 copies.

TABLE OF CONTENTS

AUTHOR'S PREFACE

Probably no term in the political vocabulary of modern times is more abused than "pacifism." To some it simply connotes, rather vaguely, an ideology which would like to see a world at peace. Others see it as a misguided attempt to cure the ills of the world by preaching. Yet another school maintains that pacifism attempts the impossible by challenging divine decrees through the mere assertion of human will. Some men make the term cover everything which might seem to be laudable or altruistic in human thought and action; while those of a contrary view make its applicability rigid, narrow, and to some degree without meaning for the world of "practical" men. The term has been used to describe beliefs which would advocate the necessity of withdrawal from the world; but it has also been held to designate methods of action in the world.

It is with this confusion in mind that *The Political Theories of Modern Pacifism* has been written. Its purpose is two-fold: first, to state as clearly as possible the distinctively modern currents of thought which might consistently and appropriately be designated "pacifist"; and second, to criticize the major arguments of this peculiarly modern pacifism insofar as they relate themselves to the world of politicis. In the pursuit of this dual purpose, numerous troublesome questions have naturally arisen. It was not easy to decide what elements could be considered characteristic of modern pacifism. Then there was considerable difficulty in choosing the theorists to be represented, since all possible discussion of the subject could not possibly be analyzed. Finally, a selection of the major critics of modern pacifism had to be made with a view to pointing up as acutely as possible the crucial questions which the pacifist thesis raises.

The author does not contend that these and other difficulties which might be mentioned have been adequately met. He realizes that misrepresentations and wrong emphases have probably occurred. But he also thinks that at this stage of pacifist intellectual effort many statements of what pacifism holds are bound to be wanting in clarity. For the plain fact is that an adequate philosophical discussion of all the implications of the pacifist argument remains yet to be written. This essay is only a brief exploratory introduction to the multifarious problems involved. As such, the author hopes it will be helpful; but he also trusts that it will be read critically and with an understanding of what it purports to do.

Several persons have read the original manuscript and to these the author wishes to extend his thanks for many helpful comments and criticisms. Professor Francis G. Wilson, Department of Political Science, University of Illinois; Mr. Harold Fey, of the *Christian Century;* Professor Douglas Steere, Department of Philosophy, Haverford College; Mr. A. J. Muste; Dr. Theodore Paullin; and the Director of the Pacifist Research Bureau, Professor Harrop Freeman—all have had a hand in the indispensable work of criticism and suggestion. But for any errors of interpretation the author is responsible.

MULFORD Q. SIBLEY
University of Illinois

THE POLITICAL THEORIES
OF MODERN PACIFISM
AN ANALYSIS AND CRITICISM

* * * *

I. INTRODUCTION

In every period of history, when the force and coercion latent in all politics assume the dramatic and overt form of international and civil war made chronic, philosophies of non-violence claim the attention of many men.[1] The twentieth century is preeminently one of those periods and the enquiring student of politics will discern three philosophies of non-violence which address themselves to the political issues of our times — Hindu pacifism, Christian pacifism, and the pacifism of the secular revolutionary movement. This study is concerned in its first part with an analysis of these three streams of modern pacifist thought, and in its second with their critical evaluation.

II. ANALYSES OF PACIFIST POLITICAL PHILOSOPHIES
A.
HINDU PACIFISM

At the heart of Hindu religious philosophy is the conception of a world in which individuals are separated from the whole, or from God. Desire and lust after things of the world constantly impede their ability to lose themselves in the Reality which this world tends to hide or make obscure. Possessing a dualistic vision of the universe, the Hindu view makes a sharp distinction between the material, which is essentially evil, and the spiritual, which is good.

Hence there runs through all its beliefs the idea that the flesh should be cast aside for the spirit, for in so doing one would be eliminating evil and embracing good. In releasing oneself from the bondage of the body, desire itself is cast out, thus breaking the fatal chain into which the soul is forced when once it becomes incarnate.

For incarnation is a punishment for past offenses or a necessary preparation for future advance. Souls are incarnated or re-incarnated in accordance with their Karma, or predestining deeds, of a previous

---

[1] In the China of the sixth century B. C. they take the form of Laotze's anarchist pacifism; in the disintegrating Roman Empire, apocalyptic Christianity and neo-Platonism; and in the ideology of Catholic Christianity, monasticism.

The substance of Part II, Sections A and B, of the present essay will be found in my article, "The Political Theories of Modern Religious Pacifism," *American Political Science Review*, (June, 1943), Vol. XXXVII, 439-454.

existence; and the guise of the incarnation will be directly dependent
upon the nature of those actions. An incarnation in beastly form is
presumably less to be coveted than is an embodiment in human flesh;
but whatever shape the body takes depends, not upon an act of will
on the part of the soul about to be condemned, but rather upon its
previous cumulative actions which inevitably and with finality point
to the kind of body which must necessarily be assumed. There is
thus an intimate cause and effect relationship between each act and
the form of incarnation, and an inter-connection, in the shape of soul-
substance, among all forms of life. Ethically, this becomes translated
in the form of a command which directs us to act in that way which
will cause the least possible rift or disturbance to this soul-substance
binding together the world of those spirits who are so unfortunate as
to suffer the pangs and hardships of incarnation.

It is at this point that the conception of violence enters the picture. Violence is the creation of a disturbance in the structure of that
soul-substance which is the common heritage of all life. It is any act
which tends to accentuate the separateness of one soul from another—
and from the God to which souls are seeking to return—separateness
which is to some degree inevitable within the realm of material incarnation but which has to be resisted.[2]

Out of these views of the universe the most eminent expounder
of Hindu pacifism, Mohandas K. Gandhi, has developed his political
theory. Its genesis will be found in his remarkable autobiography,[3]
but we are interested here not so much in how he came to hold what
he does, as in the elements of the theory itself. It may be said to involve
(1) a philosophy of history; (2) a theory of revolution; and (3) a
doctrine of the ideal State. To examine each in turn is to develop the
political philosophy of Hindu pacifism.

[2]There is a considerable body of Hindu and Buddhist religious literature in English.
The collection found in Robert O. Ballou (ed), *The Bible of the World* (New
York: Viking, 1939), is one of the most convenient. See also Paul Carus, *The
Gospel of Buddha* (Chicago: Open Court, 1905). Of the Hindu scriptures
themselves, the Upanishads as a whole are valuable. See also the *Garuda
Purana,* Sankaracharya's *Atma Bodha,* and the *Yoga Sutras* of Patanjali.

The doctrine of Karma is stated well in Ch. CXIII and CXVI of the
Garuda Purana.

[3]*The Story of My Experiments with Truth,* 2 vols., (Ahmedabad: Navajivan Press,
1927-1929).

To Gandhi, history is "an interruption of the course of nature."[4] Here Nature—the active manifestation of God in human history—is looked upon as operating or acting through what Gandhi, following many ancient Hindu texts, calls soul-force. God, through Nature, endeavors to attract man to the Truth, which, once seen, is always embraced; but God can act only through the principle of *ahimsa,* which Gandhi identifies with non-violence or love. Truth, and hence God, can engulf man only when the divine method is utilized for its discovery.[5] Historical politics negate Nature and God and are thus found worthy of note; while actions which couple *ahimsa* with *satya,* or truth, are buried beneath the *himsa*-ridden politics.

But what is *ahimsa* in terms of concrete action and how can it be recognized? Here Gandhi is not entirely clear. The problem is how to reconcile a theory of non-violence with what he asserts is an obvious fact: namely, that life, and hence politics here in the body, reposes on violence. While Nature presumably works as the agent of God through *ahimsa,* spirits bound to the body must be in part violent despite their recognition of the contrary principle.[6] Violence is the will to live; and the problem is how to thwart that will in order to approximate the divine tactic of action solely through the principle of *ahimsa.* Gandhi has finely stated this in these words:[7]

---

[4] C. F. Andrews. *Mahatma Gandhi at Work* (London: Allen and Unwin, 1931), 310, a selection from his *Hind Swaraj.*

The term "history" often has a different meaning in theological discussions than it has among historians. To the historian, "history" has no purpose, it is neither moral or immoral. It is merely man's record of all past events. Many Christian theologians accept the view of history held by MacMurray, MacGregor, Muste, Cadoux, and Niebuhr, which will be treated later in this study. In this view, history is the onward march of man's development, past, present or future, recorded or unrecorded. God is "in history" shaping it to conform to a Divine plan or nature of things. Man's acts are either in harmony or opposed to this "onward march" of "history." Gandhi and the Hindus have much the same concept of relationship between man's development and the moral order, or Truth, and hence somewhat the same philosophy of history, but they use the word "history" in a sense more nearly that of the historian. Thus they see that which is in accordance with Truth as natural and therefore not noteworthy; hence recorded "history" deals largely with man's conflicts rather than his "living-togetherness."

[8] *Ibid.,* 123: "*Ahimsa* and *satya* (truth) must always go together."

[6] "All life in the flesh exists by some violence. . . . The world is bound in a chain of destruction. In other words, violence is an inherent necessity for life in the body," Gandhi recognizes. C. F. Andrews, *Mahatma Gandhi's Ideas* (London: Allen and Unwin, 1930), 138.

[7] *Ibid.,* 138.

"None, while in the flesh, can thus be entirely free from violence, because one never completely renounces the 'will to live'. Of what use is it to force the flesh merely if the spirit refuses to cooperate? You may starve even unto death, but if at the same time the mind continues to hanker after objects of sense your fast is a sham and a delusion. What, then, is the poor, helpless slave to the 'will to live' to do? How is he to determine the exact nature and the extent of the violence *he* must commit?"

To this question the apostle of Hindu pacifism himself has given no complete answer. The closest approximation is the implication—at this time made almost explicit—that we ought, in personal and socio-political action alike, to abstain from the use of physical force against all animal life and reduce our material needs to a very bare minimum. This minimum must, of course, exclude the possibility of suicide which would itself constitute an act violative of the principle of *ahimsa*.

Thus man finds himself called to use the pure means of *ahimsa* as the sole avenue to truth and hence to an obliteration of his separateness; and yet he discovers himself imprisoned—bound by an iron law to an existence in which he cannot live without parasitism and coercion. It is as though Truth were mocking him—beckoning him with one hand to discover her by the only means possible—*ahimsa*—yet binding him with the other to what Gandhi calls a "chain of destruction."

It is at this point that the Gandhian theory of politics, as such, is developed. It centers largely around means or methods of injecting the maximum degree of *ahimsa* into the power struggles of men. Unlike Tolstoy and many others in the Christian pacifist tradition, Gandhi is not an anarchist. Political organization is essential for the coordination of community life, but the coercive element in that government must cease to be what Gandhi calls "body-force" and become "soul-force."[8]

This faith becomes embodied in the political conception of *satyagraha*—"firmness in Truth"—and in the organization and discipline of the *satyagrahis* who follow its leadership. The latter are carefully trained and disciplined warriors in the cause of Truth. Thoroughly impregnated with the doctrine of *ahmisa* until it becomes a part of the warp and woof of his life, the *satyagrahi* learns to oppose only soul-force to body-force. For body-force impedes the discovery of truth and hence that far-off event when separateness will be re-

Ibid., 193-94,

moved and oneness restored. On the other hand, the consistent use of soul-force will impart to the *satyagrahi* a sense of utter invincibility.[9] Soul-force commands abstention not only from overt violence but also from any verbally emitted untruth or distortions of fact—even in poltical struggle.[10]

The political ethics of soul-force, or truth-force (and Gandhi uses the terms interchangeably) root in a metaphysic similar to that upon which nineteenth-century Liberals based their doctrines of freedom of expression. Truth in an absolute sense is unknown to any individual or group in the community; and that community is best which, recognizing its general ignorance about the contents of Truth, encourages the widest possible discussion and mutual criticism as the sole avenues by which it is possible to approach the elusive goal. All practices and political traditions which impede this debate are, then, to be condemned.

The principle of *ahimsa* ensures the creation of a situation in which it will be possible more nearly to approach truth through debate and discussion. For by refusing to countenance the use of body-force, the intellect remains free of hatred and the corruption inevitably following upon the utilization of violence. The principle of *himsa,* on the contrary, whether it takes the form of war, verbal distortion, or revolutionary violence, can only tend to close the channels through which truth can be pursued.

But politics means struggle—and no one is more aware of this apparently immutable fact than the proponent of Hindu non-violence. Unlike nineteenth-century Liberal advocates of the idea of progress and the anarchists, he foresees no period in which politics will be eliminated, short of final reunion of man with the divine. In fact, politics are inseparable from the incarnation. Hence the problem is not so much one of politics versus no politics, as the philosophical anarchists would state it, but rather a politics which cut off all avenues to truth as over against a politics which allow them to remain relatively open. Human nature is capable of goodness, despite the "chain of destruction." The *satyagrahi* acts in politics *as if* his opponent could be trusted; and in so doing eventually evokes a response which will prove that his faith was not misplaced.[11]

But how evoke this maximum truth-discovering propensity in the opponent? How translate the idea of *ahimsa* into the arena of

---

[9]*Ibid.,* 104.
[10]*Mahatma Gandhi at Work,* 248-49.
[11]*Ibid.,* 223.

political action? Here Gandhi rephrases an old democratic dogma. For Jefferson's doctrine that only those governments are legitimate which depend upon the consent of the governed for their authority, Gandhi substitutes the assertion that government of any kind is *impossible* without the consent of those to be ruled.[12] The whole panoply of power and the armed violence and coercion of the modern State depend in the end upon the willingness of the governed to obey. A withholding of that obedience is the key to the problem of non-violent revolution.

In the area of immediate action, soul-force operates in a crisis through voluntary acceptance of suffering by the *satyagrahis*. When divisions between rulers and ruled or between separate political entities occur, the tactic is first of all to propose negotiation and, that failing, in the end to refuse obedience. This latter refusal in relation to the ruler or conqueror has for its purpose not unilateral triumph on the part of the *satyagrahis*, but rather the creation of a situation in which discussion can take place. The true *satyagrahi* will willingly receive the blows of his opponents, be they police or soldiers. As elements in the political struggle he will cheerfully bear the penalties for failure to pay taxes, or to hold office, or for obstructing traffic and public activities. Economically, he will be sustained by his ascetic diet and manner of living and by the contributions of sympathizers. Meanwhile, he will make his demands perfectly clear and leave not a shadow of doubt about his program.[13]

There will be growing up within the *satyagrahi* organizations, in the meantime, an internal government, with relationships of leadership based on this principle of *ahimsa* and consent. Leadership in the old sense of coercive imposition of rule, either through control of physical force or manipulation of the symbols of verbal expression, will be

[12]The use of soul-force, for Gandhi, is "based upon the immutable maxim that government of the people is possible only so long as they consent either consciously or unconsciously to be governed." *Mahatma Gandhi's Ideas*, 198. Cf. Anselm Bellegarrigue, the nineteenth century French radical, who, arguing in like manner, remarked "In the end, there are no tyrants, only slaves." Quoted in Barthelemy de Ligt, *The Conquest of Violence* (New York: Dutton, 1938), 109.

[13]For a detailed account of the practical implications of Gandhi's political theory, see Krishnalal Shridharani, *War Without Violence* (New York: Harcourt Brace, 1939). Romain Rolland, *Mahatma Gandhi: The Man Who Became One With the Universal Being* (London: Swarthmore, 1924); C. F. Andrews (ed.); *Speeches and Writings of M. K. Gandhi* (Madras: Natesan, 1918); Glorney Bolton, *The Tragedy of Gandhi* (London: Allen and Unwin, 1932); Haridas T. Muzumdar, *Gandhi versus the Empire* (New York: Universal, 1932) and *The United Nations of the World* (New York: Universal, 1942) are also useful.

discarded. Inherent in Gandhian pacifism is the active role played by the democratic idea.[14]

In fact, the *satyagrahi* movement and its governance constitute the alternative government. When the violent power-group dissolves due to the penetration of soul-force, the new politics takes its place. Power becomes subordinate to principle as and because the body and its force are subordinate to the soul and its coercion.

The State transformed through *satyagraha* and made politically in the image of *ahimsa* would presumably differ considerably from the modern order. The military would be eliminated; and the police, in their present form. Much machinery would have to go in accordance with Gandhi's principle of relative economic self-sufficiency. Gandhi, along with many other pacifist speculators, is distrustful of a high degree of centralization in either economics or politics—for centralization is inevitably associated with the principle of violence.

Gandhi has been much criticized on the ground that he is an enemy of progress—particularly for his attack on machinery and industrialization.[15] Some have attempted to defend him by alleging that his emphasis on a primitive agricultural and decentralized economy was a temporary expedient to facilitate immediate political objects. It is difficult to agree with that assertion. A machineless economy is his ideal and his theory of the State cannot be understood in the absence of it. "Ideally," he once said, "I would rule out all machinery, even as I would reject this very body, which is not helpful to salvation, and seek the absolute liberation of the soul. From that point of view I would reject all machinery; but machines will remain because, like the body, they are inevitable."[16]

But the State of the Gandhian visions—machineless, or largely so, coercionless (at least in the old sense of that term), and without violence—is not an end. Unlike so many theorists of Liberal progress, who assumed that they knew the end of the historical process,[17] Gandhi confesses he is without knowledge of the end in a distant and political sense. He is concerned with means, for no human organization can become an end without violating the natural law of *ahimsa,*

[14]"No one has to look expectantly at another, and there are no leaders and hence no followers. The death of a fighter, however eminent, makes not for slackness but, on the other hand, intensifies the struggle." *Mahatma Gandhi at Work,* 253.

[15]See Jawaharlal Nehru, *Toward Freedom* (New York: John Day, 1941), 313-323 and John Lewis, *The Case Against Pacifism* (London, Allen and Unwin, 1941), 99-101.

[16]*Mahatma Gandhi's Ideas,* 341-42.

[17]J. B. Bury, *The Idea of Progress* (New York: Macmillan, 1932).

So soon as it becomes the end and ceases to be the means, the politics of *himsa* are once more uppermost, power becomes the desideration, and the whole painfully constructed structure organizing the *satya-grahis* collapses. "Mankind is only able to utilize the means," Gandhi once said, "the ultimate end is beyond us. As soon as we think we have achieved one end, another arises. So all we are concerned with here are the simple means of life, the primal necessities; the rest we may leave in the hands of God."[18]

B.

CHRISTIAN PACIFISM

All theories of Christian pacifism[19] emanate from a certain emphasis on the character of God; from an interpretation of the manner in which the Divine Being manifests himself in history; and finally, from a set of political principles derivable from the former two postulates. An examination of Christian pacifism involves, therefore, an understanding of its theology, its philosophy of history, and its attitude toward the State.

The character of God is determined by the view presented in the New Testament. He is primarily a God of Love, one whose will is bent upon inducing fallen men to return to Him and then to express in human life the essence of his Godhead.

To the Christian pacifist, the signficance of the Christ lies in His statement of what God's love implies for human life and politics. That statement is the rule of non-violence which is binding upon mankind in its individual and corporate capacities alike. Christ's atone-

[18]*Mahatma Gandhi's Ideas,* 115.

[19]On the early history of Christian pacifism consult Ernst Troeltsch, *The Social Teaching of the Christian Churches,* Eng. trans., (New York: Macmillan, 1931); C. J. Cadoux, *The Early Church and the World* (Edinburgh: Clark, 1925); and several of the works of Adolf Harnack, particularly his *Militia Christi, die christliche Religion und der Soldatenstand in den ersten drei Jahrhunderten* (Tubingen: 1905).

Umphrey Lee, *The Historic Church and Modern Pacifism* (Nashville: Abingdon-Cokesbury, 1943) treats the history of Christian pacifism from a non-pacifist point of view.

For modern Catholic discussions of the questions raised by the Christian pacifist argument see John A. Ryan and Francis J. Boland, *Catholic Principles of Politics* (New York: Macmillan, 1940); Msgr. George Barry O'Toole, *War and Conscription at the Bar of Christian Morals* (New York: Catholic Worker Press, 1941); John J. Hugo, *Weapons of the Spirit* (New York: Catholic Worker Press, 1943); and, in general, the publications of the American Catholic Worker and British Pax groups. The Catholic argument may take two forms: (1) the contention that no modern war can possibly justify the conditions laid down for a just war by Saints Augustine and Thomas Aquinas and other doctors of the Church; and (2) the belief that conscientious objection to war is one of the *counsels* of perfection, although not one of the *commandments*.

ment is seen to be, not some magic propitiation of an angry God, but rather a demonstration of the means which His followers are to utilize in reconstructing human life. His ideal is a Kingdom of God to be established politically here on earth as the result of a technique which constitutes the heart of His doctrine.[20]

What is that method? A search of Christian pacifist literature reveals the following emphasis: (1) the individual character of the revolutionist and the means he is to utilize; and (2) the social and political character of the revolution.

Revolutionists must be humble, for only the meek can inherit the earth either individually or politically.[21] They must reject great possessions, because wealth is corrupting and bars any possible achievement of God's Kingdom—indeed, great possessions themselves generate violence against fellow-men and God. Finally, physical violence must be completely repudiated by revolutionists.[22]

The social and political character of the revolution is illustrated by the concrete nature of the Kingdom to be envisioned.[23] It is to be realized here in this world through the utilization of a type of power which has a positive relation to the end to be attained. Jesus in the Temptation story[24] rejected armed revolt as a means of overcoming Caesar, and his followers are bidden to do likewise under all circumstances.[25]

But if God wills only love and commands only non-violence in politics and life in general and if at the same time we believe that He reflects himself in history—and in this latter assertion Christian pacifism agrees with the general Christian position—how can we reconcile God as Love with God as presumably reflected in the violence of

---

[20]Religious groups like the Mennonites would, of course, repudiate this assertion. "Popular pacifism today. . . . is something very different from scriptural pacifism. It is essentially a political or social philosophy aiming at influencing national or international affairs and policies by any methods of propaganda or coercion short of violence and war. . . . It is humanistic rather than theistic or Biblical in its outlook. Because of this debased use of the term, non-resistant Christians avoid speaking of themselves as pacifists. . . . " Edward Yoder, Jesse W. Hoover, and Harold S. Bender, *Must Christians Fight* (Akron, Pennsylvania: Mennonite Central Committee, 1943), 62-63.

[21]A. J. Muste, *Non-Violence in an Aggressive World* (New York: Harper, 1940).

[22]John MacMurray, *The Clue to History* (New York: Harper, 1939) constitutes a good statement of the theological assumptions of pacifism.

[23]Cf. G. H. C. MacGregor, *The New Testament Basis of Pacifism* (New York: Fellowship of Reconciliation, 1940), 55.

[24]*Matthew* IV, 8.

[25]*Matthew* V, VI, and VII.

politics? This is an old question, and involves the Christian pacifist philosophy of history.[26]

The answer, briefly, is that God acts in a two-fold sense—a cosmic and a personal. In the first He is conceived as Ruler; in the second, as Father. This does not mean that He is divided, but rather that man's freedom, itself the creation of God, enters the picture. The character of politics, with its wars and exploitation, is determined by the use which man makes of his God-created freedom. The will of God is love; but the freedom of man makes it possible for him to act contrary to the divine will. Thus he learns as a child learns by acting contrary to his father's desire. In so acting, however, he meets the cosmic God which, impersonally and according to law, ultimately frustrates the acts of human wills acting contrary to the divine. God ordains a cause and effect relationship and if man chooses a course of action not "willed" by God, he reaps the inevitable consequences— he perishes as a result of his own will to power. If, on the other hand, he selects an alternative "willed" by God, he equally reaps the consequences—this time, progress toward the Kingdom of God, which, because it *is* willed by God, is inevitable.

Thus, while man is given a choice of alternative courses of action, all those choices not ultimately willed by God are frustrated; and the intention with which man begins bears a fruit different from all his expectations. This is true because the action was not compatible with the end to be achieved, or because the end itself was constitutive of means not willed by God. If an act of repentance does not take place—and here a new beginning *can* be made—man becomes involved in a chain of destruction, which, after a period, compels humility and an attitude of repentance. In the end God inevitably triumphs and man is educated as a result of frustration of his own means and ends to see that his real will, not apprehended before, is the will of God.[27]

Now Christian pacifist literature reads human history in terms of man's rebellion against God's will. That rebellion is the assertion of man's own will to power. Always it has been frustrated in the end, whether it take the guise of intellectual arrogance, of bloody inquisition, of verbal misrepresentation, or of physical violence. History is the record of man's search for the Kingdom of God by means which,

---

[26]See footnote 4. Interpretations of the Christian pacifist philosophy of history include MacMurray, Muste, MacGregor, *op. cit.*, and *The Relevance of an Impossible Ideal* (New York: Fellowship of Reconciliation, 1941); and C. J. Cadoux, *Christian Pacifism Re-Examined* (Oxford: Blackwell, 1940).

[27]And thus a celestial determinism is reconciled with a terrestrial "free will."

in the first place, vitiate the end because they are of such a nature as inevitably to make power the end, and, in the second, turn in upon themselves and destroy those who utilize them.

God thus moved in Hebrew history when Israel and Judah were punished by Assyria and Babylonia for their will to power through violence; and Assyria and Babylonia in turn fell because they, too, had lived by the sword. The mission of Jesus was not to point to a "spiritual" kingdom in Heaven, as contrasted with a "temporal" Kingdom on earth; rather was it to indicate the way to a conquest of power on earth by means which would not generate the will to power and hence result in a persistence of the chain of destruction maintained by man's failure to discover his own real will. It was this mission which led to the repudiation by Jesus of violence.[28]

Similarly, God is seen moving in non-Hebrew history. The Kingdom of God is a world of non-violence characterized by two qualities —freedom and equality. Both are implicit in the ideal of non-violence, freedom implying a political order in which it is possible for the individual to choose the good without penalty, and equality the absence of that coercion created by the existence of class.[29] But the ideal must be implicit in the means selected, or the will to power will exhibit itself despite a verbal statement of the idea; and, asserting itself, will frustrate the ideal, turn in upon the power-holders, and destroy them. This was true of the Roman Empire. It was likewise the fruit of the schemes of Richelieu, which, proclaimed as proposals for the pacification of Europe, were disguises for the will to power in the French State and its rulers—and the result was overthrow of the monarchy and a chain of destruction the end of which has not yet been seen.[30] In recent politics, this philosophy of history is illustrated in the history of abolitionism in the United States, which, intending to abolish slavery, used means which produced the will to power and created evils perhaps greater than those against which it had originally protested.[31] The so-called Russian Revolution is another instance in point: with ends not differing widely from traditional Christian ends, the

---

[28]"If my Kingdom were of this world" (were created as past political societies have been constructed) "then would my servants fight." *John*: XVIII, 36.

[29]This is particularly emphasized throughout MacMurray.

[30]Aldous Huxley, *Grey Eminence* (New York: Harper, 1941).

[31]See, for example, Mary Katherine Reeley's review of Avery Craven's *The Coming of the Civil War*, in *Fellowship*, December, 1942, 215. Of the Abolitionists she remarks, "They were so noble-souled, so high-minded, so consecrated in their zeal for good, and they wrought such havoc."

means utilized were such as to produce ends utterly at variance with the avowed objective.[32]

The whole history of the human race, in short, is seen by the Christian pacifist as a vast educational endeavor carried on by the Divine Being to teach a being possessed of freedom that the creature cannot attain the political Kingdom of God by means contrary to the Divine Nature as revealed in the New Testament. The creature is free to try force; he is permitted to attempt coercion; he can choose exploitation and class stratification—but he will discover in every case that the divine end, freedom and equality, which in his lucid moments he can intuitively discern, will always escape him. Instead he will become oblivious of his own intention, which is also God's intention, and make his means his end. But eventually the power which he has grasped and held will fall from him as a result of attacks from the political agents of God's wrath.

The philosophy of history associated with Christian pacifism constitutes the basis for its view of the State. Here there are two main lines of thought—the anarchism of Tolstoy and his followers and those theories which attempt to distinguish between coercion on the one hand and violence on the other, and thus to permit a continuance of the State.

To Tolstoy, the ablest representative of Christian anarchist pacifism, "the words 'a Christian State' resemble the words 'hot ice.' The thing is either not a State using violence, or it is not Christian."[33] Violence and coercion are one, and since the State would dissolve without its coercive mechanism, the most efficacious way to strike at the persistence of a violent ethic in human affairs is to attack its citadel —the State.[34] Out of this general view proceeds Tolstoy's repudiation of private property which rests upon the protection of violence.[35] The true pacifist must be a communist.[36] Armies, navies, property, the judicial system, police, law, voting—all are devices to perpetuate a world

[32]Richard B. Gregg is particularly emphatic at this point. *The Power of Non-Violence* (Philadelphia: Lippincott, 1935).

[33]Leo Tolstoy, "Church and State," *Essays, Letters, Miscellanies*, in *Works* (New York: Scribner, 1929), Part I, 150.

[34]"Government is violence, Christianity is meekness, non-resistance, love. . . . Government cannot be Christian. A Christian cannot serve government." "Letter to Dr. Schmitt," *Ibid.*, Part II, 45. Tolstoy's novel *Resurrection* is, of course, an elaboration of this theme.

[35]"A Letter from Tolstoy to the Canadian Doukhobors," in Aylmer Maude, *A Peculiar People*: The Doukhobors (New York: Funk and Wagnalls, 1904), 272.

[36]*Ibid.*, 272.

where the essential canons of the Gospel are contradicted. The politics of Tolstoy are, then, those of an ascetic Christianity which seeks escape from power-struggles altogether; which interprets the will to power as the desire to use power even as a means; and which calls for an existence on a bare subsistence level.[37]

Tolstoy's principles of non-violence take him much further than do those of Gandhi. There is less of humor in the former than in the latter—less disposition to relieve the tension by laughter when the point is inevitably reached where to push the principle of non-violence further would itself generate violence; less inclination to see with a twinkle the fact, as Gandhi understands it, that every breath of life involves in a measure an act of violence.[38]

A non-violent ethic implies for Tolstoy, not only a repudiation by the individual of politics and the State, but also many elements of what has come to be called civilization.[39] The true Christian must repudiate service on the jury, in the police, in the army and navy, in courts of justice, and in legislative bodies. He must refuse to pay taxes to a coercive order. Personally, he must be chaste; must eat no meat, lest he violate animal life; and he must give up his possessions. If nominal Christians would act in this manner they would cut through the destructive violence to which this world is bound, the State would collapse, and with the State would go all impediments to the establishment of the Kingdom of God.

But the main stream of Christian pacifist thought has not accepted Tolstoyan anarchism. It may prefer at times, with Aldous Huxley, to sit "on the fringe" of the political arena,[40] lest its ends be corrupted by the violences inherent in the politics of this world. At points, indeed, it skirts amazingly close to Tolstoy's position—for all pacifist doctrines are anti-authoritarian. But for the most part it attempts to steer clear of anarchism.

The dominant schools of Christian pacifism have been concerned with three problems: (1) distinguishing between the mere use of power and the will to power; (2) transformation of a non-pacifist political order into one approved by the Christian pacifist ethic; and (3) the nature of a State based upon pacifist principles.

---

[37]Leo Tolstoy, *My Religion* (New York: Crowell, 1885), 196.

[38]For an instructive analysis of the relationship between Tolstoy and Gandhi see Milan I. Markovitch, *Tolstoï et Gandhi* (Paris: H. Champion, 1928).

[39]Thus emphasizing his repeated contention that even the so-called non-political aspects of the modern world repose on violence.

[40]*Grey Eminence.*

Whereas for the Christian anarchist pacifist any coercion is to be condemned, the non-anarchist pacifist attempts to set up criteria for discriminating between permissible and non-permissible coercion. Professor MacGregor, for example, draws a line between what he calls "redemptive" and "non-redemptive" power. Some means—such, for example, as the surgeon's knife and part of the discipline of the home —are capable of being controlled in the interest of, and subordinated to, ethically approved ends. Other power, however—for example, the naked and irresponsible force of war—cannot be so controlled and hence is "non-redemptive."[41]

The most elaborate attempt to establish a sharp contrast between power and the will to power has been made by Professor Cadoux.[42] Substituting "pressure" for the term "force," he defines "pressure" as "*all* methods whereby we endeavor to cause our neighbor to act or refrain in a certain way."[43] There are two types of pressure—non-coercive (examples of which are telepathy, kindness, trust, intercessory prayer, and spoken or written arguments and appeals) and coercive,[44] which in turn might be either non-injurious or injurious. The first variety of coercion would include threats, refusal to cooperate, mild punishment, strikes, school discipline, and humane police administration; the second, "the police truncheon, prolonged imprisonment, threats, capital punishment, armed rebellion, war, medieval persecution, oriental penalties, and gratuitous massacre."[45] It is the injurious coercive devices for which no Christian ethical warrant can be discovered; and with Cadoux's analysis most of the apologists for Christian pacifism, such as Gregg,[46] Muste,[47] and Holmes,[48] would apparently agree. For them, all coercion is suspect, but "injurious coercion" is absolutely barred.

These principles would be conformable to the major doctrines taught by those two individualists in the modern stream of Christian pacifism—Gerald Heard and Aldous Huxley. The will to power is for them either with Heard, a "mechanomorphic" cosmology[49]—principles which see the universe and life simply as machines; or with

[41]*The New Testament Basis of Pacifism.*
[42]Cadoux, *Christian Pacifism Re-Examined,* especially Ch. II.
[43]*Ibid.,* 15.
[44]*Ibid.,* 20.
[45]*Ibid.,* 45.
[46]*The Power of Non-Violence.*
[47]*Non-Violence in an Aggressive World.*
[48]John Haynes Holmes, *Out of Darkness* (New York: Harper, 1942).
[49]*The Third Morality* (New York: Morrow, 1937), 148-49.

Huxley, the absence of what he terms "non-attachment"[50]—that is to say, the absence of that spirit which can view with utter indifference loss of fame, fortune, friends, exclusive loves, social position, and nation. For to Huxley attachment to anything less than the ultimate reality at the center of the universe is of the essence of violence.[51] With Heard, then, mechanomorphic cosmologies are associated with the will to power; with Huxley, attachment to all powers less than God. In fact, these two statements complement Cadoux's analysis—"injurious" coercion always, and "non-injurious" coercion often, lead to and accentuate "attachment," just as an ethical ideal of "attachment" will inevitably associate itself with violence.

But what theory of political action does Christian pacifism erect upon these foundations? Its initial difficulty is one of fitting its own theory of social revolution into its assumptions. It holds that God operates in history and that the corporate calamities of mankind are the result of its corporate disregard of divine law. War, for example, is God's judgment on man for his past offenses. The question, then, becomes: If human politics are foredoomed to destruction because of their violation of the eternal law, is it not presumptuous for those about to share in the corporate punishment to try to avert it by taking thought or to try to resist it once it comes? Can they really escape divine judgment and ought they not really to cooperate heartily in it?[52]

MacGregor sees this problem, as all pacifist theologians must, for he asks "May not war . . . be regarded as society cooperating with God in affirming the moral order?" In reply, he admits with orthodox Christian political philosophers that the social and political order is ethically justified in establishing "certain restrictive and even forcible social sanctions."[53] Just as the moral order contains within itself the pains and penalties applied to those who violate its commands, so must society establish rules which contain appropriate penalties for their infraction. But to the Christian pacifist any such restrictions must

---

[50]Aldous Huxley, *Ends and Means: An Enquiry Into the Nature of Ideals and Into the Methods Employed for their Realization* (New York: Harper, 1937). See also his novel *Eyeless in Gaza* (New York: Harper, 1936).

[51]*Ends and Means*, 4.

[52]This is the line of argument taken by Charles Clayton Morrison in *The Christian and the War* (Chicago: Willett, Clark, 1942), where the Christian pacifist interpretation of politics is vigorously criticized. No alternative but war-making remains once war comes, Morrison maintains; and he seems to contend that any conception of politics which makes possible organized opposition to it is an act of sheer and futile rebellion against the historical process itself.

[53]*The New Testament Basis of Pacifism*, 86.

be conformable to the basic principle of the moral order, which is love. What Cadoux would call "injurious coercion" is thus excluded, even though the effect of man's corporate stupidity is to produce just such violence.[54] MacGregor also argues that while God may be looked upon as using class or national violence for His own ends—in that these flourish because man, given freedom, rebels against the divine law and hence suffers the penalty—it does not follow that man, imprisoned in the historical process, should use them. His refusal to do so is a part of that act of repentance whereby he is permitted, by divine grace, to break the vicious circle of violence and the will to power in which he finds himself enmeshed.

The implications of Christian pacifist social action, as critics such as Reinhold Niebuhr have pointed out,[55] tend to be sternly suspicious of what are ordinarily termed political methods. This suspicion reaches its extreme form in Tolstoyan anarchism, of course, but is in no wise lacking elsewhere. Thus, Father Joseph, the collaborator of Richelieu, failed to produce a good society, according to Aldous Huxley, precisely because he thought political action would constiute a short-cut to the peace and harmony so desirable.[56] He failed to see, even though a mystic, that "Good is a product of the ethical and spiritual artistry of individuals. It cannot be mass-produced."[57]

Nevertheless, political action for the non-anarchist pacifist is necessary, and the chief problem is to make certain that its end will not be distorted in the process. This is to be ensured by the full acceptance of the philosophy of non-violence and by adequate training for those who are to constitute the vanguard of the non-violent army. One element in that training will be the development of a mystic consciousness of God.[58] Then, to some, the discipline of non-violence requires a re-examination of the problem of diet. Many pacifists tend to be vegetarians, the belief being based either upon the general doc-

---

[54]Or, as MacGregor finely puts it, "We shall never 'affirm' to a man that the moral order in which we live is one of love by blowing him in pieces with high explosive, however we may have first represented to him that our action is the inevitable consequence of his own previous wrongdoing." *Ibid.*, 87.

[55]In, for example, Reinhold Niebuhr, *Christianity and Power Politics* (New York: Scribner, 1940). Niebuhr was himself a pacifist until in the 1930's he developed the theory that Jesus' ethic was not within the stream of history—thus denying one Christian view of history.

[56]*Grey Eminence.*

[57]*Ibid.*, 303.

[58]Note particularly Gerald Heard, *The Third Morality* and *Pain, Sex and Time* (New York: Harpers, 1939); the publications of the Fellowship of Reconciliation; and *The Catholic Worker* (New York). To some pacifists this element is overemphasized by Heard.

trine of non-violence, or upon the contention that a non-protein diet aids in developing what Gerald Heard calls "the reflective controlled," as contrasted with "the impulsive and impatient" type of personality.[59] Particular emphasis is given by some theorists to manual training as a disciplinary device.[60] Such training is said to be valuable in developing "faith, self-confidence, imaginative power, dignity, and self-respect."[61] It is supposed also to stimulate an *esprit de corps,* to encourage a "sense of order and cooperation,"[62] and to be conducive to certain attitudes important for the non-violent leader—humility, love of truth, and faith in human nature. Training along these lines would be far more exacting even than military discipline, and would at the same time promote a sense of social unity.

Pacifist ideology is prone also to emphasize the fickleness and unreliability of "great men," whether they be men of action or academicians.[63] The revolution to freedom and equality, if and when it comes, must arise from below through a well-disciplined and spiritually integrated mass of men, ready and able to utilize non-violent approaches.

Modern pacifism thinks of itself as essentially a rebel movement—one whose aim is to shake the modern State to its very foundations. Ultimately its ideology entails, if necessary, organized civil disobedience and non-cooperation as methods alike of preventing future war and of overthrowing those who control and dominate the State. Paul's conceptual foundation of authority found in the thirteenth chapter of Romans, does not disturb most pacifists. They interpret Paul's words admonishing all souls to obey the existing powers as making the principle of "ordered government for the protection of justice" a divine ordinance;[64] but when particular governments promote the contrary, when they utilize means which can only develop a will to power that will eventually destroy the political community, there the divine ordinance requires widespread and organized disobedience. The ideology of the general strike is not far from pacifist conceptions of means; but any such endeavor will be unsuccessful unless accompanied by the

---

[59]*The Third Morality,* 277; See the position of Lew Ayres, *Fellowship,* May, 1944, 93.
[60]R. B. Gregg, *A Discipline for Non-Violence* (Wallingford, Pennsylvania: Pendle Hill, 1942).
[61]*Ibid.,* 5.
[62]*Ibid.,* 13.
[63]Huxley, *Ends and Means,* 373.
[64]MacGregor, *The New Testament Basis of Pacifism,* 118.

severe disciplines recommended and the training suggested.[65] Non-violence is powerful precisely because it discards the usual methods of politics and resorts to the unexpected. Heaping coals of fire upon the "enemy's" head by feeding him "moral jiu jitsu" as Gregg has it,[66] will generate far greater power than armies or navies or penal sanctions. And it will do so by encouraging, rather than disrupting, the sense of community. If in the process voluntary mass-suffering and jail-going are necessary, the social power will be even greater.

Granted that the dominant note in Christian pacifist thinking is not anarchism, although some have interpreted it in that way, how will the non-violent order differ from the modern State? It will be a State whose nature is implicit in the means used for its attainment. It will believe profoundly in the virtues of decentralism, for it holds that violence and centralization of power are inseparable. As in Hindu pacifism, there is strong criticism and suspicion of a machine age which de-personalizes men and society and hence contributes to the ubiquity of violence in the modern world. The fundamental basis of the pacifist State must be the small community and the world will then become a federation of small communities. But even in such an order coercion and inequality will be embryonic. Unlike Marxian theory, Christian pacifism still believes in the idea of fallen man. While a polity more nearly in accord with Christian pacifist ethics is possible, that polity, too, will be subject to the seeds of decay and corruption and must be perpetually called to account. The conception of pacifist struggle is permanent on the plane of history.

C.

REVOLUTIONARY SECULAR PACIFISM

Nineteenth century liberalism at no time constituted a creed of non-violence. It is true that its political ideal was an harmonious world of supposedly liberated men, each of whom spoke and wrote freely in the ever-widening search for truth. Again, it is true that the inevitable progress to a peaceful, non-exploitative order which it envisioned was an important element in its whole view of politics.[67] But even

---

[65]Pacifist argument is so suffused with this theme that it seems superfluous to cite particular passages. But see Gregg, *The Power of Non-Violence*, 51, for a good example.

[66]"The art of jiu jitsu is based on a knowledge of balance and how to disturb it. In a struggle of moral jiu jitsu the moral balance seems to depend upon the qualities of one's relationship to moral truth. Hence part of the superior power of the non-violent resister seems to lie in the nature of his character." *Ibid.*, 51.

[67]See *Bury, op. cit.*, and Guido de Ruggiero, *The History of European Liberalism* (London: Oxford, 1927).

so, the political ethics of Liberalism were not pacifist. There was nothing to be condemned in wars for national liberation, nor was the violent revolt of repressed peoples morally reprehensible. Kossuth, Mazzini, and the instigators of the several Polish revolts were heroes to Victorian libertarians—Gladstone praised them, and the Liberals of Great Britain wished them well. The extreme form of violence, war itself, might to them be a liberating force.[68]

For the most part, the Marxian revolutionary creeds fall into the same pattern. Whatever Marx really meant by Revolution, his belief could hardly be termed a philosophy of non-violence. It is true that in his historic struggle with Bakunin it was he who denounced terrorism as a revolutionary device—it was "romantic" and ineffective; but it was primarily against acts of individual terrorism that his invectives were directed.[69] The very conception of the dictatorship of the proletariat is a utilization of bourgeois methods for the eventual elimination of the bourgeoisie.[70]

In general, the whole range of what might be termed proletarian revolutionary literature witnesses the same phenomenon. When Alexander Berkman was about to shoot Henry Clay Frick, Emma Goldman mentally questioned the ethics, not so much of the act itself, as of a possible miscarriage of it.[71] Similarly, Georges Sorel, the theoretician of syndicalism, has no compunctions. Violence—and he confines the term to acts of revolt, reserving "force" for the means by which a minority imposes its will on the mass of individuals[72]—is seen as the method whereby the gulf between bourgeoisie and proletarian can be maintained; by it the workers "reply by blows to the advances of the propagators of social peace."[73] For Trotsky, the theoretical defense of violence in the Russian Revolution needs little justification—indeed, its necessity is obvious;[74] while for Lenin the proletarian order is

---

[68]After all, the "liberations" of the past century have been largely a release of political nationalism; and with nationalism both war and Liberalism have been intimately associated. See Carlton J. H. Hayes, *Essays on Nationalism* (New York: Macmillan, 1926) and *The Historical Evolution of Modern Nationalism* (New York: R. R. Smith, 1931).

[69]Robert Hunter, *Violence and the Labor Movement* (New York: Macmillan, 1914).

[70]Nicolai Lenin, *The State and Revolution* (New York: Vanguard Press, 1929), 127.

[71]Emma Goldman, *Living My Life* (Garden City: Garden City Publishing Company, 1934), 88.

[72]*Reflections on Violence,* trans. by T. E. Hulme (New York: Peter Smith, 1941), 195.

[73]*Ibid.,* 88-89.

[74]Leon Trotsky, *My Life* (New York: Scribner, 1930), 475.

merely, in the beginning, the substitution of one regime of violence
for another, although later that violence is somehow to disappear.[75]
Considerations involving the sacred character of human personality
are of no concern because the idea of personality itself is the result of
a chain of revolutionary violence whose end is not yet. Trotsky is
not concerned as to the "goodness" or "badness" of violence "from
the viewpoint of normative philosophy"—but he does think that it
is the only method which past politics has confirmed to be efficacious.[76]

But while the major stream of Western non-religious revolutionary
tradition has not been pacifist, there has always been a dissenting
current, both anarchist and socialist.[77] Illustrative of non-religious
anarchist pacifism are the politics of Alexander Berkman and the Dutch
writer Barthelemy de Ligt;[78] while John Middleton Murry may be
taken to represent the political theory of socialist pacifism. Let us
examine each in turn.

Means, for the revolutionary anarchist pacifist,

"have their own abiding end, proceeding from the function
for which they came into being, which can only be subordinated to other loftier ends as far as the latter are attuned to
the essential, and, as it were, innate end. Besides, every end
suggests its own means. To transgress this law inevitably
brings about a tyranny of the means. For if these lead away
from their intended goal, then the more people use them, the
farther they get from their objective and the more their actions are determined by them. For example, it is impossible
to educate people in liberty by force, just as it is impossible
to breathe by coal gas."[79]

[75]Lenin, op. cit., 129.
[76]Trotsky, My Life, 474. The sharp dichotomy which secular revolutionists create
  between ends and means is further illustrated in Trotsky's observation that "A
  revolutionary organization is not the prototype of the future state, but merely
  the instrument for its creation. An instrument ought to be adapted to fashion-
  ing the product; it ought not to include the product. Thus a centralized organization can guarantee the success of a revolutionary struggle—even where the
  task is to destroy the centralized oppression of nationalities." Leon Trotsky,
  History of the Russian Revolution, 3 vols. (New York: Simon and Schuster,
  1932), III, 38.
[77]Among socialist leaders of the twentieth century, perhaps Eugene V. Debs and
  Keir Hardie most nearly agreed with the pacifist view of politics. See David
  Karsner, Debs (New York: Boni and Liveright, 1919); Eugene V. Debs,
  Walls and Bars (Chicago: Socialist Party, 1927); and William Stewart, J. Keir
  Hardie (London: National Labour Press, 1921). George Lansbury would also
  fall into this category.
[78]Berkman, What is Communist Anarchism? (New York: Vanguard, 1929); DeLigt,
  The Conquest of Violence: An Essay on War and Revolution (New York:
  Dutton, 1938). The career of Berkman is interesting because it begins with
  a belief in the achievement of the anarchist society through violence and ends
  with an avowal of what may be called, as in the text, anarchist pacifism. A
  similar evolution took place in Emma Goldman.
[79]DeLigt, 72.

Or again, "The means are the seeds which bud into flower and come to fruition. The fruit will always be of the nature of the seed you planted. You can't grow a rose from a cactus seed."[80]

Now violence has been characteristic of all previous civilization in that all hitherto existing societies have been composed of small groups of privileged men who acquire their power and splendor only because they possess the means for exploiting the vast mass of mankind. The history of mankind has been largely the story of the "vertical violence" of the exploiters and the counter-violence used at times by the exploited, together with the "horizontal" violence known as war. In fact the State up to now can best be defined in terms of the violence it encourages and the exploitation it protects.[81]

With this general view of history, the anarchist pacifist doctrine proceeds to examine the modern State. That political order has been dominated by the bourgeoisie, which of all ruling classes in history has been perhaps the most violent. The whole of modern culture is suffused with the idea of violence—in school, church, literature, and the arts.[82] Without the use of violence neither the domestic positions nor the colonial empires of Western ruling classes could be maintained.[83] Parasites upon the mass of mankind, the ruling orders use the method so bound up with all parasitism.

Because the use of violence can only result in the enhancement of exploitation, and not in its elimination, the anarchist pacifist argues, it can never constitute the means of liberation.[84] But the revolutionist must repudiate vertical and horizontal violence under all circumstances not only because of the general principle enunciated, but also because the nature of modern violence particularly makes any other course suicidal. For the revolutionist to compete with the mechanized armed power of the twentieth century is to spell the doom of every revolutionary endeavor.[85]

If, then, any revolutionary violence whatsoever is incompatible with the achievement of the Revolution itself, wherein lies the possible success of the Revolution? Berkman suggests it is to be found "in the shop, in the mine and factory."[86] DeLigt and other anarchist pacifists agree with him. Workers are to rely upon a collective with-

---

[80]Berkman, 168.
[81]DeLigt, 27-29.
[82]Ibid., 48.
[83]Ibid., 101.
[84]Ibid., 75.
[85]Berkman, 247.
[86]Ibid., 247.

drawal of labor for their attainment of power. Approaching current politics with a philosophy of history which associates the class system with the utilization of violence, they can only attack that system through repudiation of its characteristic method. By mass organization they must withdraw their labor from production for war, and, when the revolutionary time is ripe, must in united fashion withhold it from the governing elite. If that elite has neither the labor necessary to support its exploitative social system, nor soldiers and war workers to sustain the wars in which it engages to preserve its own order, the system itself must inevitably collapse. When the State shall no longer be able, by reason of organized refusal of workers to serve in its armies, to wage war or extend violence, the whole organization of mass exploitation will crumble and a classless society will be possible.

And not only the classless society in a vague and ambiguous sense, but specifically the anarchist world will be achieved. That world is a universal and voluntarist cohesive confederation of materially independent communities.[87] It is a vast decentralized order, in which not only individuals but also the tiny communities cooperate, spontaneously and freely without coercion. Violence has ceased to be the order of the day because, cooperating in communities where each man is intimately acquainted with his fellows, men have no need of the violence found essential in an exploitative regime.

From the socialist viewpoint, this general thesis of revolutionary pacifism has been perhaps most clearly affirmed in the writings of J. Middleton Murry.[88] He argues that the question of revolution in a highly integrated capitalist democracy cannot be solved in accordance with the old ideal of a self-conscious working class seizing the reins of power and if necessary retaining them by force. That solution is impossible if only because the very interdependence of men causes working-class parties to distrust a violent "solution."[89] Hence, even before it attained power, a genuine Socialist movement would be virtually paralyzed, and tend to conform to the rules of "democratic" capitalist politics. Such was true of the Socialists of Germany, Italy,

---

[87] *Ibid.*, 284.

[88] Murry might with equal validity be placed within the stream of Christian pacifism. In this essay his views are examined at this point because it seems to me that his most significant discussion has used the language of a "non-religious" or secular socialism.

[89] J. Middleton Murry, *The Necessity of Pacifism* (London: Cape, 1937), 29. Subconsciously, if not explicitly, Murry argues, working-class groups see that civil war could result only in "plague, pestilence, famine, chaos, and barbarism." See also his *The Necessity of Communism* (London: Cape, 1932).

and Austria. But conformity in the modern State means agreement in all fundamentals with the power groups which control the democratic capitalist order, for modern capitalism can no longer maintain itself except in a war economy and those who attained power under a Socialist label would already have had to assent in every important respect to the formulae of the war State. All political activity within the framework of the existing order must, therefore, be essentially war activity; and only when groups with revolutionary ends break utterly with that order in terms of means can they expect to realize their goals.[90]

The radical, then, according to the socialist pacifist, is confronted with two equally unpalatable alternatives—either he attempts to transform national loyalty into class loyalty, and international war into civil war, as a method of escaping the necessity of a meaningless political conflict within the existing order; or he frankly surrenders to "democratic" politics, plays the game, and necessarily supports the war and exploitative ideology of the integrated State. If he selects the first alternative, he is merely erecting a new tribal morality in place of the old and running the very great risk of dissolving the community itself; while if, rejecting the former, he chooses the latter, he ceases to be radical.

Murry finds the answer, of course, in a pacifism very closely resembling that of Berkman and DeLigt. Socialists must first learn to be socialistic in a non-political sense of living in small communities and sharing the work equally. Individual training and discipline, resolute refusal to contribute personal service and taxes to the State in time of war, and the deliberate outlawry of himself from society during the same period—these are the duties incumbent, according to Murry, on the socialist-pacifist. He must see the illusion "that the class-struggle, which is a social and economic fact, can be posited as an ethical and political dynamic."[91] In so acting and speculating, he will be able to create a new dynamic genuinely revolutionary because eschewing both the blind alley of civil war and the equally futile endeavor to overthrow the present order by acting wholly within its

---

[90]*The Necessity of Pacifism*, 45. "Politics," he goes on, "means war; because the politics of an integrated capitalist society is compelled to conform to the economic reality of national unity. That national unity acts on the instinctive level: against a threat to its life, its possessions, or its interests, it prepares to defend itself."

[91]*Ibid.*, 97.

framework. The political theories of anarchist pacifism and those of
socialist pacifism thus join hands at this point and merge into the general
stream of revolutionary pacifism.[92]

III. CRITICAL EVALUATION OF PACIFIST
POLITICAL PHILOSOPHIES

Any critical evaluation of the political theories of modern pacifism must begin with an emphasis on the divergencies in content and
varieties of approach within those theories themselves. As is true of
any vital tendency in political thought, differences of statement and
emphasis within the pacifist stream seem only less great than those
which separate it from other analyses. Hindu pacifism roots in presuppositions which see "matter" as evil and "spirit" as good; and in
its statement there remains an acute tension produced by the idea,
perfectly consistent with its own assumptions, that even the process
of living in a "material" body is an act of violence and hence to be
condemned. Christian pacifism, in contrast, is in the main non-dualistic.
It sees good, as well as evil, attached to the "material" and evil, as
well as good, inhering in "spirit." But even in Christian pacifism there
is a dualistic strain, which becomes particularly marked in Christian
anarchists such as Tolstoy, for whom any physical force — that is,
"matter" — is in essence evil.

As for non-religious revolutionary pacifism, it roots itself in a
kind of utilitarianism for which problems of natural and divine law,
so vital to the Hindu and Christian pacifist, do not exist. Violence is
to be condemned and a theory of revolutionary action developed with
that condemnation as its base, not because violent action is contrary
to the will of God or to the rational nature of man, but rather because
violence produces undesired results. This utilitarian approach is not
lacking in Hindu and Christian pacifism, which can easily be understood since both are in fact revolutionary, but it constitutes only part
of the religious approach.

Then again, within the whole broad current of modern pacifist
thought there is a constant difficulty in regard to the problem of differentiation between non-resistance and non-violent resistance. Some
emphases contend that the two are to be sharply distinguished, the
former implying renunciation of power in any form, the latter an
endeavor to change "the world" by a "right" method of acquiring

---

[92]Fruitful insights into many of the questions raised by pacifist politics will be found
    in A E (George Russell), *The Interpreters* (New York: Macmillan, 1923).

and using power. Yet other analyses would minimize the distinction, and some even deny it altogether. On the whole, "non-violent resist-ance" has tended to eliminate "non-resistance" in the ideology of modern pacifism.

This latter tendency may be due to the fact that modern pacifism is much more explicitly political than were doctrines of non-violence before the twentieth century. Many in the historic current of pacifist thought have looked upon the ethics of pacifism as essentially personal and without any particular relation to the problem of conquest of power. Non-resistance was associated with the idea of renunciation of the "world," not with the conception of a conquest of the city of Man by methods characteristic of the city of God. One became a non-resistant, not with the hope of attaining political power, but in a sense for the contrary reason: a Christian was not interested in political power—had he been so interested, he would have fought and used all the methods of this world. This conflict between an individualistic pacifism, which holds to the belief that political power is to be totally rejected, and a political pacifism, which seeks to attain political power for the purpose of changing "the world," is very much alive in twen-tieth-century pacifist thought.[93] It accounts in considerable measure for many inconsistencies which appear in the political doctrines which we have, in a rather broad sense, denominated "pacifism."

Finally, there is a sharp conflict between those who adopt frankly anarchistic views with reference to the State and those who, while at-tacking the modern State, would yet retain it and with it a measure of coercion within strictly prescribed limits. Within very wide limits, indeed, it might be said that all pacifism is tinged with anarchism; but those limits are so far apart that it would be grossly mis-representative to fail to make very specific distinctions. Most pacifists would un-doubtedly repudiate the anarchism of Berkman and DeLigt. Yet the anarchist eddy in the current of modern pacifism is extremely impor-tant and cannot be neglected in a critical evaluation.

But these widely varying interpretations of meaning and implica-tions should not blind the analyst to unifying elements. The general tendency of pacifist political philosophies moves in one direction, in

---

[93]Most Mennonites stand in the "non-resistant" individualistic pacifist stream of thought. Their theology is one which holds that society, and particularly the State, is essentially and irretrievably corrupt and that believers in non-violence should withdraw from it as much as possible, confining their social acts to works of personal mercy. See C. H. Smith, *The Story of the Mennonites* (Berne, Indiana: Mennonite Book Concern, 1941), and Don Smucker, "The Mennonite Stand," *Conscientious Objector,* February, 1943. See also footnote 20.

negative and positive senses alike. There are a large number of common arguments, particularly at the political level. And even where the divergence is so sharp that it is impossible to discern any common ground, it is often possible to examine the predominating thesis and then turn to the dissents.

Thus, on the theological level, Hindu and Christian pacifism seem far apart at points. But a close examination will disprove this appearance. For Hindu doctrine feels constrained, in the political area at least, to modify its strict dualism by accepting as inevitable a large element of the "material" and admitting the impossibility of disassociating "spirit" from "body"; while Christian pacifism, refusing to admit the essentially evil character of the "material," is yet led to agree that sensual corruption as well as "pride of spirit" is a factor in the problem of violence. The "body-force" which Hindu pacifism attempts to repudiate completely in its dualistic presuppositions is accepted over a certain area in its ethics and politics; while Christian distrust of any sharp dichotomy between body and spirit does not lead it to deny that there is an ethical distinction between types of pressure associated with what Gandhi calls "body force" and methods of coercion termed "soul force." In the political area, the problem for both Hindu and Christian pacifism thus becomes one of allocating to both "body force" and "soul force" their proper spheres of action.

Again, while most secular pacifism is utilitarian or pragmatic in approach, and religious pacifism has non-pragmatic elements, this difference should not blind one to their essential likenesses on the social level. Some religious pacifist doctrines do, indeed, deny that non-violence has anything to do with success in this world, but most affirm that the pragmatic criterion is entirely legitimate when used as an element in the validation of a tentative religious insight.

Similar observations could be made in relation to the controversy between those who advocate non-resistance and those who see the pacifist ethic fructifying in non-violent resistance. While differences between the two interpretations should not be minimized, there is at least one unifying factor: both non-resistance and non-violent resistance deny the ethical right of any State to claim complete and unquestioning obedience. When the non-resistant refuses to be conscripted for war service, he is, in the very act of refusing to fight the "enemy," resisting the demands of the State that he do so. At this point, at least, he is not acquiescing, any more than the non-violent resister. And on this common ground, if on no other, the two approaches—one ostensibly an extreme attempt to renounce power of all kinds, and the other an effort to gain power by methods which will more nearly frustrate the will to power—can unite.[94] Some renunciation of "this world" is implicit in both doctrines. But at the same time, neither view can avoid the problem of power and its use—the non-violent resistant not attempting to do so; the non-resistant forced by the exigencies of life in society to concede the inevitability of power in the very act of choosing to resist the State rather than the State's "enemy." For even individual disobedience of political authority is a very real act of power; and unless the non-resistant is to become an exponent of passive obedience to all the commands of all those who assume authority over him, he must join the non-violent resister in acts of resistance.

More specifically, the main currents of modern pacifist thought which have been examined in this essay hold five propositions in common. A critical examination of each will reveal most clearly both the strength and weakness of pacifism considered as a political theory. The tenets are:

A.

TENET ONE: Violence Hinders the Achievement of a Democratic and Peaceful Order

Violence—including war, violent revolt, verbal misrepresentation, and much of the characteristic activity of the modern State— can never hasten, but only hinder, the achievement of a democratic and peaceful order. This principle is seen to be valid regardless of the fact that violence may be administered by those who look forward to a coercionless order. It is applicable in all instances and is not a matter of mere expediency. In larger perspective, violence is seen to inhere in any political system or action which hinders the free expression of divergent views of truth. Implicit in this conception, in turn, is the idea that a society which, either because of its defective organization or by reason of the ideologies of its rulers, fails to make possible a free and unhampered expression of clashing views of truth is a society reposing on violence. Reversing the statement, the existence of violence in its obvious political expressions—as in war and State propaganda— is evidence that the rulers of that society either fear the truth or believe that they have complete knowledge and therefore possess the ethical right to impose their views on others.

---

[94]As the non-resistant Mennonites have united with non-violent resistance groups to form the National Service Board for Religious Objectors.

The pacifist is contending that violence is power which can never be controlled and which always "corrupts," not only its user but also the end for which it was ostensibly used. A society in which violence is utilized to maintain public authority, whether in the form of war, or suppression of "revolt" or the habitual violence of a ruling caste against its "subjects," can never consider the public welfare, if only because the means which constitute its weapons swallow up the end to be attained. The means cannot be isolated from the end to be achieved. They *determine* the end. Spanish progress was impeded not only by the violence of General Franco and the Nazis, but also by that of Largo Caballero and the Stalinite communists.[95]

This view has been criticized on two grounds. In the first place, it is said to lack validation in history. History clearly demonstrates, so the critics assert, that violence has played a prominent role in achieving ends which both pacifist and non-pacifist would agree were desirable. In support of this argument, a leading British critic of the pacifist thesis instances the defeat of the Persians by the ancient Greeks; the battle of Tours in which the Mohammedans were struck down by the French; the repulsion of the Turkish Sultan before Vienna in 1529 and in 1683; the expulsion of the Spaniards by the rising Dutch Republic; the English Civil Wars which "preserved British parliamentary liberties"; the American War of Independence ("for a just cause" and "entirely successful"); the American Civil War—clearly seen "to have been both necessary and right"; and the resistance offered by the Soviet Union to Allied invasions and White insurrections. Without the violent resistance of those who were ultimately victorious in these conflicts, the progress of the world toward a free and equal society would have been irretrievably injured. In no instance, moreover, did the victorious party take on the political character of its opponent, as pacifist arguments like to maintain.[96]

It is not within the scope of this essay to examine in detail the relation of violence to history and to what is called "progress." Questions of this type have been dealt with elsewhere.[97] Whether specific wars or particular military victories have been "good" or "bad" for

---

[95]DeLigt, 189 ff.

[96]Lewis, *The Case Against Pacifism*, 139-141.

[97]See, for example, Walter Bagehot, *Physics and Politics* (New York: Appleton, 1898); Jacques Novicow, *War and Its Alleged Benefits* (New York: Henry Holt, 1911); P. Chalmers Mitchell, *Evolution and War* (London: John Murray, 1915); G. F. Nicolai, *The Biology of War* (New York: Century, 1918); and Pitirim Sorokin, *Contemporary Sociological Theories* (New York: Harper, 1928).

the human race as a whole will probably continue to be a subject for endless debate. Violence, both pacifist and non-pacifist would probably agree, has, in the past, always tended to brutalize. On the other hand, it can be argued that war has to some extent been associated with "progress" in that violent conflicts have broken up what Walter Bagehot called old "cakes of custom" and liberated individuals from subservience to the group mind, thus bringing the critical faculty into play.[98] One can even accept Lewis' statement that in the conflicts he mentions it was better for the world that victory was vouchsafed to those who actually won rather than to their opponents. There is no small measure of support for the view that historically violence has served to impede spiritual and artistic development. Its brutalizing effects in the past have been admitted by the critics of pacifism. It may have served to destroy rigid social systems and thus to promote individual consciousness. Yet its service in this latter case was always largely negatived in that the habit of violence itelf was more firmly established than ever and probably tended to create further individual subordinations to the group.

Moreover, in relation to Lewis' specific instances, while it would be entirely legitimate to maintain that, within the framework of power politics, a "victory" by the Franks at Tours was relatively better than a triumph by sons of the Prophet, yet at the same time, and without any inconsistency, the pacifist may well attack the very citadel of power politics itself, and, from a position outside the presuppositions of that system, deny that the outcome at Tours was "good" for the world. This is certainly what the political doctrine of pacifism maintains.[99]

Lewis quite rightly criticizes some pacifist statements that "war and violence have never accomplished anything in history." Historically, war and violence have contributed to the accomplishment of many things, some of them incidentally good. That, any sound pacifist philosophy of history will have to admit. But the good that was pro-

---

[98]Such is the contention, for example, of Frederick J. Teggart; see his *Theory and Processes of History* (Berkeley: University of California Press, 1941), 271-72; 291-92.

[99]The "rightness" or "wrongness" of any particular "victory" in history is itself a matter for endless debate. While most "Christian" commentators seem to take it for granted, for example, that it was desirable for the Christians to oppose by violence and defeat the Moslems at Tours, equally competent Moslem observers argue the contrary. See, to take one instance, Ameer Ali, *A Short History of the Saracens* (London: 1899), 111, where the author comments on the fact that because the Moslems were not victorious at Tours, Europe had to endure eight hundred years of barbarism!

The whole point is that the "rightness" of the cause, if existing at all, tends to be wiped out by the violent method employed.

duced always flourished in a scheme of things which made it subordinate to a higher end—namely, power. The will to power is always engendered by war, and all non-power values become its ministers. Nor does Mr. Lewis' observation answer the question whether this "good" might not otherwise have been better achieved.

Moreover, the thrust of all modern politics, the pacifist contends, is in the direction of making violence the ethical norm of existence. Always in past history power has tended to be the end, but there have been areas in which one might escape the ubiquity of violence. In the twentieth century, on the other hand, those areas are rapidly closing because of a centralized economic order and a politics associated with it.

This is the appropriate place to examine the general basis for the pacifist discussion of ends and means, for it is here that the whole framework of the argument focuses. This fact is recognized by the critics, and of the critics Max Lerner has been one of the most persistent. He denies that all means must necessarily be either "good" or "bad" ethically. Some means, he maintains, may be "ethically neutral" —that is, they may be used for either "good" or "bad" ends. There is nothing in their nature which necessarily tends to corrupt either their manipulators or the ends for which they are being manipulated. He instances bombing planes and time-table wars and the systematic use of propaganda and espionage as examples of ethically neutral means;[100] and he contrasts these means with those which, like political terrorism and the one-party system, are ethically reprehensible. "The plane," Lerner writes, "for all its connotations of death, is ethically neutral. In the service of those who are seeking the triumph of totalitarian ideals, it takes on the over-tones of totalitarian ethics. In the service of democratic defense, it takes on democratic overtones."[101]

Lerner's distinction would seem to be of very doubtful validity. It is somewhat forced, and from the context in which it occurs it is not too difficult to believe that Lerner himself remains uncertain about its validity. No doubt a bombing plane does not have to be used to bomb—it can carry freight or passengers on a pleasure cruise. No doubt a planned time-table war does not have to be waged—it may remain in the blue-print stage, and the paper upon which the plans are sketched may be used for the packing of chinaware. No doubt, also, systematic propaganda and espionage may continue in the phase

[100]Max Lerner, *Ideas for the Ice Age* (New York: Viking, 1941), 40.
[101]*Ibid.*, 41.

of adumbration. In this way, all these contrivances may, perhaps, be termed "ethically neutral." But once bombs are falling, or a time-table war is being waged, or the usual distortions of truth are proceeding from government propaganda ministries, men are being blown to bits, community is being disrupted, and havoc is made of intellectual honesty. The bombing plane ceases to be a bombing plane if no longer used for bombing. The same is true of time-table wars and espionage.

By what legerdemain, moreover, can these acts be distinguished ethically from the use of terrorism or the one party system? The pacifist would appear to be on solid ground when he argues that no real differentiation is possible. No espionage system can function without organized deception, which is of the essence of violence. To discern an ethical distinction between planned deceit, moreover, and a one-party system, would appear to be a curious example of analysis. Implicit in the former is always the latter. The purpose of organized deception is quite obviously to prevent open and frank discussion of differences and to force the will of the deceiver upon the deceived. A one-party political system is simply the extension of this principle: politics become a matter of the party holding a political monopoly manipulating opinion and data in such a way as to prevent any embarrassing challenge of its position. Power considered as an end cannot afford the luxury of genuine criticism; and to prevent any such disturbance, it utilizes the only appropriate means, violence, to sustain itself. That violence may be either physical or intellectual; and of the latter, deception is certainly a prime example.

But even if this refutation of Lerner's contentions be valid, it does not in itself answer another major objection to the pacifist thesis. When Aldous Huxley maintains in the course of his argument that "the end cannot justify the means, for the simple and obvious reason that the means employed determine the nature of the ends produced,"[102] he subjects himself to several critics, of whom Lerner is again one. "If the end does not justify the means," Lerner demands, "then what does?"[103] It is a legitimate question and one about which the pacifist argument has been all too ambiguous. A not infrequent answer is to contrast the principle "the end justifies the means" with the dictum "the means determine the ends." The assumption often seems to be that one principle is the antithesis of the other. On close examination, however, no such contradiction can be seen to exist. The

[102]*Ends and Means,* 10.
[103]Lerner, 37.

end justifies the means only if and when the end is actually achieved—
then, indeed, the means selected can receive approval. But a projected
end, as contrasted with one achieved, can never "justify" any and all
means. The very statement of an end automatically excludes certain
types of means.[104]

It would be more nearly correct to say that a projected end dictates its own means just as our desire to see a forest of oak trees flourish
on what is now bare earth dictates that we plant acorns and only
acorns. The acorn is not the oak nor the oak the acorn. But the oak
is embryonic in the acorn; and, with proper conditions, the acorn will
always become an oak and never a beech or pine. In politics, of course,
the problem is extremely complex, due to the multiplicity of factors
involved. But the principle would seem to be the same.

Nor are the objections of K. S. Shelvankar, who argues the question from the viewpoint of the materialist dialectic, more solidly based.
Pacifists argue, he contends, that the good society can be achieved only
by the devoted efforts of what Huxley calls "non-attached" individuals
—that is, pacifists. But, he says, the good society itself is defined by
pacifists as a community of "non-attached" individuals. Thus, Shelvankar concludes, pacifism is involved in a constant tautology; "ends,
means, and starting-points are all the same—only more so."[105] The
ideal is a community of independent, equal, and non-attached men.
It can come about only through the efforts of independent, equal, and
non-attached men, in accordance with the pacifist ends-means postulate. Yet how can the independent, equal, and non-attached men arise,
given the same postulate, in a society composed of subservient, unequal,

---

[104]"Thus an end entirely just, holy, and pure," observes the Jesuit Father Rickaby,
"purifies and sanctifies the means, not formally, by investing with a character
of justice means in themselves unjust, for that is impossible—the leopard cannot change his spots—but by way of elimination, removing unjust means as in-
eligible to my purpose, and leaving me only those means to choose from which
are in themselves just." Joseph Rickaby, S. J., *Moral Philosophy* (New York:
Longmans, Green, 1908), 37.

See also Jacques Maritain, "On the Purification of Means," in *Freedom in
the Modern World* (London: Sheed and Ward, 1935), 139-192, for an excellent discussion of the whole problem from the viewpoint of Christian humanism.

Perhaps the best documentation for the pacifist case is to be found in
Gerald Brenan, *The Spanish Labyrinth* (New York: Macmillan, 1943). This
study is a detailed analysis of the social and political background of the Spanish
Civil War; and the theme most recurrent is one of political parties, which,
with ideals of a non-exploitative order, were yet eager to use violence to bring
that order about. "The troubles of Spain," Brenan observes succinctly, "come
from the belief, shared by almost every element in the country, in violent
remedies." 148.

[105]K. S. Shelvankar, *Ends Are Means* (London: Lindsay Drummond, 1938), 44.

and attached human beings? This seems to be the burden of Shelvankar's objection.

This criticism misreads the pacifist argument. It fails to consider the idea of growth. A careful perusal of the pacifist case does not disclose any implication that a given situation can only perpetuate itself. On the contrary, pacifism adopts a Socratic teleology—all things strive to attain their true nature, which is only incipient at any given moment in history. "Man" is only incipient in the child of eight and "oak tree" in the acorn but newly planted. But the character of the incipient form will provide the framework of the mature structure. The acorn does not lie in the ground only to demonstrate that it is itself, as Shelvankar implies the pacifists would argue, but rather to exhibit the oak within. The non-attached, non-violent men of a pacifist social philosophy do not themselves constitute the good society, but rather that embryo which embraces within itself the potentiality of the good society. But politics are always mixed, and in any one historical situation the potentialities for both a society of "attached" individuals and one of "non-attached" men exist side by side. At no given moment in time are the possibilities wholly on the side of "attachment" or "non-attachment." Even in a war situation, in which the lopsidedness becomes greatest, there are saving remnants of "non-attachment" from which any future good society will have to be born. It is this saving remnant which the pacifist desires to encourage, while pointing out in the meantime the tendency in modern politics for the "attached" side to assume hegemony.

At another point Shelvankar seems to discern this line of argument, for he criticizes Huxley vigorously for what he sees as the latter's sharp dualism between good and evil. He contends that Huxley's analysis is defective, since he fails to account for the presence of evil.[106] Shelvankar suggests that the only answer within the framework of the pacifist argument is some theological dogma of Original Sin and the Fall of Man. He maintains, however, that Huxley is not explicit here, pretending to have evolved a "modern" political philosophy, while in reality operating within the traditional Christian analysis. Shelvankar is essentially correct in this latter view. Huxley does carry on his analysis within the traditional theological assumptions regarding the nature and destiny of man—although at times he seems to deny it—and in this his ideas fall within the main stream of many philosophies of non-violence. Man, for not a few pacifists, symbolically became

---

[106]Shelvankar, 47.

separated from God through the Fall. His search for goodness, and hence God, has since been wholly a quest for means, for in terms of the ultimate and final end, all political "ends" are mediate—are themselves only means. The power of evil is constantly attempting to erect means into the ultimate end—to make gods of human institutions. But it is never wholly successful in this endeavor, for making ends of human institutions always leads to the destruction of the power which they possess, the nominal directors of those institutions being corrupted by the very gods they have exalted.

Man, moreover, according to this particular interpretation of pacifist theory, has not fallen so low as to be entirely determined in his actions by evil. There is an autonomy, a "free will," which enables him to discover the method whereby he can free himself from the power of evil. To the pacifist this method is non-violence. Through its development in all areas of life, the non-attached and devoted individuals met with in pacifist literature will, because of their understanding of the character of power, be able to break through the vicious circle of evil in which the world is engulfed. They possess the lever by which the whole can be moved.

In some such way, the Huxleyan pacifist would dispose of Shelvankar's demand that the presence of evil must be accounted for. Whatever the ultimate "origin" of evil, such a pacifist frankly admits its presence in human life and endeavors to show how its operations might be checked. He sees evil as that ever-present force which attempts to induce men to consider their means as an end in themselves, thus transforming the relative into the absolute. In other words, to the Huxleyan, evil is the tendency to establish one particular system of human judgments as so final that those who accept that system may legitimately attack the supporters of other systems, in a spirit of intolerance, and even by means of violence.

B.

TENET TWO: Modern States Are Built on Violence and Only Revolution Can Effect A Pacifist Order

Any sober analysis of modern political and economic history would seem to corroborate a second commonly held assertion of pacifist doctrine: that all modern states are built upon a large substratum of violence and that only a political and economic revolution can effect a pacifist world-order. The whole literature of Marxian speculation also is an assertion of the validity of this contention. What Barthelemy de Ligt called the "horizontal violence" of international war and the "vertical violence" implicit in, modern class structure are phenomena so obvious as scarcely to require comment. Whether the State be looked upon as dominated by capitalists or by a rising class of bureaucrats or "managers," as Burnham[107] would have it, the use of naked bayonets or officially sponsored verbal manipulations is indispensable to any minority domination. That the degree to which this statement is applicable varies from State to State doe$ not alter its fundamental conformity to fact. The ultilization of violence may be more overt in States like Germany and Japan than in political structures like those of Great Britain and the United States, where economic exigencies have thus far not called for its more brutal manifestations But that the modern State *per se*, however the expression may vary in particular instances, is suffused with violence, is surely difficult to deny. Even so-called democratic States exhibit increasingly what Michels once so aptly termed "the iron law of oligarchy"[108]—the tendency in an ostensibly democratic society for the forms of democracy alone to remain, the substance of power shifting to small groups of self-designing men whose end is power. The movement of history seems to be inevitably in that direction, unless checked by an almost super-human capacity for resistance and a widespread knowledge of the structure and dynamics of society.

To a degree never surpassed in any former age the State today tends to approach St. Augustine's conception of a commonwealth without justice. Such a "State," the bishop of Hippo avowed, more nearly resembled a robber band than an ordered polity.[109] The modern State, on the whole, does more to promote disorder than to destroy it, any order it achieves ministering strictly to the disorder characteristic of war. Internally, it elicits obedience often by overt, more often by covert, violence; and when its subjects become restive despite its propaganda ministries, economic doles, private police systems, industrial use of tear gas, and elaborate bureaucracies, it opens up an avenue for human energy externally by engaging in war. In either case its essential aim is to destroy as much as necessary for retention of power by its rulers and to cloak its motives in as much plausible deception

---

[107] James Burnham, *The Managerial Revolution* (New York: John Day, 1941).

[108] Robert Michels, *Political Parties* (New York: Hearst's International Library, 1916).

[109] *The City of God,* translated by John Healy, 3 volumes (London: J. M. Dent, 1903), Bk. XV., Ch. 20 and 21.

as possible. Within what other framework is it possible to explain the Second World War? Here the pacifist argument would appear to be buttressed by an amazing amount of evidence.

C.
TENET THREE: This Revolution Must Develop and Employ a Technique Embodying a Non-Violent Ethic

There is a powerful argument to be made out, then, for the third proposition common to the most articulate stream of twentieth-century pacifist thought. That is a plea for a technique of revolution which will conform and conduce to the end of a non-violent political order. Pacifism discovers the answer to this problem in the conscious infusion of politics with a non-violent ethic. Specifically, it asks for the adoption of a technique modeled on that of modern Hindu pacifism. A highly disciplined body of relatively ascetic individuals, inured to suffering and ready to undergo death or imprisonment in the process of civil disobedience as non-cooperators—such is the picture presented.

The critics of pacifism have to a considerable degree centered their attention on this aspect of the pacifist thesis. Their attack alleges, in the first place, that pacifist literature offers no reliable criterion for distinguishing between violent and non-violent action. Lewis, for example, criticizes De Ligt by remarking that "His constructive proposals do not go beyond a general strike, which seems inconsistant with his rejection of economic sanctions against aggressor nations on the ground that this would deprive non-combatants of food."[110] Is a boycott of the cloth manufactured by men who rule a State by violence, itself an act of violence against those wage-earners who are deprived of their livelihood? In the case of a general strike, is provision to be made for a feeding of those who are deprived of their regular supplies?[111] Voluntary acceptance of hardship is well and good, but, in the interests of a presumably higher political ethic, what is the ethical status of an act of non-violent resistance which results in hardship on those who belong neither to the ruling class nor to the group of resisters?

[110]Lewis, 95.
[111]Jack London in his essay "The Dream of Debs" portrays with remarkable vividness problems such as this. Here the general strike results in wholesale starvation for members of the ruling class. Lack of food reduces economic and political oligarchs alike to a state of primitive savagery. London, *Essays of Revolt* (New York: Vanguard, 1928), 33-34. Unfortunately, while London raises the issues, at least implicitly, he does not offer a solution. See also his *The Iron Heel* (New York: The Daily Worker, 1934).

To these questions the answers of most pacifist thinkers are not satisfactory. For many, the queries do not seem to have arisen in serious form. The distinction between violence and non-violence is probably most carefully considered by Cadoux,[112] but even his answers leave much to be desired. Gandhi himself is not at all clear as to his answer, although he does at least see the problem. The critics are hypercritical at times, of course—apparently failing to see that for many purposes and at many points the distinction is quite obvious. Nevertheless, this remains perhaps the weakest link in the whole pacifist chain.

The critics of pacifism not only deny that it has formulated an adequate basis for distinguishing between violence and non-violence, but go further and maintain that any such distinction is impossible on the level of political action. To be effective, they continue, all supposedly "non-violent" action must be coercive, and hence violent. Thus Lewis[113] holds that strikes and refusals to pay taxes cannot be differentiated in quality from war or violent revolt. Even saintliness constitutes "moral coercion," and hence violence. If, then, violence is evil and can lead only to evil ends, the same must be true of all schemes for non-violent resistance.

On first consideration, Lewis' theory seems plausible. But a more careful examination will make it difficult to accept. To make all forms of coercion tantamount in nature to violence seems to be a rather arbitrary erasure of very real distinctions. Without going into the vexing philosophical problem as to whether truth, once seen, is always embraced, there is certainly a basis for maintaining that truth itself is coercive, as Cadoux emphasizes. Socrates drinking the hemlock and Jesus on the cross were highly coercive in compelling men, against what was formerly their "better judgment," to act in certain ways.[114] While other factors were no doubt involved, the cruel sufferings accepted by the early Quakers played a large part in securing what little religious toleration there is in the modern State. Surely "coercion" of this type cannot be equated with the deliberate manipulations of words and symbols and the outright physical violence characteristic of most politics. That the coercion of a Nehru in prison for civil disobedience or the power wielded by an unarmed Las Casas in the Central Ameri-

---

[112]C. J. Cadoux *Christian Pacifism Re-Examined,* 1-45.

[113]Lewis, 110.

[114]Bertrand Russell: "The Great War, and its aftermath of dictatorships, has caused many to underestimate all forms of power except military and governmental force. This is a short-sighted and unhistorical view. If I had to select four men who have had more power than any others, I should mention Buddha and Christ, Pythagoras and Galileo." *Power* (New York: Norton, 1938).

can jungles are ethically indistinguishable from the violence of ma-
chine-guns and bayonets is a doctrine pernicious in the extreme and
one impossible to accept.

In sooth, if all pressure (what Lewis would call "coercion") were
to be eschewed—that of voluntarily accepted suffering as well as what
Cadoux calls "injurious coercion"—there would seem to be but little
hope of ever attaining a "moral" politics. For in such an event, those
who disavowed power altogether—granting for the moment the possibility of such action—would be clearly at the disposal of men who
had no qualms regarding the utilization of all types of pressure.
"Morality" then would be meaningless for it would be defined as that
type of action, or perhaps inaction, which allowed the "immoral" to
rule. However, the answer to the problem of politics cannot be found
in any philosophy of passive obedience and the attempted renunciation of power—first, because any approximation to that ideal would
be to give up hope for a moralization of politics, and for the minimiza-
tion of power as an end; and second, because power can never be completely renounced. On the other hand, the solution cannot be discovered in any system which makes no distinctions between types of
pressure and considers all species equally legitimate. The answer must
be discerned in a philosophy which, on the one hand, admits the inevitability and necessity of power, and yet, on the other, holds that a
nice discrimination between types of power is necessary if power itself
is not to become the end. This approach has been that of modern pacifism, and it makes out a powerful argument for its case.

There is a second major criticism of non-violent resistance which
merits at least passing notice. It has to do with the alleged paucity of
historical examples demonstrating the efficacy of non-violent action. In
reply, the pacifist statement points out that history affords more examples than is generally recognized. The separation of Norway from
Sweden; the defeat of the abortive Kapp putsch of 1920; the movement which induced the French to evacuate the Ruhr region; and the
two great non-cooperation campaigns of Gandhi in India;—all these
largely non-violent political endeavors were at least partially successful.[115] While in many of them it could hardly be claimed that the

---

[115]Clarence M. Case, *Non-Violent Coercion: A Study in Methods of Social Pressure*
(New York: Century, 1923); Gregg, *The Power of Non-Violence;* and
DeLigt, are replete with examples. What, indeed, was the great withdrawal of
the plebs in ancient Rome—so fraught with consequences for the Roman Constitution—but an example of non-violent resistance? The forthcoming Pacifist
Research Bureau publication, *An Introduction to Non-Violence,* analyzes other
examples to be found in history.

campaign of non-violence was the only factor involved, yet it would be equally false to maintain that it was not partially responsible.

Two decades ago, indeed, a sociological examination of the question seemed to show vast possibilities. Professor Case not only instanced countless historical examples of the utilization of non-violence in both private and public affairs, but defended it theoretically. It is true that it is subject, he continues, to the danger of degenerating into violence, on the one hand, or of ebbing away into apathy, on the other.[116] But what political technique, one might well ask, is not subject to perils equally great? Frustration of ends is ubiquitous in political life.

D.

TENET FOUR: Decentralization in Politics and in the Economic Order is Sought

Another element common to all pacifist political thought is its emphasis on decentralization in politics and the economic order. Accompanying this tendency is a strong distrust of industrialism and a parallel belief in a semi-agrarian society. Gandhi, as our analysis of Hindu pacifism showed, is strongly in favor of a large degree of economic self-sufficiency and local autonomy for all political entities—not primarily, as has been so frequently asserted, because he is a political and economic reactionary (however "conservative" his politics may be),[117] but rather because he sees in centralization and extreme industrialization great impediments to a non-violent order. Complex organization loses sight of the individual and, because it is intricate, necessitates a large number of experts, who in the end become a ruling class using violence and terrorism to sustain their power. Huxley reinforces this argument by emphasizing the dangers of large-scale reform, which likewise plays always into the hands of the violent unless rigorously checked by a group embracing a definitive philosophy of non-violence.

---

[116]Case, 406-7.

[117]Lewis, among others, makes this charge. It is true that Gandhi has emphasized the importance of a return to a pre-industrial condition, but so, after all, did William Morris, and few would hurl "reactionary" against him. When the term is used in reference to Gandhi, it is usually with the implication that he desires to sustain an existing economic oligarchy. But such is far from true. This is not said by way of defending Gandhi's economic ideas as a body— many of them are curiously naive and some of them, from my point of view, positively dangerous—but rather in order to correct certain misconceptions about his general approach.

"Organization *per se*," remarks Evan Thomas, a leading American pacifist, "seeks short cuts and immediate results. Therefore, it demands authoritative leadership and uniformity of action. Because it recognizes success only in terms of power it imposes its will by coercion and organized violence. Once successful, it invariably seeks to become an end in itself."[118] The problem for him is how to prevent organization from becoming an end. Decentralization and a partial return to an agrarian mode of life are methods for reducing the power of organization, the menace of centralized control, which the pacifist sees associated, both as cause and effect, with violence in the modern world. Democracy, in this view, is the logical prelude to a kind of anarchy. It is, as Evan Thomas again points out, "a compromise which seeks to avoid the absolutism of organization. Its goal is not government as an end in itself but the withering away of the state through voluntary cooperation."[119]

This aspect of the political theory of pacifism is an endeavor to wrestle with one of the most persistent of the problems of politics—how to order political life in such a way as to minimize the apparently inevitable tendency for oligarchies to control societies, whatever the political form might be. In another connection, this essay has already emphasized the issues connected with this phenomenon—but they bear re-emphasis. Pareto,[120] Mosca,[121] Michels,[122] and the Marxists have shown that without much doubt the thrust of politics is always to throw up a ruling class, which, consolidating and centralizing its power, corrupts those who, in the name of popular control, seek to overthrow it. Always there is the tendency for the subjects to assume the vices of their rulers, as well as to aspire after their governors' wealth, power, and privileges. Great political parties, classes which have tasted, or are about to taste, power "find it very difficult to tolerate the utterances of inconvenient truths," remarks Michels.[123] Political theorists of pacifism understand these phenomena, at least implicitly, and their whole analysis of bureaucracy and centralism in the modern State reflects that understanding.

---

[118]Evan Thomas, *The Positive Faith of Pacifism* (New York: War Resisters League, 1942), 6.

[119]*Ibid.*, 8.

[120]Vilfredo Pareto, *The Mind and Society*, 4 volumes (New York: Harcourt Brace, 1935).

[121]Gaetano Mosca, *The Ruling Class* (New York: McGraw-Hill, 1939).

[122]*Political Parties.*

[123]*Ibid.*, 269.

Closely allied to the general pacifist criticism of life and politics is its attack on urban civilization and the values which that civilization presumably exalts. This attack is epitomized in a remark of Arthur Sheehan. "It is one of the startling facts of a city's idea of order," he writes, "that it places . . . policemen at the doors of banks to protect them from the people when a right order should have the policemen at the doors of poor persons to protect them from the banks."[124] Violence is seen to inhere in the very essence of urbanism; for city life breaks down the family, destroys the intimacy of the home, subjects political life to domination by huge boss-dominated machines, becomes part of the pattern of centralized control, and, in the end, because the basis of free consent is destroyed, makes force and violence inevitable.

But this emphasis on decentralization and agrarianism should be looked upon as a current in the much larger stream of modern political thought which has attacked the whole basis of the twentieth-century State. There has arisen already a considerable literature outlining this assault and the pacifist analysis constitutes only one segment of the whole.[125] In a broader sense, modern conceptions of decentralization and agrarianism stand in an historic tradition represented in British political thought by Sir Thomas More, in French by the early Rousseau, and in American by Jefferson and his followers. With Spengler in the twentieth century, they see the spread of a "megalopolitan" civilization as a sharp indication of decadence, and the extension of centralization as the precursor of ruin. With Austin Tappan Wright, whose huge nostalgic novel of an agrarian utopia[126] represents the same current of political thought, they would question the modern world's tendency to identify speed and complicated machinery with progress.[127]

---

[124]*The Catholic Worker*, January, 1943, 8.

[125]To refer to the whole mass of decentralist and agrarian literature would obviously be beyond the legitimate scope of a short footnote. However, the following might well be mentioned as illustrations: Ralph Borsodi, *This Ugly Civilization* (New York: Harper, 1929) and *Flight from the City* (New York: Harper, 1933); W. J. Marx, *Mechanization and Culture* (St. Louis: Herder, 1942); Arthur E. Morgan, *The Small Community, Foundation of Democratic Life* (New York: Harper, 1943); and Willis J. Nutting, "On Freedom and Reform: Some Agrarian Views," *The Review of Politics*, IV, October 1942.

[126]*Islandia* (New York: Farrar and Rinehart, 1942).

[127]"Speed," one of Wright's heroes is made to ask, "is that progress? Anyway, why progress? Why not enjoy what one has? Men have never exhausted present pleasures. . . . Doesn't progress create the very situation it seeks to cure— always changing the social adjustment so that someone is squeezed out?" *Ibid.*, 76.

What can be said of such an ideal, particularly as it is related to pacifist conceptions? The answer will be found in a somewhat qualified approval. Undoubtedly the fetishes of bigness, of universal planning and centralized organization, have blinded many social reformers to the very real dangers inherent in such methods. The benefits which might be reaped from large-scale organization should not shut our eyes to the probability that the whole structure will become corrupt and lead to tyranny. The more complicated the political and economic organization, the more centralized the polity, the less difficult it is for dictatorship and rule by force to fasten themselves upon a whole society, no areas remaining free from their violent impact.

Nor is it sufficient to reply that "democratic control" will ensure responsibility and hence an avoidance of tyranny. What became of the "democratic controls" existent over a large part of Western society at the beginning of the twentieth century? Everywhere they are being subjected, with scarcely a murmur, to domination by autocrats or near-autocrats; and if it be replied that they were insufficient because of deficiency in organization or because they were not applied to all areas of life, both of which may be true, there still remains the question as to whether all organs for democratic supervision, in a highly centralized and complex society, must not give way, in the absence of some such scheme as that proposed by pacifist decentralists, to tyrannical and violent management.

But pacifist thought at this point contributes a note of its own, which any adequate criticism of its doctrine must appreciate. Being distrustful of all organization, it combines with its plea for decentralization and simplicity the proposal for a systematic education in non-violence and in all that non-violence implies politically. It sees, as so much modern political speculation has not, that while the system may and does manipulate the individual, no genuine revolution is possible in the absence of regenerated individuals.

But although it is thus true that pacifist theory in its decentralist and agrarian phases contributes not a little to a well-rounded criticism of life and politics in the twentieth century, there are undoubtedly certain dangers in its emphases. The first is that it will tend to over-idealize rural life and forget that for the most part an agrarian existence has in the past been considered intolerable by vast multitudes of human beings. And justifiably so. To some, the reek of manure, days of grinding toil, and the sheer boredom involved in much rural living, are far from conducive to the development of those qualities of mind and heart which pacifist doctrine exalts. No wonder many of the most intelligent have sought refuge in the over-crowded cities and chained themselves to machines in order to escape the monotony of farm life. It is true that technological developments promise to make an agrarian existence far more preferable. But technology is the very phenomenon against which pacifist agrarians so often protest.

Then, again, greater autonomy for small communities and regions can be grossly exaggerated. The pacifist, whether anarchist or non-anarchist, is right in protesting against the swallowing up of the individual personality by the Leviathan State. His is a valid criticism, both implicit and explicit, of what Hilaire Belloc, in the opening years of the twentieth century, called the "servile State"—one where the individual increasingly becomes a slave dependent upon the State for his very existence, whether he be a recipient of the State's doles, or takes the State's old age pensions and "unemployment insurance," or simply becomes one more member of an ubiquitous State bureaucracy which battens upon the land.[128] Such a State can govern only by chicane, force, and violence. Quite often the pacifist does not see, however, that the very evils which he discerns in the modern State because of its centralization and emphasis on technology would arise were the contrary principles, decentralization and agrarianism, pushed too far. A world in which the binding tie of political cohesion is practically severed would be a poor setting for social harmony and non-violence. Yet that is exactly where the argument of anarchist, and even of some non-anarchist, pacifism, ultimately would lead us.

A balanced view of the problem of violence would seem to warn us against both the Scylla of extreme centralization and industrialization and the Charybdis of extreme social and political decentralism and agrarianism. The first course would separate most men from the primary means of subsistence, enhance their dependence upon central political authority, and hence minimize chances of effective resistance to any tyranny which might gain control of the political machinery. The second course, if pushed to extremities, would tend to eliminate the principle of order and planning altogether, and in so doing give birth to a violence of chaos as destructive as the violence of centralization. It would be the story of fourteenth and fifteenth century Italian City-States repeated. It is the situation of the twentieth-century inter-

[128]Hilaire Belloc, *The Servile State* (London: T. N. Foulis, 1912).

national order, a fact well recognized in pacifist writings.[129] From one point of view, indeed, twentieth-century politics may be looked upon as an interacting of both first and second courses—the first reflected in the internal structure of the national State, while the latter is manifest in its external relations. The violence inherent in each principle stimulates the other so that the effect is cumulative. The tendency toward internal oligarchy in all areas of life is reflected most dramatically in that oligarchy's manipulation of its subjects for purposes of external war; and the power thus exemplified in war is utilized as a springboard for perpetuation of the oligarchy's power internally. Peace becomes the problem of so articulating centralizing and decentralizing elements as to allow neither to become the paramount principle. The answer in terms of statesmanship is not an easy one.

If pacifist speculation could elaborate a new synthesis of the two principles, in terms of political organization, it would be contributing vastly to the major problem of twentieth-century politics. Starting from its premise of non-violence, it could attempt to show in specific terms, how, given the facts of industrialism, the structure of the modern State, and the development of an ethos of violence, the political world might be transformed. It would show, perhaps in the form of a utopia, how the balance between central planning and local autonomy is to be maintained. It would re-emphasize what Alexander Hamilton and James Madison pointed out long ago—that political entities as such cannot by arms be effectively coerced.[130] It would attempt to blend the virtues of an agrarian existence with the very real contributions made by industrial technology. It would understand that a non-violent order can never be attained and preserved, in the last analysis, solely by a reconstructed social and political organization; that such an order, once approximated, is always made immediately subject to destruction once more through the eruption of violence. It would refine and develop its doctrine of non-violent resistance, so that the weapons of non-violence could be brought to bear effectively at any point in the social and political structure where the principles of a non-violent and non-parasitic social order were disregarded. A positive statement of this kind would go far in answering those who maintain that pacifist criticism of centralism and the industrial order is merely negative and unconstructive.

---

[129]See for a most recent expression Harrop Freeman (ed.), *Peace is the Victory,* (New York: Harper, 1944).

[130]An emphasis found in such works as Harrop Freeman and Theodore Paullin, *Coercion of States: In Federal Unions* (Philadelphia: Pacifist Research Bureau, 1943); Harrop Freeman, *Coercion of States: In International Organizations* (Philadelphia: Pacifist Research Bureau, 1944).

E.

TENET FIVE: The Ideology of Non-Violence Has a Direct Relevance to Politics

A fifth element underlying most modern pacifist philosophy, one implicit in the previous four, is the belief that an ideology of non-violence has a direct relevance to politics. Pacifism, its proponents aver, is not an endeavor to escape from a sordid world—a pietistic or neo-platonic aloofness from the power struggles of the human race. It believes, whether it be Hindu, Christian, revolutionary, anarchist, or non-anarchist, that its conception of the universe is pertinent to history here and now. It holds that, if acted upon, its philosophy of politics can constitute the basis of a framework within which power will more often, if not always, remain subordinate to non-power values. It argues that seemingly impossible ideals are the very ones which often, on closer inspection, reveal the only strategies of political action which can possibly be successful. It maintains, indeed, that the very width of the gulf subsisting between an "impossible" ideal and the practice of the world will not infrequently generate the power that will make ideal and practice more nearly coincident.

It is these fundamental assertions of twentieth-century pacifist doctrine which have constituted the target for its most redoubtable critic's charges. For Reinhold Niebuhr has maintained that pacifist political theory falls within the category of what he terms "ethical utopianism."[131] Perfectionist, it does not understand that an ethics such as it advocates cannot be operative in the political sphere. The political area is one in which power is the keynote. Here the love-ethic of the New Testament can find but little place; and to attempt to practice it, as pacifist political theory would have us do, can result only in giving power to autocrats and tyrants.[132] Niebuhr criticizes pacifist doctrine on the ground that it would attempt to emancipate reason from force. It assumes, he contends, the separation of spirit from body. It upholds the thesis that reason, freed, can act without the implementation of force. Failing in this endeavor, as he asserts it must fail, pacifism tends to be escapist and to renounce politics altogether. Indeed, Niebuhr apparently holds that there can be no middle ground between complete world-renunciation, on the one hand, and a willingness to see all types of power without distinction as ethically legitimate.

[131]*Reflections on the End of an Era* (New York: Scribner, 1934), 224.
[132]Niebuhr, *The Nature and Destiny of Man*, 2 volumes (New York: Scribner, 1941 and 1943), II, 88.

This latter element in his argument seems to be specifically confirmed in his analysis of the nature of God and of God's relation to history. The characteristic feature of the Divine is for him a "perfect coincidence of power and goodness." Divine love is selfless love. But no love on the plane of history can be selfless or disinterested. It must always be concerned about its own. If expressed at all, it expects reciprocation. Justice on the level of history is a nice balancing of mutually contradictory interests, and any love which was genuinely selfless would soon find itself extinguished in politics. Men, in other terms, who deliberately refuse to participate in the power struggles of history—who give and do not seek, and who offer no resistance—will find their lives ending "tragically."[133]

The non-resistance taught in the Sermon on the Mount is, therefore, the only way by which this conception of divine love can be realized in history—but the essence of history is negated if the ethics of non-resistance be exalted. The pacifist theory of politics, on the other hand, believes it is possible to embody the principles of non-resistance in history. In this, being necessarily and inevitably frustrated, it emerges with an entirely different principle: non-violent resistance. But this latter is not to be differentiated ethically from all politics—it, too, is power seeking and a repudiation of the Sermon on the Mount.

In its political theory, Niebuhr maintains, pacifism is afflicted with the same disease as Marxism, which he denounces as "too superficial to plumb the depths of evil illumined by a profound religion."[134] No perpetual guarantee of peace or justice in society is possible, because of the tendency to oligarchical control and because no self can be disinterested without surrendering its ability to live on the plane of history.[135] From this phenomenon proceed revolts and violence; and while a time of relative peace may some day be assured, always there will be "periods of decay and destruction, such as our own, in which it is necessary to risk the very destruction of civilization for the sake of preventing a tyrannical unification of western Christendom."[136] Force can be the only answer to those who would seek the reins of power for tyrannical purposes, although that force, as Niebuhr admits, may itself create greater destruction than the havoc wrought by tyrants.

---

[133]*Ibid.*, II, 72.
[134]*Reflections on the End of an Era*, 224.
[135]*Ibid.*, 246-47.
[136]Niebuhr, *Christianity and Power Politics* (New York: Scribner, 1940), 62.

Niebuhr's philosophy of history is not one, however, which repudiates the idea of progress. Discussing the problem within the
categories of Christian thought, he admits that progress in the direction of the Kingdom of God is possible. But he charges that pacifist
thought fails to see that at each new level of achievement, dire perils
of a new order occur. Pacifism, he maintains, is one of a number of
creeds which see evil being conquered progressively—without understanding that such conquests merely reveal in altered form the pre-
carious nature of all human justice. Any interpretation of the Kingdom of God which views it as a possibility within the domain of human
history is false. Pacifism, by implying that suffering love can conquer
the kingdoms of this world and create an equilibrium of power which
will make force no longer necessary, is thus engaging in a utopian
illusion which, if acted upon, would cause its proponents to fall a
complete prey to the sinful proclivities of human nature.[137]

No one can read even this brief account of Niebuhr's views and
fail to be impressed by the fact that he has here touched upon some of
the most glaring deficiencies of modern political thinking—pacifist
and non-pacifist. Events in the twentieth century should long ago have
caused us to question the nineteenth's widespread belief in the idea of
inevitable and continuous progress. Yet implicit in much twentieth-
century American, British, and French political thought, not to speak
of the broad stream of Marxist speculation, is still an underlying faith
in the old beliefs. After the First World War there was to have been
a new political order; after the Russian Revolution, many kindly
spirits and serious students of politics looked for the rapid germina-
tion of a coercionless and classless world; while following the Second
World War, which to some would seem merely an interlude in the
onrushing progress of mankind, certain men think they see emerging
a social and political order in which the tears of the present are forgotten in the approaching brotherhood of mankind.

Against all this shallow optimism Niebuhr points his acute criticism. History is not, he tells us, simply an express train of progress.
It is also tragedy in the old Greek sense of the term—a school which
compels men to choose between several courses of action, all of which

---

[137]This is the thesis of practically all of Niebuhr's writing since the publication, in
1932, of his *Moral Man and Immoral Society* (New York: Scribner). His
political doctrines cannot be understood unless it is remembered that pacifism
is only one of several systems which he categorizes as "perfectionist" and
"utopian." Among others are Marxism and certain types of Liberalism. See
his *Beyond Tragedy: Essays on the Christian Interpretation of History* (New
York: Scribner, 1937), particularly Ch. IX.

fall far short of the ideal of divine love and reveal the essentially
"sinful" character of man. Any historical achievement has always to
be judged not only by the degree to which it constitutes progress as
compared with what preceded it, but also by the ever greater dangers
of will to power and chaos which always accompany it. The creation
of every new possibility for "good" is inevitably paralleled by an
equally great potentiality for "evil." Such, for example, has been the
whole history of technological advance. Twentieth-century politics
seem to validate only too well these propositions of the Niebuhrian
argument.

But all this has to do with the general climate of political thinking. In relation specifically to much pacifist thought, Niebuhr is also
in some degree correct. The anarchist pacifism both of Tolstoy and
the secularists would seem to be a good example of that perfectionism
against which he has protested so vociferously. All too easily, as another critic[138] has remarked of Tolstoy's theories in particular, evil
tends to be identified with the use of physical force. Such an identification may be said to be defective because it is both too narrow and too
broad: too narrow, in that it excludes a whole group of acts which on
any reasonable interpretation must be looked upon as exhibitions of
violence, although not issuing in physical force; too broad, because all
acts of physical force do not necessarily constitute violence against
personality. To make evil co-terminous with violence is one thing;
to identify violence with physical force and all physical force with
violence is something entirely different. Insofar as pacifist conceptions
of politics are responsible for the latter identification they would seem
to be erroneous. As Niebuhr quite rightly points out, "spiritual" force
can be just as self-centered, as egoistic, and therefore as violent, as
physical force.[139] There is no hope for a just polity if we make the
use of physical force as such tantamount to injustice, and the utilization
of non-physical power equivalent automatically to justice.

Not only do some statements of the pacifist argument, particularly
the anarchist, tend to err in a too easy identification of physical force
with violence; they also often seem to agree with the general idea of
inevitable, rapid progress. This is again true primarily of anarchist
views and not of most religious pacifism. But insofar as it creeps into
the structure of general pacifist philosophy—and it does, in some expressions—it falls under the same condemnation as that which Niebuhr directs against all doctrines of nineteenth and twentieth century

[138]Maude, *The Doukhobors*, 281.
[139]*The Nature and Destiny of Man*, II, 261.

political optimism. Myths about the supposed efficacy of a non-violent general strike in bringing about an entirely new social order fall within this category. Non-violence may create the best and probably the only context in which to discover the road to a new polity—it is the thesis of this essay, indeed, that here the pacifists are on strong ground. But to move from that assertion to the further statement that it is possible to obtain a wholly non-violent situation is to neglect the very factors which, as Niebuhr rightly maintains, are present in every collective act of mankind.[140]

Finally, there is not a little validity in a constantly recurring Niebuhrian argument which holds that the pacifist thesis tends in many of its statements to be blind to the broader social and political implications of its own philosophy. It fails all too often to state concretely what a pacifist theory would mean in positive terms. Much of the pacifist approach to politics takes its point of departure from the admitted phenomena connected with the more obvious forms of violence in the modern world, and all too frequently ends where it began. As Niebuhr correctly argues, any doctrine of non-violence deserving to be called a philosophy must see the problem of violence in an extremely broad setting. It must understand that the phenomena against which it is protesting cannot be exorcised by being isolated from the general problems of politics. And this, all too often, the political doctrine of pacifism fails to see.

Niebuhr's attack on the politics of pacifism ought, then, to be regarded as in some measure sustained. He emphasizes with great force its ambiguities, inconsistencies, and not infrequent narrowness of vision. That conceded, it remains to point out why, on the whole, the criticisms of Niebuhr can be looked upon as frequently invalid. Professor MacGregor has elaborated this theme within the context specifically of Christian pacifism and New Testament theology.[141] It remains for this essay to criticize Niebuhr from a more general vantage-point in political thought.

When Niebuhr terms pacifist political theory "perfectionist" or "ethically utopian," he is undoubtedly correct, if by those terms he means to say that no conduct in the world of political relativity can possibly measure up to the ideal. Whether expressed in religious or

[140]Cf. Niebuhr, "Politics will, to the end of history, be an area where conscience and power meet, where the ethical and coercive factors of human life will interpenetrate and work out their tentative and uneasy compromises." *Moral Man and Immoral Society,* 4.

[141]MacGregor, *The Relevance of an Impossible Ideal.*

non-religious terms, the pacifist ideal of conduct in politics represents an "impossible" goal in one sense. It implies the liquidation of politics as it has been understood in history. It is, as Gandhi emphasizes, the negation of that history. But from all this Niebuhr draws the wrong inference. He implies that because the ideal has not been embodied in the politics of the present, men ought to discard it and not so act as to protest historic political ethics. To follow that advice, however, would be to remove completely the tension between the "city of the world" and the "city of God"—a tension indispensable if power politics are to be controlled at all. Niebuhr, in general, would admit that this tension is essential if the political world is to remain under judgment for failure to raise its ethical practice to a higher level; and yet, inconsistently, he denies to pacifism any role in making this gulf between the ideal and the real vivid and meaningful. Pacifist apologetics would not contend that individual "perfection" in political and social action could be attained so long as the contemporary political structure subsists; but that does not mean that a "perfectionist" ideal, frustrated as it may be in a political order where men do not follow it, should not be laid down as the standard for action of those who wish to see it ultimately prevail in all areas. The social role of utopias is exactly this—to constitute the ideological cement for those small groups who refuse to identify prevalent practice with ideal right and who hold that, at points, they should deliberately dissociate themselves from those acts of a society which most clearly and unequivocally violate the ideal.

Niebuhr objects that the pacifist statement concentrates upon the problem of violence, that its political theory is lop-sided, and that it consequently fails in an over-emphasis of "perfectionism" in one area, while neglecting it in others. It does not completely dissociate itself from private ownership of capital, for example, even while attempting to "contract out" of the more dramatic forms of violent State coercion. But MacGregor answers, with considerable force, that it is because of the very ubiquity of obvious violence, and particularly war, in modern politics, that the pacifist is warranted in regarding it as the "eruption point" where the tension between the ideal and the actual has become greatest.[142] In former ages the same point could be identified with the institution of chattel slavery and the ethical issues raised by its existence; the focus of the ethical problem in divers epochs of history is located at different centers; but that fact does not eliminate all other

---

[142]*Ibid.*, 30-32.

political issues—it merely subordinates them to the most crucial contemporary question of morals and politics. Pacifism does not always
see this clearly, but this conclusion is at least implicit in its approach.
The nature and ubiquity of overt war, moreover, are such that to adopt
the pacifist outlook will inevitably, if taken seriously, imply a reorienta-
tion in relation to the whole gamut of problems raised in the politics
of social reform.[143]

For to question the ethical justification of overt violence is to raise
immediately the problem of all the covert violences which stand at the
very center of modern life. Disparities in power as among individuals
and groups can no doubt be defended so long as those disparities have
some relation to function performed in the community; but if no such
relation can be clearly shown, they become acts of sheer violence.[144]
Now any cursory investigation of the contemporary State will show
an astounding array of examples illustrating this non-functional, and
hence violent, quality of power in twentieth century politics and
economic organization. War is merely the most vivid and dramatic
destruction of the finer qualities of human personality and the values
which all the universal religious and humanist philosophies have
exalted. The grinding toil of the tenant farmer, the wage slavery of
the city worker, the forcible surrender of political privileges by the
minor civil servant, the persistence of a profit economy placing the
emphasis on scarcity rather than abundance, and the increasing subjec-
tion of the "lower orders" of men to a State machine which patronizes
them through doles and "social security" in lieu of genuine justice—
all these phenomena, when seen clearly, indicate a wide infusion of
the ethos of violence. It is precisely against this all-pervasiveness of
the cult of violence in the modern world that pacifism directs its
criticism.

But all this means that any political analyst who has the slightest
regard for consistency and coherence and who begins with pacifist
assumptions, cannot possibly emerge with any other than a radical
social philosophy. Implicit in the pacifist view of things is always the
anarchist, socialist, or communist world outlook. The fact that some
pacifist thinkers have not pushed their argument to its furthermost
limits does not argue against the contention that every pacifist is implicitly either an anarchist, or a socialist, or a communist; it merely

[143]Murry, *The Necessity of Pacifism.*
[144]Cf. R. H. Tawney, *The Acquisitive Society* (London: Harcourt Brace and Howe,
1920).

raises the further query as to why some pacifists and not a few of their critics have failed to see this.[145]

From the other side, it would seem that any anarchist, socialist, or communist social theory would have to embody the pacifist perspective as a part of its own. The goals laid down for an anarchist, socialist, or communist society dictate the means which the pacifist insight exalts, just as the pacifist emphasis on means would seem clearly to indicate the ends of socialism or communism.

An adequate social and political philosophy, then, would see with pacifism the dangers lurking in centralization of power and would question the possibility, given the raw human stuff upon which political and economic structures must repose, of any lasting resolution of the problem of power becoming violence. It would maintain, again with pacifism, that the imminence of violence will confront any future society; but that it is possible through the development of training for non-violent resistance to keep the tendency to violence within much narrower limits than in the past. It would give emphatic assent to the pacifist analysis of the problem of ends and means in politics. But it would also insist, with socialism and communism, upon a radically altered perspective in relation to the phenomena of property. With socialism and communism, it would argue that no world of peace and harmony can be even approximately achieved in the absence of an economic organization whose whole thrust is in the direction of econo-

---

[145]These are hard sayings for many in the historic tradition of non-violence as well as for not a few modern critics of pacifism. There has been a tendency among some pacifists to see the problems of politics largely in terms of overt war or its absence; and the critics—e.g., Lewis and Shelvankar—have in many instances seized upon this over-simplification to cast ridicule upon pacifism as a whole.

What precisely do we mean when we say "every pacifist is implicitly either an anarchist, or a socialist, or a communist"?

(1) A radical view of property relations is implicit in pacifist theory. Pacifists cannot be consistent without holding out as a goal the ideal "from each according to his ability, to each according to his need." Any other distributive theory is bound to mean exploitation and violence. Need can be the only criterion of distribution if we agree with the pacifist postulate that all men ought to live as brothers, without war and all that war connotes.

(2) Whether this general view would envision ultimate abolition of the State, which, of course, is the anarchist view, is a question into which we cannot go here. But certainly this peculiar contribution of anarchism cannot be ignored. In the immediate sense, however, it is the contention of this paper that the maintenance of the State is compatible with the pacifist ethic. To think of pacifism in terms of elimination of all types of pressure seems to me unrealistic. Wherever two or more men live together a power relation arises— and the twin questions of authority and obedience are posed. Then the problem becomes one of defining spheres of authority and obedience and delimiting the types of sanctions permissible.

mic equality—not necessarily exact equality in incomes (although a much more powerful argument for this can be made out than is generally assumed), but equality in the sense that every human being shall be equally assured that he will have the material goods essential to perform his proper function in society.[146]

It is the thesis of this essay that just such a philosophy is clearly' implicit, and often explicit, in the leading doctrines of twentieth-century pacifism. When Niebuhr criticizes the pacifist argument because it places violence, and particularly war, in the central place of its analysis, it is not difficult to reply, then, that such an emphasis is perfectly legitimate. If the State could be prevented by organized effort such as pacifists advocate from engaging in the wholesale and dramatic form of violence called war, it could not long maintain the covert and often more insidious violences which stand at the base of modern society. For the modern State and its ruling oligarchy, war is an escape from the constant pressure from below which menaces all oligarchs. The twentieth century State cannot live without exploitation and to attack it at the point of most obvious violence would be to remove the props upholding the whole system.

But Niebuhr also fails to apprehend clearly the theological assumptions of at least non-anarchist religious pacifism. They are much closer to his own beliefs than he will admit. It is precisely because it is aware of what he terms the "demonic" element in human nature—the tendency, under all conditions to glorify force and seek power as an end in itself[147]—that the ethical and political theory of pacifism is so concerned about the quality of the means used to implement political ideals. Its object is to make more nearly certain that those means do not encourage and enhance this very tendency which Niebuhr so rightly discerns in the very nature of human society.

Political theories of non-violence do indeed envision the possibility of a measure of progress, in the sense that they do not believe it beyond the wit of man to make more shallow the valleys of "decay and destruction" and to level down the peaks of power. Therein they constitute an attempt to refute the contention of Niebuhr and Oswald Spengler that because the past seems with regularity to demonstrate cycles of progress and decay, the future must also necessarily exhibit such a pattern. Pacifism is a belief that it is possible to break into what

---

[146]R. H. Tawney, *Equality* (New York: Harcourt Brace, 1931), has a penetrating discussion of this problem.
[147]*Christianity and Power Politics,* 62.

Gandhi has called this "chain of destruction," by invoking a political
ethic, which, if valid at all, is revolutionary in its implications. By
seeking to base its politics upon the systematized use of what it looks
upon as an ethically higher and politically more efficacious type of
power—while recognizing with Niebuhr that at any level power contains within itself "demonic" qualities—it believes it has discovered the
key to this revolution.

But with non-anarchistic pacifist approaches at least, it is the key
to partial success in the future inevitable struggles of political society
—not the open sesame to the elimination of struggle, as with the
Marxian and many Liberal views of progress. For the struggle will
remain, as with Niebuhr. On this hard inner core of human nature
and destiny, a large body of pacifists and their critics will agree. Contrary to Niebuhr's whole interpretation of what it holds, there is no
evidence that the main stream of religious pacifism, with the exception
of Tolstoyan currents, looks forward to an easy triumph of that divine
love or *agape,* which it seeks to infuse into politics. Certainly there is
nothing in Gandhi's doctrine to support such a contention. There is to
be no apocalyptic descent of the Kingdom of God, no swift transformation of the whole into a classless society, no imminent end of history.

IV. RECAPITULATION AND CONCLUSION

Recapitulating, this essay has attempted to show that, within the
broad stream of modern pacifist speculation, there are wide variations
as to assumptions and considerable differences in statements of objectives. The ultimate philosophical presuppositions of Hindu, Christian,
and secular revolutionary pacifism cannot be equated exactly with one
another; there is a difference between those who see pacifist political
principles issuing forth in "non-resistance" and those who find them
exemplified in "non-violent resistance"; and the distinction between
anarchist and non-anarchist analyses cannot by any standard be minimized.

But despite these divisions, five underlying bases of modern pacifist political theory receive general assent:

(1) the emphasis given to the ends-means problem in politics;

(2) the view that the modern State is essentially an engine of
violence and tends to infuse its *ethos* throughout all life;

(3) an elaboration of a method whereby at least one large segment of pacifist thought seeks to keep the will-to-power proclivities of most men subordinate to ideal ends in the political arena;

(4) a deep and abiding distrust of industrialism and of a centralized economic and political order; and

(5) an assumption that its ideal of action is relevant to the political order here and now—an order which still apparently believes that bombing is compatible with political harmony and espionage with a cooperative society.

But the politics of pacifism are not without serious deficiencies and omissions. Summarily, they are:

(1) A lack of clarity as to the precise distinction between violence and non-violence.

(2) A frequently recurring ambiguity about the nature of power. This in itself is not unusual since we are concerned here with an area of political theory where, if one can go even that far, the problems only have been stated by non-pacifists as well as pacifists, with no attempt at an adequate solution.[148] But this general deficiency should not excuse the lack of an adequate pacifist analysis, for the problem of power is central to its whole thesis.

(3) A not infrequent failure to see the full implications of its own philosophy of non-violence. It often does not see, for example, that individual objection to violence—even to the extent of jail or the gallows—does not necessarily mean effective political objection. In this respect, Hindu and secular revolutionary pacifism are far more penetrating than most emphases of Christian pacifism; for the former see that in politics mass action based upon previous agreement is essential if the power of the State is to be effectively challenged.

Or again, how would government be organized in a society more nearly conformable to the pacifist ethic? If some types of coercion be accepted, how would they be related to the general political structure? In the modern world, pacifism is largely a creed of revolt and rebellion. Suppose that it should gain new adherents and be called upon to furnish a handbook for governors instead of marching orders for social rebels? Such questions cannot be ignored with impunity; yet pacifist literature is amazingly vague and uncertain in the answers it gives.

---

[148]Cf. Charles E. Merriam, *Political Power* (New York: McGraw-Hill, 1934) and Bertrand Russell. *Power* (New York: Norton, 1938).

(4) Where the political ends of pacifism are made more explicit, as they are in its widespread acceptance of the decentralist-agrarian thesis, there is often a tendency to over-simplification of the economic and political problems involved.

(5) Finally, some currents of pacifist thought seem to be affected by nineteenth century illusions of inevitable progress; by an implicit assumption that the whole world is about to be won over to the ethics of non-violence.

This essay cannot reconstruct and revise the social and political philosophy of pacifism. But such an effort is urgently needed and might well prove to be one of the most significant intellectual efforts of our time.

NON-VIOLENT ACTION
IN TENSION AREAS:
Series III: Number 1
July 1944.

INTRODUCTION
TO
NON-VIOLENCE

By
THEODORE PAULLIN

THE PACIFIST RESEARCH BUREAU
1201 CHESTNUT STREET
PHILADELPHIA 7, PENNSYLVANIA

MEMBERS OF THE PACIFIST RESEARCH BUREAU

FINANCIAL SUPPORT

The Pacifist Research Bureau is financed entirely by the contributions of organizations and individuals who are interested in
seeing this type of research carried on. We trust that you may desire
to have a part in this positive pacifist endeavor to aid in the formulation of plans for the world order of the future. Please make contributions payable to The Pacifist Research Bureau, 1201 Chestnut Street,
Philadelphia 7, Pennsylvania. Contributions are deductible for income
tax purposes.

DIRECTOR'S FOREWORD

"When I use a word," Humpty Dumpty said, in a rather scornful tone, "it means just what I choose it to mean—neither more nor less."

"The question is," said Alice, "whether you *can* make words mean different things."

In the writings of pacifists and non-pacifists concerning theories of and experiences with non-violence, there is a clear lack of uniformity in the use of words.

The present booklet, introducing the Bureau's new series on *Non-Violent Action in Tension Areas,* distinguished by green covers, critically examines pacifist terminology. But it does more, for it analyzes various types of non-violence, evaluates examples of non-violence referred to in previous literature, and points to new sources of case material.

Dr. Theodore Paullin, Assistant Director of the Bureau, is the author of this study. The manuscript has been submitted to and reviewed by Professor Charles A. Ellwood and Professor Hornell Hart, both of the Department of Sociology, Duke University; and by Richard B. Gregg, author of several works on the philosophy and practice of non-violence. Their criticisms and suggestions have proved most helpful, but for any errors of interpretation the author is responsible.

The Pacifist Research Bureau frankly bases its work upon the philosophy of pacifism: that man should exercise such respect for human personality that he will employ only love and sacrificial good will in opposing evil and that the purpose of all human endeavor should be the creation of a world brotherhood in which cooperative effort contributes to the good of all. A list of pamphlets published or in preparation appears on the back cover.

HARROP A. FREEMAN,

Executive Director

Any organization ordering 500 or more copies of any pamphlet published by the Pacifist Research Bureau may have its imprint appear on the title page along with that of the Bureau. The prepublication price for such orders is $75.00 for each 500 copies.

TABLE OF CONTENTS

PREFACE

The purpose of the present study is to analyze the various positions found within the pacifist movement itself in regard to the use of non-violent techniques of bringing about social change in group relationships. In its attempt to differentiate between them, it makes no pretense of determining which of the several pacifist positions is ethically most valid. Hence it is concerned with the application of non-violent principles in practice and their effectiveness in achieving group purposes, rather than with the philosophical and religious foundations of such principles. It is hoped that the study may help individuals to clarify their thinking within this field, but the author has no brief for one method as against the others. Each person must determine his own principles of action on the basis of his conception of the nature of the universe and his own scale of ethical values.

The examples chosen to illustrate the various positions have been taken largely from historical situations in this country and in Europe, because our traditional education has made us more familiar with the history of these areas than with that of other parts of the world. It also seemed that the possibilities of employing non-violent methods of social change would be more apparent if it was evident that they had been used in the West, and were not only applicable in Oriental societies. It is unfortunate that this deliberate choice has eliminated such valuable illustrative material as the work of Kagawa in Japan. The exception to this general rule in the case of "Satyagraha" has been made because of the wide-spread discussion of this movement in all parts of the world in our day.

I want to acknowledge with great appreciation the suggestions I have obtained from the preliminary work done for the Pacifist Research Bureau in this field by Russell Curtis and Haridas T. Muzumdar.

THEODORE PAULLIN

July 1, 1944

INTRODUCTION TO NON-VIOLENCE

I. INTROUCTION: ON TERMS

"In the storm we found each other." "In the storm we clung together." These words are found in the opening paragraphs of "Hey!
Yellowbacks!" The War Diary of a Conscientious Objector. Ernest L.
Meyer uses them to describe the psychological process by which a
handful of men—a few professors and a lone student—at the University of Wisconsin grew into unity because they opposed the First
World War, when everyone around them was being carried away
in the enthusiasm which marked the first days of American participation. If there had been no storm, they might not have discovered
their affinity, but as it was, despite the disparity of their interests and
backgrounds, they found themselves in agreement on the most fundamental of their values, when all the rest chose to go another way. By
standing together they all gained strength for the ordeals through
which each must go, and they were filled with the spirit of others
before them and far removed from them, who had understood life
in the same way.[1]

The incident may be taken as symbolic of the experience through
which pacifists have gone in this Second World War, too. Men and
women of many creeds, of diverse economic backgrounds, of greatly
divergent philosophies, with wide variations in education, have come
together in the desire to sustain one another and aid one another in
making their protest against war. Each in his own way has refused
to participate in the mass destruction of human life which war involves, and by that refusal has been united by the strongest bonds
of sympathy with those of his fellows who have done likewise. But
it is the storm that has brought unity. When the skies clear, there will
be a memory of fellowship together, but there will also be a realization that in the half light we have seen only one aspect of each other's
being, and that there are enormous differences between us. Our future
hope of achieving the type of world we want will demand a continuation of our sense of unity, despite our diversities.

At present pacifism is no completely integrated philosophy of
life. Most of us would be hard pressed to define the term "pacifist"
itself. Despite the fact that according to the Latin origins of the word
it means "peace maker," it is small wonder that our non-pacifist friends
think of the pacifist as a negative obstructionist, because until the
time came to make a negative protest against the evil of war we ourselves all too often forgot that we were pacifists. In other times, if

[1]Ernest L. Meyer, "Hey! Yellowbacks!" (New York: John Day, 1930), 3-6.

we have been peace-makers at all, we have thought of ourselves merely as doing the duty of citizens, and, in attempting to overcome some of the causes of conflict both within our domestic society and in the relations between nations, we have willingly merged ourselves with other men of goodwill whose aims and practices were almost identical to ours.

Since the charge of negativism strikes home, many pacifists defend themselves by insisting that they stand primarily for a positive program, of which war-resistance is only a pre-requisite. They oppose war because it is evil in itself, but they oppose it also because the type of human brotherhood for which they stand can be realized only when war is eliminated from the world. Their real aim is the creation of the new society—long and imperfect though that process of creation may be. They share a vision, but they are still groping for the means of moving forward towards its achievement. They are generally convinced that some means are inappropriate to their ends, and that to use such means would automaticaly defeat them; but they are less certain about the means which *will* bring some measure of success.

One section of the pacifist movement believes that it has discovered a solution to the problem in what it calls "non-violent direct action." This group derives much of its inspiration from Gandhi and his non-violent movement for Indian independence. For instance, the Fellowship of Reconciliation has a committee on non-violent direct action which concerns itself with applying the techniques of the Gandhi movement to the solution of pressing social issues which are likely to cause conflict within our own society, especially discrimination against racial minorities. As a "textbook" this group has been using Krishnalal Shridharani's analysis of the Gandhi procedures, *War Without Violence*.[2] The advocates of "non-violenct direct action" believe that their method can bring about the resolution of any conflict through the ultimate defeat of the forces of evil, and the triumph of justice and goodwill. In a widely discussed pamphlet, *If We Should Be Invaded*, issued just before the outbreak of the present war, Jessie Wallace Hughan, of the War Resisters League, maintained that non-violent resistance would be more effective even in meeting an armed invasion than would reliance upon military might.[3]

---

[2] Krishnalal Shridharani, *War Without Violence* (New York: Harcourt Brace, 1939); *Selections from War Without Violence* was published by the Fellowship of Reconciliation, 2929 Broadway, New York, as a pamphlet, in 1941.

[3] Jessie Wallace Hughan, *If We Should Be Invaded: Facing a Fantastic Hypothesis* (War Resisters League, New York, 1939). A new edition with the title *Pacifism and Invasion* was issued in 1942.

Many pacifists have accepted the general thesis of the advocates of non-violent direct action without analyzing its meaning and implications. Others have rejected it on the basis of judgments just as superficial. Much confusion has crept into the discussion of the principle and into its application because of the constant use of ill-defined terms and partially formulated ideas. It is the purpose of the present study to analyze the positions of both the friends and opponents of non-violent direct action within the pacifist movement in the hope of clarifying thought upon this vitally important question.

Before we can proceed with our discussion, we must make a clear distinction between non-violence as a principle, accepted as an end in itself, and non-violence as a means to some other desired end. Much of the present confusion in pacifist thought arises from a failure to make this distinction.

On the one hand, the absolute pacifist believes that all men are brothers. Therefore, he maintains that the supreme duty of every individual is to respect the personality of every other man, and to love him, no matter what evil he may commit, and no matter how greatly he may threaten his fellows or the values which the pacifist holds most dear. Under no circumstances can the pacifist harm or, destroy the person who does evil; he can use only love and sacrificial goodwill to bring about conversion. This is his highest value and his supreme principle. Though the heavens should fall, or he himself and all else he cherishes be destroyed in the process, he can place no other value before it. To the pacifist who holds such a position, non-violence is imperative *even if it does not work.* By his very respect for the personality of the evil-doer, and his insistence upon maintaining the bond of human brotherhood, he has already achieved his highest purpose and has won his greatest victory.

But much of the present pacifist argument in favor of non-violence is based rather upon its expediency. Here, we are told, is a means of social action that *works* in achieving the social goals to which pacifists aspire. Non-violence provides a moral force which is more powerful than any physical force. Whether it be used by the individual or by the social group, it is, in the long run, the most effective way of overcoming evil and bringing about the triumph of good. The literature is full of stories of individuals who have overcome highwaymen, or refractory neighbors, by the power of love.[4] More recent treatments

---

[4] Many later writers have selected their examples from the large number presented by Adin Ballou, *Christian Non-Resistance: In All Its Important Bearings* (Philadelphia: Universal Peace Union, 1910); first published in 1846,

such as Richard Gregg's *Power of Non-Violence*[5] present story after story of the successful use of non-violent resistance by groups against political oppression. The history of the Gandhi movement in India has seemed to provide proof of its expediency. Even the argument in Aldous Huxley's *Ends and Means,* that we can achieve no desired goal by means which are inconsistent with it, still regards non-violent action as a *means* for achieving some other end, rather than an *end* in itself.[6]

So prevalent has such thinking become among pacifists, that it is not surprising that John Lewis, in his closely reasoned book, *The Case Against Pacifism,* bases his whole attack on the logic of the pacifist position upon the theory that pacifists *must,* as he does, hold other values above their respect for individual human personalities. Even in speaking of "absolute" pacifism he says, "The most fundamental objection to war is based on the conviction that violence and the taking of human life, being themselves wrong, cannot lead to anything but evil."[7] Thus he defines the absolute pacifist as one who accepts the ends and means argument of Huxley, which is really an argument based upon expediency, rather than defining him correctly as one who insists that violence and the taking of human life are the greatest evils, under any conditions, and therefore cannot be justified, even if they could be used for the achievement of highly desirable ends.

Maintaining as Lewis does that respect for every human personality is not their highest value, non-pacifists attack pacifism almost entirely on the ground that in the present state of world society it is not expedient—that it is "impractical." Probably much of the pacifist defense of the position is designed to meet these non-pacifist arguments, and to persuade non-pacifists of goodwill that they can really best serve *their* highest values by adopting the pacifist technique. Such reasoning is perfectly legitimate, even for the "absolutist," but he should recognize it for what it is—a mere afterthought to his acceptance of non-violence as a principle.

The whole absolutist argument is this: (1) Since violence to any human personality is the greatest evil, I can never commit it. (2) But, at the same time, it is fortunate that non-violent means of overcoming evil are more effective than violent means, so I can serve my highest value—respect for every human personality- and at the same

---

[5]Richard B. Gregg, *The Power of Non-Violence* (Philadelphia: Lippincott, 1934). A new and revised edition of this book is to be published by Fellowship Publications, N. Y., 1944.

[6]Aldous Huxley, *Ends and Means: An Inquiry into the Nature of Ideals and the Methods Employed for Their Realization* (New York: Harpers, 1937).

[7]John Lewis, *The Case Against Pacifism* (London: Allen and Unwin, 1940), 23.

time serve the other values I hold. Or to say the same thing in positive terms, I can achieve my other ends *only* by employing means which are consistent with those ends.

On the other hand, many pacifists do in fact hold the position that John Lewis is attacking, and base their acceptance of pacifism entirely on the fact that it is the best means of obtaining the sort of social or economic or political order that they desire. Others, in balancing the destruction of violent conflict against what they concede might be gained by it, say that the price of social achievement through violent means is too high—that so many of their values are destroyed in the process of violence that they must abandon it entirely as a means, and find another which is less destructive.

Different as are the positions of the absolute and the relative pacifists, in practice they find themselves united in their logical condemnation of violence as an effective means for bringing about social change. Hence there is no reason why they cannot join forces in many respects. Only a relatively small proportion, even of the absolutists, have no interest whatever in bringing about social change, and are thus unable to share in this aspect of pacifist thinking.

Definition of Terms

Both in pacifist thought and in the criticisms of pacifism, a great deal of confusion arises because of the inexact use of terms. We have already seen that pacifists of many shades of opinion are united in their refusal to participate in war. In this objection there is a negative quality. The very word "non-violence" used in the title of this study suggests this same negative attitude, and it was not long ago that pacifists were generally known as "non-resistants." Although some of those who oppose participation in war still insist upon calling themselves "non-resistants"[8] many of the modern pacifists disclaim the term because it is negative, and insist that the essence of pacifism

---

[8]Guy F. Hershberger makes a definite distinction between non-resistance and pacifism. He says that the former term describes the faith and life of those "Who cannot have any part in warfare because they believe the Bible forbids it, and who renounce all coercion, even nonviolent coercion." He goes on to say, "Pacifism, on the other hand, is a term which covers many types of opposition to war. Some modern so-called pacifists are opposed to all wars, and some are not. Some who oppose all wars find their authority in the will of God, while others find it largely in human reason. There are many other differences among them." "Biblical Nonresistance and Modern Pacifism," *The Mennonite Quarterly Review*, XVII, (July, 1943), 116.

Hershberger is here defining pacifism broadly to include the European meaning of opposition to war, but not necessarily a refusal to take part in it. In the United States, and generally in Great Britain, the term is ordinarily applied only to those who actually refuse participation in war.

is the element of active goodwill toward all men.[9] Yet when confronted with evil, even he who thinks of his pacifism as a positive attitude must decide not only what means he *will* use to oppose evil, but what means he *will not* use. At the moment when the society of which he is a part insists that every one of its members participate in an enterprise to employ these proscribed means, the pacifists of all shades of opinion become "conscientious objectors." To what is it exactly that they object?

Most answers to this question would say that they oppose "the use of force," "violence," "coercion," or in some cases, any "resistance" to evil whatever. But pacifists themselves have not been agreed upon the meanings and implications of these terms, and the opponents of pacifism have hastened to define them in such a way as to deny validity to the pacifist philosophy. Before we can proceed with our discussion we must define these terms for ourselves, as we shall use them in the present study.

Force we may define as physical or intangible power or influence to effect change in the material or immaterial world. *Coercion* is the use of either physical or intangible force to compel action contrary to the will or reasoned judgment of the individual or group subjected to such force. *Violence* is the willful application of force in such a way that it is physically or psychologically injurious to the person or group against whom it is applied. *Resistance* is any opposition either physical or psychological to the positive will or action of another. It is the negative or defensive counterpart of coercion.

The very diversity of terms used to describe the pacifist position shows that none of them satisfactorily expresses the essence of the pacifist philosophy. Among those commonly used are: (1) non-resistance, (2) passive resistance, (3) non-violent resistance, (4) super-resistance, (5) non-violent non-cooperation, (6) civil disobedience, (7) non-violent coercion, (8) non-violent direct action, (9) war without violence, and (10) Satyagraha or soul force.[10]

Of these terms only "non-resistance" implies acquiescence in the will of the evil-doer; all the rest suggest an approval of resistance. Every one of them, even "non-resistance" itself, contemplates the use of some intangible moral force to oppose evil and a refusal to take an active part in committing evil. At least the last five indicate the positive desire to change the active policy of the evil-doer, either by

[9] See Devere Allen, *The Fight for Peace* (New York: Macmillan, 1930), 531-540.
[10] On the origins of these terms see Haridas T. Muzumdar, *The United Nations of the World* (New York: Universal, 1942), 201-203.

persuasion or by compulsion. As we shall see, in practice they tend to involve a coercive element. Only in their rejection of violence are all these terms in agreement. Perhaps we are justified in accepting *opposition to violence* as the heart of the pacifist philosophy. Under the definition of violence which has been suggested, this would amount to virtually the same thing as saying that the pacifist has such respect for every human personality that he cannot, under any circumstances whatsoever, intentionally inflict permanent injury upon any human being either physically or psychologically. This statement deserves further examination.

All pacifists approve the use of "force," as we have defined it, and actually do use it, since it includes such things as "the force of love," "the force of example," or "the force of public opinion."[11] There are very few pacifists who would draw the line even at the use of *physical* force. Most of them would approve it in restraining children or the mentally ill from injuring themselves or others, or in the organized police force of a community under the proper safeguards of the courts and law.[12]

Many pacifists are also willing to accept coercion, provided it be non-violent. The strike, the boycott, or even the mass demonstration involve an element of coercion as we have defined that term. Shridharani assures us that despite Gandhi's insistence to the contrary, "In the light of events in India in the past twenty years as well as in the light of certain of Gandhi's own activities, . . . it becomes apparent that Satyagraha does contain the element of coercion, if in a somewhat modified form."[13] Since to some people "coercion" implies revenge or punishment, Shridharani would, however, substitute the word "compulsion" for it. Gandhi himself and many of his followers would claim that the techniques of Satyagraha are only a marshalling of the forces of sympathy, public opinion, and the like, and that they are persuasive rather than coercive. At any rate a distinction, on the basis of the spirit in which they are undertaken, between types of action which are outwardly similar seems perfectly valid.

There are other pacifists who would even accept a certain element of violence, as we have defined it, provided it were not physical in

---

[11] John Haynes Holmes, using the older term rather than "pacifist," has said, "The true non-resistant is militant—but he lifts his militancy from the plane of physical, to the plane of moral and spiritual force." *New Wars for Old* (New York: Dodd, Mead, 1916), xiii.

[12] Cecil John Cadoux, *Christian Pacifism Re-examined* (Oxford: Basil Blackwell, 1940), 15-16; Leyton Richards, *Realistic Pacifism* (Chicago: Willett, Clark, 1935), 3.

[13] Shridharani, *War Without Violence*, 292.

nature. Some persons with boundless good will feel that even physical violence may be justified on occasion if it is not accompanied by hatred toward its object.[14] However, there would be few who consider themselves pacifists who would accept such a position.

We are again forced to the conclusion that it is violence as we have defined it to which the pacifist objects. At this point, the chief difference between the pacifist and the non-pacifist is that the latter defines violence as does Clarence Case, as "the *unlawful* or *unregulated* use of destructive physical force against persons or things."[15] Under such a definition, war itself, since it is sanctioned by law, would no longer involve violence. Thus for the non-pacifist it is ethically acceptable to use lawful violence against unlawful violence; for the pacifist, violence against any personality is never ethically justified.[16]

On the other hand, a very large group of pacifists insist upon discarding these negative definitions in favor of one that is wholly positive. Maurice L. Rowntree has said: "The Pacifist way of life is the way that brings into action all the sense and wisdom, all the passion of love and goodwill that can be brought to bear upon the situation."[17]

In this study, no attempt will be made to determine which of the many pacifist positions is most sound ethically. Before any person can make such a determination for himself, however, it is necessary that he understand the differences between the various approaches to the problem of influencing other people either to do something which he believes should be done, or to refrain from doing something which he feels ought not to be done.

It might be helpful for us in our thinking to construct a scale at one end of which we place violence coupled with hatred, and at the other, dependence only upon the application of positive love and goodwill. In the intermediate positions we might place (1) violence without hatred, (2) non-violence practiced by necessity rather than because of principle, (3) non-violent coercion, (4) Satyagraha and non-violent direct action, and (5) non-resistance.

---

[14]John Lewis says, "We must draw a sharp distinction between the use of violence to achieve an unjust end and its use as police action in defence of the rule of law." *Case Against Pacifism*, 85.

[15]Clarence Marsh Case, *Non-Violent Coercion* (New York: Century, 1923), 323. Italics mine.

[16]C. J. Cadoux has clearly stated his position in these words: "He [the pacifist] will confine himself to those methods of pressure which are either wholly non-coercive or are coercive in a strictly non-injurious way, foregoing altogether such injurious methods of coercion as torture, mutilation, or homicide: that is to say, he will refrain from war." *Christian Pacifism*, 65-66.

[17]Maurice L. Rowntree, *Mankind Set Free* (London: Cape, 1939), 80-81.

We need, at the outset, to recognize that we are speaking primarily of the relationships between social groups rather than between individuals. As Reinhold Niebuhr has so ably pointed out, our ethical concepts in these two areas are greatly at variance with one another.[18] The pacifist principles are already widely accepted as ideals in the affairs of individuals. Every ethical religion teaches them in this area, and the person who rejects them is definitely the exception in our western society, until the violent man is regarded as subject to the discipline of society in general.

Our real concern in this study is with non-violent means of achieving group purposes, whether they be defensive and conservative in character, or whether they be changes in the existing institutions of the social order. The study is not so much concerned with the religious and ethical bases of these techniques as it is with a consideration of their application in practice, and their effectiveness in achieving the purposes which the group in question has in view. We shall begin at one end of our scale and proceed to discuss each type of action in turn.

II. VIOLENCE WITHOUT HATE

Occasions may arise in which a man who genuinely abhors violence confronts an almost insoluble dilemma. On the one hand he may be faced with the imminent triumph of some almost insufferable evil; on the other, he may feel that the only available means of opposing that evil is violence, which is in itself evil.[19]

In such a situation, the choice made by any individual depends upon his own subjective scale of values. The pacifist is convinced that for him to commit violence upon another is itself the greatest possible evil. The non-pacifist says that some other evils may be greater, and that the use of this lesser evil to oppose them is entirely justified. John Lewis bases his entire *Case Against Pacifism* upon this latter assumption, and says that in such a coniflct of values, pacifists "continue to be pacifists either because there is no serious threat, or because they do not expect to lose anything, or perhaps even because they do not value what is threatened."[20] The latter charge is entirely unjustified.

---

[18] Reinhold Niebuhr, *Moral Man and Immoral Society* (New York: Scribner's, 1932). See especially his consideration of coercion and persuasion in the two realms of individual and social conduct, pages xxii-xxiii.

[19] As Cadoux puts it, "Broadly speaking, almost the whole human race believes that it is occasionally right and necessary to inflict injurious coercion on human beings, in order to prevent the perpetration by them of some intolerable evil." *Christian Pacifism Re-examined,* 97.

[20] Lewis, 62.

The pacifist maintains his opposition to violence in the face of such a threat, not because he does not value what is threatened, but because he values something else more.

Cadoux has phrased it, "Pacifism is applicable only in so far as there exist pacifists who are convinced of its wisdom. The subjective differences are of vital importance, yet are usually overlooked in arguments on the subject."[21] This means that our problem of considering the place of violence and non-violence in human life is not one of purely objective science, since the attitudes and beliefs of pacifists (and non-pacifists) themselves become a factor in the situation. If enough people accepted the pacifist scale of values, it would in fact become the true basis for social interaction.[22]

In our western society, the majority even of those who believe in the brotherhood of man, and have great respect for the dignity of every human personality, will on occasion use violence as a means to attempt the achievement of their goals. Since their attitude is different from that of the militarist who would place violence itself high in his scale of values, it would pay us to consider their position.

Revolutionary Anarchism

The revolutionary Anarchists belong essentially in this group. As Alexander Berkman has put it, "The teachings of Anarchism are those of peace and harmony, of non-invasion, of the sacredness of life and liberty;" or again, "It [Anarchism] means that men are brothers, and that they should live like brothers, in peace and harmony."[23] But to create this ideal society the Anarchist feels that violence may be necessary. Berkman himself, in his younger days, was able to justify his attack upon the life of Frick at the time of the Homestead Strike in 1893 in these words:

> "But to the People belongs the earth—by right, if not in fact. To make it so in fact, all means are justifiable; nay advisable, even to the point of taking life. . . . Human life is, indeed, sacred and inviolate. But the killing of a tyrant, of an enemy of the People, is in no way to be considered as the taking of a life. . . . To remove a tyrant is an act of

[21]Cadoux, *Christian Pacifism Re-examined,* 116-117.
[22]The way in which a whole social order can differ from that of the West, merely because it chooses to operate on the basis of different assumptions concerning such things as the aggressive nature of man is well brought out in the study of three New Guinea tribes living in very similar environments. Margaret Mead, *Sex and Temperament in Three Primitive Societies* (London: Routledge, 1935).
[23]Alexander Berkman, *What Is Communist Anarchism?* (New York: Vanguard, 1929), x-xi, 176.

liberation, the giving of life and opportunity to an oppressed people."[24]

Later, Berkman insisted that a successful revolution must be non-violent in nature. It must be the result of thoroughgoing changes in the ideas and opinions of the people. When their ideas have become sufficiently changed and unified, the people can stage a general strike in which they overthrow the old order by their refusal to co-operate with it. He maintains that any attempt to carry on the revolution itself by military means would fail because "government and capital are too well organized in a military way for the workers to cope with them." But, says Berkman, when the success of the revolution becomes apparent, the opposition will use violent means to suppress it. At that moment the people are justified in using violence themselves to protect it. Berkman believes that there is no record of any group in power giving up its power without being subjected to the use of physical force, or at least the threat of it.[25] Thus in effect, Berkman would still use violence against some personalities in order to establish a system in which respect for every personality would be possible. Actually his desire for the new society is greater than his abhorrence of violence.

Abraham Lincoln

Abraham Lincoln represented the spirit of moderation in the use of violence. He led his nation in war reluctantly and prayerfully, with no touch of hatred toward those whom the armies of which he was Commander-in-Chief were destroying. He expressed his feeling in an inspiring way in the closing words of his Second Inaugural Address, when the war was rapidly drawing to a victorious close:

> "With malice toward none; with charity for all; with firmness to do the right, as God gives us to see the right, let us strive on to finish the work we are in; to bind up the nation's wounds; to care for him who shall have borne battle, and for his widow, and his orphan—to do all which may achieve and cherish a just and lasting peace among ourselves, and with all nations."

The Church and War

The statements of British and American churchmen during the present war call to mind these words of Lincoln. At Malvern, in 1941, members of the Church of England declared: "God himself is the

---

[24]Alexander Berkman, *Prison Memoirs of an Anarchist* (New York: Mother Earth Publishing Association, 1912), 7.

[25]Berkman, *Communist Anarchism*, 217-229, 247-248, 290.

sovereign of all human life; all men are his children, and ought to be
brothers of one another; through Christ the Redeemer they can become
what they ought to be." In March, 1942, American Protestant leaders
at Delaware, Ohio, asserted: "We believe it is the purpose of God
to create a world-wide community in Jesus Christ, transcending nation, race and class."[26] Yet the majority of the men who drew up
these two statements were supporting the war which their nations
were waging against fellow members of the world community—
against those whom they professed to call brothers. Like Lincoln
they did so in the belief that when the military phases of the war
were over, it would be possible to turn from violence and to practice
the principles of Christian charity.[27]

There is little in human history to justify their hope. There is
much to make us believe that the violent attitudes of war will lead
to hatred and injustice toward enemies when the war is done. The
inspiring words of Lincoln were followed by the orgy of radical reconstruction in the South. There is at least as grave a doubt that the
spirit of the Christian Church will dominate the peace which is concluded at the end of the present war.

The question arises insistently whether violence without hate
can long live up to its own professions.

III. NON-VIOLENCE BY NECESSITY

The use of non-violent resistance does not always denote devotion to pacifist principles. Groups who would gladly use arms against
an enemy if they had them often use non-violent means simply because
they have no others at their disposal at the moment. In contrast to
the type of action described in the preceding section, such a procedure
might be called "hate without violence." It would probably be better
to call it "non-violence by necessity."

---

[26]A number of these religious statements are conveniently brought together in the
appendix to Paul Hutchinson's *From Victory to Peace* (Chicago: Willett, Clark,
1943). For a statement of a point of view similar to the one we are discussing
here, see also Charles Clayton Morrison, *The Christian and the War* (Chicago:
Willett, Clark, 1942).

[27]Bernard Iddings Bell has expressed the attitude of such churchmen: "Evil may
sometimes get such control of men and nations, they have realized, that armed
resistance becomes a necessity. There are times when not to participate in
violence is in itself violence to the welfare of the brethren. But no Christian
moralist worth mentioning has ever regarded war *per se* as other than mon-
strous, or hoped that by the use of violence anything more could be accomplished than the frustration of a temporarily powerful malicious wickedness.
War in itself gives birth to no righteousness. Only such a fire of love as leads
to self-effacement can advance the welfare of mankind." "Will the Christian
Church Survive?" *Atlantic Monthly,* Vol. 170, October, 1942, 109.

The group using non-violence under such circumstances might have in view one of three purposes. It might hope through its display of opposition and its own suffering to appeal to the sense of fair play of the group that was oppressing it. However, such a hope can exist only in cases where the two opposing parties have a large area of agreement upon values, or homogeneity, and would have no basis when the oppressing group looked upon the oppressed as completely beneath their consideration. It is unlikely that it would have much success in changing the policy of a nation which consciously chose to invade another country, although it might affect individual soldiers if their cultural background were similar to that of the invaded people.[28]

An invader usually desires to gain something from the invaded people. In order to succeed, he needs their cooperation. A second way of thwarting the will of the invader is to refuse that cooperation, and be willing to suffer the penalties of such refusal. Since the invaded territory would then have no value, the invader might leave of his own accord.

A third possibility is for the invaded people to employ sabotage and inflict damage upon the invader in the belief that his invasion can be made so costly that it will be impossible for him to remain in the conquered territory. Such sabotage easily merges into violence.

In the preceding paragraphs, the enemy of the group using non-violence has been referred to as the "invader," because our best examples of this type of non-violent opposition are to be found in the histories of conquered people opposing the will of occupying forces. A similar situation may exist between a colonial people and the home government of an imperial power, since in most cases their position is essentially that of a conquered people, except that their territory has been occupied for a longer period of time.

Non-Violent Resistance to Invaders

Stories of the use of this sort of non-violence occur in our press every day, as they find their way out of the occupied countries which are opposing the Nazi invaders with every means at their disposal. In these countries the vast majority of the people are agreed in their determination to rid themselves of Nazi control. Such common agreement is the first requisite for the success of this method of resistance.

[28]Franklin H. Giddings said, "In a word, non-aggression and non-resistance are an outcome of homogeneity." "The Gospel of Non-Resistance," in *Democracy and Empire* (New York: Macmillan, 1900), 356. See also Case, *Non-Violent Coercion*, 248; Lewis, *Case Against Pacifism*, 185-186.

When the people of the territory refuse to inform the police about individuals who are committing unlawful acts against the invaders, it is virtually impossible for the latter to check the expansion of non-cooperation or sabotage. Similarly, if the whole population refuses to cooperate with the invader, it is impossible for him to punish them all, or if he did, he would be destroying the labor force whose cooperation he desires, and would have defeated himself in the very process of stamping out the opposition to his regime.

Hitler himself has discovered that there is a difference between military occupation and actual conquest. In his New Year's proclamation to the German people in 1944, he attempted to explain the Nazi reverses in North Africa and Italy in these words:

> "The true cause of the difficulties in North Africa and the Balkans was in reality the persistent attempts at sabotage and paralyzation of these plutocratic enemies of the fascist people's State.
>
> "Their continual sabotage not only succeeded in stopping supplies to Africa and, later on, to Italy, by ever-new methods of passive resistance, thus preventing our soldiers and the Italians standing at their side from receiving the material wherewithal for the conduct of the struggle, but also aggravated or confused the situation in the Balkans, which had been cleared according to plan by German actions."[29]

Opposition to the German invader has taken different forms in different countries. In Denmark, where there was no military resistance to the initial invasion, the subtle opposition of the people has made itself felt in innumerable ways. There are many stories such as that of the King's refusal to institute anti-Jewish laws in Denmark on the ground that there was no Jewish problem there since the Danes did not feel themselves to be inferior to the Jews. Such ideological opposition makes the Nazis angry, and it also makes them uncomfortable, since they do hold enough values in common with the Danes to understand perfectly the implications of the Danish jibes. Such psychological opposition merges into sabotage very easily. For instance when the Germans demanded ten torpedo boats from the Danish navy, the Danes prepared them for delivery by taking all their guns and equipment ashore, and then burning the warehouse in which these were stored. The Nazis even forbade the press to mention the incident, lest it become a signal for a nationwide demonstration of solidarity.[30]

[29] *New York Times,* Jan. 1, 1944, page 4, columns 2-7.
[30] C. H. W. Hasselriis, "Nothing Rotten in Denmark," in *The New Republic,* June 7, 1943, Vol. 108: 760-761.

Other occupied countries report the same type of non-violent resistance. There are strikes of parents against sending their children to Nazi-controlled schools, strikes of ministers against conforming to Nazi decrees, demonstrations, malingering, and interference with internal administration. Such events may appear less important than military resistance, but they make the life of an occupying force uneasy and unhappy.[31]

Calls for non-violent preparation for the day of delivery go out constantly in the underground press. While urging solidarity in illegal acts among the French population at home, one French appeal even gave instructions to Frenchmen who might go to work in Germany:

> "If you respond to Laval's appeal, I know in what spirit you will do so. You will wish to slow down German production, establish contacts with all the Frenchmen in Germany, and create the strongest of Fifth Columns in the enemy country."[32]

Over a long period of time such action cannot help having an effect upon the success of the invader. Since the grievance of the peoples of the occupied countries is a continuous one, there is no prospect that their resistance will relax until they have freed themselves of their oppressors.

Chinese Boycotts Against Foreigners

We can find many other examples of the use of these non-violent methods under similar circumstances. The Chinese made use of the boycott repeatedly to oppose foreign domination and interference in their internal affairs in the years before the outbreak of the present war against Japan. Clarence Case lists five significant Chinese boycotts between 1906 and 1919. The last one was directed against foreigners *and the Chinese government* to protest the action of the Peace Conference in giving Japan a predominant interest in Shantung. As a result the government of China was ousted, and the provisions of the treaty revised. Japan felt the effects of the boycott more than any other country. Case says of the Japanese reaction:

> "As for the total loss to Japanese trade, various authorities have settled upon $50,000,000, which we may accept as a close approximation. At any rate the pressure was great

---

[31]The publications of the various governments in exile are filled with such stories. See such periodicals as *News of Norway* and *News from Belgium*, which can be obtained through the United Nations Information Service, 610 Fifth Avenue, New York City.

[32]*Resistance*, Feb. 17, 1943, reprinted in *Free World*, July, 1943, Vol. 6, 77.

enough to impel the Japanese merchants of Peking and Tientsin, with apparent ruin staring them in the face, to appeal to their home government for protection. They insisted that the boycott should be made a diplomatic question of the first order and that demands for its removal should be backed by threats of military intervention. To this the government at Tokio 'could only reply that it knew no way by which the Chinese merchants, much less the Chinese people, could be made to buy Japanese goods against their will.' "[33]

This incident calls to mind the experience of the American colonists in their non-violent resistance to Great Britain's imperial policy in the years following 1763, which we shall discuss more at length in the next section.

Egyptian Opposition to Great Britain

Another similar example is that of the Egyptian protest against British occupation of the country in 1919. People in all walks of life went on strike. Officials boycotted the British mission under Lord Milner, which came to work out a compromise. The mission was forced to return to London empty handed, but finally an agreement was reached there with Saad Zagloul Pasha, leader of the Egyptian movement, on the basis of independence for the country, with the British retaining only enough military control to safeguard their interest in the Suez Canal. After the acceptance of the settlement in 1922, friction between Egypt and Great Britain continued, but Egypt was not sufficiently united, nor were the grievances great enough to lead to the same type of successful non-cooperation practiced in 1919.[34]

It must be recognized that in most cases such as those we have been considering, violence would be used by the resisters if they had it at their disposal. However, the occasional success of non-violence even under such circumstances is proof of the possible expediency of

---

[33]Case, *Non-Violent Coercion*, 330-339. The last sentence is quoted from *The Christian Science Monitor*, April 7, 1920.

[34]A. Fenner Brockway, *Non-Co-operation in Other Lands* (Madras: Tagore and Co., 1921), 25-39; Charles E. Mullett, *The British Empire* (New York: Holt, 1938), 622-627.

Pacifist literature has also made much of the Hungarian independence movement in the 1860's under Francis Deak, which refused to pay taxes to the Austrian government, or to co-operate in other ways. However, it would appear that outside pressures were as important in the final settlement establishing the Dual Monarchy in 1867 as was the Hungarian movement of non-cooperation. The pacifist writers generally follow the account in Brockway, *Non-Co-operation*, 1-24. He in turn follows the book of Arthur Griffith, *The Resurrection of Hungary*, published in 1904 in order to induce the Irish to use non-co-operation in their struggle against the English. For some of the other factors involved see A. J. P. Taylor, *The Hapsburg Monarchy 1815-1918* (London: Macmillan, 1941), 101-151.

this method. When it has failed, it has done so because the resisters were not sufficiently committed to their purpose to carry it out in the face of possible death. It appears from this experience that complete solidarity and commitment is required for the success of non-violent methods when used in this way, just as they are if such methods are used as a matter of principle. It must be recognized that the self-discipline necessary for the success of a non-violent movement must be even more rigorous than the imposed discipline of a military machine, and also that there is a chance that the non-violent resisters will fail in their endeavor, just as there is a virtual certainty that one side in a military conflict will be defeated.[35]

IV. NON-VIOLENT COERCION

In the last section we were considering the non-violent resistance of groups which had no choice in their means of opposing the will of an invader, but who would have chosen violence if the weapons of violence had been available to them. In those cases there was no question but that the choice rested upon the expediency of the moment rather than upon principle. In the cases of non-violence by necessity the purposes of the resisting groups were defensive and negative, designed to induce the withdrawal of the invader rather than to induce him to follow actively a different policy.

In this section we are concerned with the action of groups designed to modify the conduct of others in order to promote their own ideals. We are concerned with people who presumably have a possible choice of methods to accomplish their purposes. They might rely upon persuasion and education of their opponents through emotional or intellectual appeals; but such action would have no coercive element in it, so we shall consider it in a later section. Or they might attempt to coerce their opponents, either by violent or non-violent means. For the present we are interested only in the latter through its usual manifestations: the strike, the boycott, or other organized movements of non-cooperation.[36]

---

[35]On the discipline required see Gregg, *Power of Non-Violence*, 266-294. Lewis, to prove the ineffectiveness of non-violence, quotes Joad: "There have been only too many occasions in history in which the meeting of violence by non-violence has led not to the taming of the violent, but to the extinction of the non-violent." *The Case Against Pacifism*, 184.

[36]Clarence Marsh Case, "Friends and Social Thinking" in S. B. Laughlin (Ed.), *Beyond Dilemmas* (Philadelphia: Lippincott, 1937), 130-137; Cadoux, *Christian Pacifism Re-Examined*, 24-25, and the chart on page 45.

At first sight such methods do not appear to be coercive in nature, since they involve merely an abstention from action on the part of the group offering the resistance. Actually they are coercive, however, because of the absolute necessity for inter-group cooperation in the maintenance of our modern social, economic, and political systems. Under modern conditions the group against whom the resistance is directed must have the cooperation of the resisting group in order to continue to survive. When that cooperation is denied, the old dominant group is forced to make concessions, *even against its will*, to the former subordinate group in order to regain the help that they have refused to render under the old conditions.[37]

The non-violent resisters themselves are also dependent upon inter-group cooperation. Hence the outcome of this type of struggle usually depends upon which of the two parties to the conflict can best or longest dispense with the services of the other. If the resisters are less able to hold out than the defenders, or if the costs of continued resistance become in their eyes greater than the advantages which might be gained by ultimate victory, they will lose their will to resist and their movement will end in failure.

In all such struggles, both sides are greatly influenced by the opinions of parties not directly concerned in the immediate conflict, but who might give support or opposition to one side or the other depending upon which could enlist their sympathies. Because of the deep-seated dislike of violence, even in our western society, the side that first employs it is apt to lose the sympathy of these third parties. As E. A. Ross has put it:

> "Disobedience without violence wins, *if it wins,* not so much by touching the conscience of the masters as by exciting the sympathy of disinterested onlookers. The spectacle of men suffering for a principle *and not hitting back* is a moving one. It obliges the power holders to condescend to explain, to justify themselves. The weak get a change of venue from the will of the stronger to the court of public opinion, perhaps of world opinion."[38]

The stakes in such a struggle may be great or small. They range all the way from the demand of a labor union for an increase of five cents an hour in wages, to that of a whole people demanding political independence from an imperial master, or a revolutionary change in the economic or political power of the community.

---

[37] Case, *Non-Violent Coercion,* 330. John Lewis says, "Non-violence can be as completely coercive as violence itself, in which case, while it has the advantage of not involving war, it cannot be defended on spiritual grounds." *Case Against Pacifism,* 110.

[38] In his "Introduction" to Case, *Non-Violent Coercion.*

The decision of the resisters to use non-violent means of opposition to gain their ends may be based either upon principle or upon expediency. In the former case they would say that the purposes they have in mind would not be worth attaining if their achievement were to involve physical violence toward other human beings; in the latter they would act on the basis of the conclusion that in view of all the factors involved their purposes could best be served by avoiding violence. These factors would include the likelihood of counter-violence, an estimate of the relative physical strength of the two parties to the conflict, and the attitude of the public toward the party that first used violence. In practice the action of those who avoid violence because they regard it as wrong is very little different from that of those who avoid it because they think that it will not serve their ends. But since there is a moral difference between them, we shall postpone the consideration of Satyagraha, or non-violent direct action on the basis of principle, until the next section. It would deserve such separate treatment in any case because of the great amount of attention which it commands in pacifist circles all over the world.

At the outset it is necessary to dispel the idea that non-violent resistance is something esoteric and oriental, and that it is seldom used in western society. This type of action is used constantly in our own communities, and the histories of western peoples present us with a large number of examples of the use of non-violent action in political and revolutionary conflicts. In the following discussion, the point of view is that of the West.

The Labor Strike

The most common type of non-violent conflict is the ordinary labor strike. In a strike, the workers withdraw their cooperation from the employer until he meets their demands. He suffers, because as long as they refuse to work for him it is impossible for him to produce the goods or services upon the sale of which his own living depends. Usually he is fighting for no principle during such a strike, so that he is apt to calculate his monetary loss from it against the advantages he would have to surrender in order to reach an agreement. When he concludes that it would be cheaper to give in, it is possible for the management and the strikers to arrive at a settlement. If the employer does feel that the principle of control of an enterprise by its owner is at stake, he may hold out longer, until he actually loses more by the strike than he would by conceding the demands of the strikers, but even then he balances psychological cost against monetary cost, and when the latter overweighs the former he becomes receptive to a settlement.

During the strike the workers are going through much the same process. A strike from their point of view is even more costly than it is to the employer. It is not to be entered upon lightly, since their very means of sustenance are at stake. They too have to balance the monetary costs of their continued refusal to cooperate against the gains that they might hope for by continued resistance, and when the cost becomes greater than the prospective gain they are receptive to suggestions for compromise. They too may be contending for the principle of the right of organization and control over their own economic destinies, so that they may be willing to suffer loss for a longer period than they would if they stood to gain only the immediate monetary advantages, but when immediate costs more than overweigh ultimate psychological advantages, they too will be willing to capitulate.

In the meantime the strikers have to see to it that the employer does not find someone else with whom he can cooperate in order to eliminate his dependence upon them. Hence they picket the plant, in an attempt to persuade others not to work there. If persuasion is not effective, they may resort to mass picketing, which amounts to a threat of violence against the persons who would attempt to take over their jobs. On occasion the threat to their jobs becomes so great that in order to defend them they will resort to violence against the strikebreaker. At this point, the public, which is apt to be somewhat sympathetic toward their demands for fair wages or better working conditions, turns against them and supports the employer, greatly adding to his moral standing and weakening that of the strikers, until the strikers, feeling that the forces against them are too great, are apt to give way. The employer will find the same negative reaction among the public if he tries to use violence in order to break the strike. Hence, if he does decide to use violence, he tries to make it appear that the strikers are responsible, or tries to induce them to use it first. It is to their advantage not to use it, even when it is used against them. Labor leaders in general understand this principle and try to avoid violence at all costs. They do so not on the basis of principle, but on the basis of expediency.[39]

In the great wave of enthusiastic organization of labor that swept over the United States in 1936 and 1937, American labor copied a

[39] A. J. Muste, *Non-Violence in an Aggressive World* (New York: Harper, 1940), 70-72.

variant of the strike, which had been used earlier in Hungary and in France.[40] Instead of leaving the property of the employer and trying to prevent others from entering it to take their places, workers remained on a "sit down strike" within the plants, so that the employer would have been forced to use violence to remove them in order to operate the factory. These strikes were based in part upon the theory that the worker had a property right to his job, just as the employer did to his capital equipment. Such strikes were for a time more successful than the older variety, because strike-breaking was virtually impossible. However, it was not long before public opinion forced the abandonment of the technique. It was revolutionary in character, since it threatened the old concept of private property. The fear of small property holders that their own possessions would be jeopardized by the success of such a movement, made them support the owners of the plants against the strikers, who were then forced to give way. In this case the public's fear of revolutionary change was greater than their dislike of violence, so they even supported the use of physical force by the employers and the police authorities to remove the strikers from the plants. The very effectiveness of the method which labor was employing brought about its defeat, because the public was not yet persuaded to accept the new concept of the property right of the laborer to his job.

The Boycott

The boycott is a more indirect type of non-cooperation than the strike, in most cases.[41] This word originated in Ireland in 1880 when a Captain Boycott, an agent for an Irish landlord, refused the demands of the tenants on the estate. In retaliation they threatened his life, forced his servants to leave him, tore down his fences, and cut off his food supplies. The Irish Land League, insisting that the land of Ireland should belong to its people, used this method of opposition in the years that followed. Its members refused to deal with peasants or tradesmen who sided with the government, but they used acts of violence and intimidation as well as economic pressure. The government employed 15,000 military police and 40,000 soldiers against the people, but they succeeded only in filling the jails. The struggle might well have won land for the Irish peasant, if Parnell, who had

---

[40]Barthelemy de Ligt, *The Conquest of Violence: An Essay on War and Revolution* (New York: E. P. Dutton, 1938), 131-132.

[41]"The boycott is a form of passive resistance in all cases where it does not descend to violence and intimidation. The fact that it is coercive does not place it beyond the moral pale, for coercion . . . is a fact inseparable from life in society." Case, *Non-Violent Coercion*, 319.

become leader of the Irish movement, had not agreed to accept the Gladstone Home Rule Bill of 1886 in exchange for calling off the opposition in Ireland. The Bill was defeated in Parliament and the Irish problem continued.[42]

In later usage, the word "boycott" has been applied almost exclusively to the refusal of economic cooperation. Organized labor in America used the boycott against the goods of manufacturers who refused to deal with unions, and it is still used in appeals to the public not to patronize stores or manufacturers who deal unfairly with labor.

The idea of economic sanctions, which played so large a part in the history of the League of Nations in its attempts to deal with those who disregarded decisions of the League, is essentially similar to the boycott. In fact much of the thinking of the pacifist movement between the two wars maintained that economic sanctions would provide a non-violent but coercive substitute for war, in settling international controversies.[43]

Non-Violent Coercion by the American Colonies

The western world has repeatedly employed non-violent coercion as a political as well as an economic technique. Strangely enough, many Americans who are apt to scoff at the methods of the Indian independence movement today forget that the American colonists used much the same methods in the early stages of their own revolt against England. When England began to assert imperial control over the colonies after 1763, the colonists answered with protests and refusals to cooperate. Against both the Stamp Act of 1765 and the Townshend Duties of 1767, they adopted non-importation agreements whereby they refused to import British goods. To be sure, the more radical colonists did not eschew violence on the basis of principle, and the direct action by which they forced colonial merchants to respect the terms of the non-importation agreements was not always non-violent. The loss of trade induced British merchants to go to Parliament on both occasions and to insist successfully upon the repeal of the Stamp Act in 1766 and the Townshend Duties in 1770. In the face of non-cooperation practiced by the vast majority of

---

[42]De Ligt, 114-117; Carleton J. H. Hayes, *A Political and Cultural History of Modern Europe* (New York: Macmillan, 1936), II, 496,
[43]De Ligt, 218-241,

the colonists, the British government had been forced to give way in order to serve its own best interests.[44]

In 1774, when the Continental Congress established the Continental Association in order to use the same economic weapon again, the issues in the conflict were more clearly drawn. Many of the moderate colonists who had supported the earlier action, denounced this one as revolutionary, and went over to the loyalist side. The radicals themselves felt less secure in the use of their economic weapon, and began to gather arms for a violent rebellion. The attempt of the British to destroy these weapons led to Lexington and Concord.[45] What had been non-violent opposition to British policy had become armed revolt and civil war. It was a war which would probably have ended in the defeat of the colonists if they had not been able to fish in the troubled waters of international politics and win the active support of France, who sought thus to avenge the loss of her own colonies to Great Britain in 1763. We have here an example of the way in which non-violent resistance, when used merely on the basis of expediency, is apt to intensify and sharpen the conflict, until it finally leads to war itself.[46]

Irish Opposition to Great Britain After 1900

After centuries of violent opposition to British occupation, the Irish tried an experiment in non-violent non-cooperation after 1900. Arthur Griffith was inspired to use in Ireland the techniques employed in the Hungarian independence movement of 1866-1867. His Sinn Fein party, organized in 1906, determined to set up an independent government for Ireland outside the framework of the United Kingdom. When the Home Rule Act of 1914 was not put into operation because of the war, Sinn Fein gained ground. In the elections of 1918, three fourths of the successful Irish candidates were members of the party, so they met at Dublin as an Irish parliament rather than proceeding to Westminster. In 1921, after a new Home Rule Act had resulted only in additional opposition, the British government negotiated a

---

[44]Curtis Nettels says of the Stamp Act opposition, "The most telling weapons used by the colonists were the non-importation agreements, which struck the British merchants at a time when trade was bad." *The Roots of American Civilization* (New York: Crofts, 1938), 632. Later he says, "The colonial merchants again resorted to the non-importation agreements as the most effectual means of compelling Britain to repeal the Townshend Acts." *Ibid.*, 635.

For a good account of this whole movement see also John C. Miller, *Origins of the American Revolution* (Boston: Little, Brown, 1943), 150-164, 235-281.

[45]Miller, 355-411.

[46]Case, *Non-Violent Coercion*, 308-309.

settlement with the representatives of the "Irish Republic," which set
up the "Irish Free State" as a self-governing dominion within the
British Commonwealth. The Irish accepted the treaty, and the Irish
problem was on its way to settlement, although later events were to
prove that Ireland would not be satisfied until she had demonstrated
that the new status made her in fact independent. Her neutrality in
the present war should dispel all doubts.[47]

Strikes with Political Purposes

British workers themselves have made use of strikes with political
significance. In 1920, transport workers refused to handle goods
destined to be used in the war against the Bolshevik regime in Russia,
and thus forced Britain to cease her intervention.[48] In 1926, the general
strike in Britain had revolutionary implications which the Government and the public recognized only too well. Hence the widespread
opposition to it. The leaders of the strike were even frightened themselves, and called it off suddenly, leaving the masses of the workers
completely bewildered.[49]

In Germany, non-cooperation has also been used successfully.
In 1920, a general strike defeated the attempt of the militarists to
seize control of the state in the Kapp Putsch. In 1924, when the
French Army invaded the Ruhr, the non-violent refusal of the German
workers to mine coal for France had the support of the whole German
nation. As the saying was at the time, "You can't mine coal with
bayonets." Finally the French withdrew from their fruitless adventure.[50]

Non-Violence in International Affairs

In the international field, we also have examples of the use of
non-violent coercion. Thomas Jefferson, during the struggle for the
recognition of American neutral rights by Britain and France, attempted to employ the economic weapons of pre-revolutionary days.
His embargo upon American commerce and the later variants on that
policy, designed to force the belligerents to recognize the American
position, actually were more costly to American shippers than were
the depredations of the French and the British, so they forced a re-

[47]Brockway, Non-Co-operation, 71-92; William I. Hull, The War Method and the
   Peace Method: An Historical Contrast (New York: Revell, 1929), 229-231;
   Hayes, Modern Europe, II, 498-501, 876-879, 952-953.
[48]Allen, Fight for Peace, 633-634; Huxley, Ends and Means, 169-170.
[49]Berkman, Communist Anarchism, 247-248.
[50]Oswald Garrison Villard's "Preface" to Shridharani, War Without Violence,
   xiv-xv.

versal of American policy. The war against England that followed did not have the support of the shipping interests, whose trade it was supposedly trying to protect. It was more an adventure in American imperialism than it was an attempt to defend neutral rights, so it can hardly be said to have grown out of the issues which led to Jefferson's use of economic sanctions. The whole incident proves that the country which attempts to use this method in international affairs must expect to lose its own trade in the process. The cause must be great indeed before such undramatic losses become acceptable.[51]

The same principle is illustrated in the attempt to impose economic sanctions on Italy in 1935 and 1936. The nations who made a gesture toward using them actually did not want to hinder Italian expansion, or did not want to do so enough to surrender their trade with Italy. The inevitable result was that the sanctions failed.

The success of non-violent coercion is by no means assured in every case. It depends upon (1) the existence of a grievance great enough to justify the suffering that devolves upon the resisters, (2) the dependence of the opposition on the cooperation of the resisters, (3) solidarity among a large enough number of resisters, and (4) in most cases, the favorable reaction of the public not involved in the conflict. When all or most of these factors have been present, non-violent coercion has succeeded in our western society. On other occasions it has failed. But one who remembers the utter defeat of the Austrian socialists who employed arms against Chancellor Dolfuss in 1934 must admit that violent coercion also has its failures.[52]

V. SATYAGRAHA OR NON-VIOLENT DIRECT ACTION

There is a distinction between those who employ non-violent methods of opposition on the basis of expediency and those who refuse to use violence on the basis of principle. In the minds of many pacifists the movement for Indian independence under the leadership of Mohandas K. Gandhi stands out as the supreme example of a political revolt which has insisted on this principle, and hence as a model to be followed in any pacifist movement of social, economic, or political

---

[51]Louis Martin Sears, *Jefferson and the Embargo* (Durham, N. C.: Duke University, 1927); Julius W. Pratt, *Expansionists of 1812* (New York: Macmillan, 1925).

[52]De Ligt, 131. For other statements concerning the virtual impossibility of violent revolution today see De Ligt, 81-82, 162-163; Horace G. Alexander, "Great Possessions" in Gerald Heard, *et. al.*, *The New Pacifism* (London: Allenson, 1936), 89-91; Huxley, *Ends and Means*, 178-179; Lewis, *Case Against Pacifism*, 112-113.

reform. Gandhi's Satyagraha, therefore, deserves careful analysis in the light of pacifist principles.

Western critics of Gandhi's methods are prone to insist that they may be applicable in the Orient, but that they can never be applied in the same way within our western culture. We have already seen that there have been many non-violent movements of reform within our western society, but those that we have examined have been based on expediency. Undoubtedly the widespread Hindu acceptance of the principle of *ahimsa*, or non-killing, even in the case of animals, prepared the way for Gandhi more completely than would have been the case in western society.

The Origins of Satyagraha

Shridharani has traced for us the origins of this distinctive Hindu philosophy of *ahimsa*. It arose from the idea of the sacrifice, which the Aryans brought to India with them at least 1500 years before Christ. From a gesture of propitiation of the gods, sacrifice gradually turned into a magic formula which would work automatically to procure desired ends and eliminate evil. In time the Hindus came to believe that the most effective type of sacrifice was self-sacrifice and suffering, accompanied by a refusal to injure others, or *ahimsa*.[53] Only the warrior caste of *Kshatriyas* was allowed to fight. In his autobiography, Gandhi brings out clearly the pious nature of his home environment, and the emphasis which was placed there upon not eating meat because of the sacred character of animal life.[54]

It is not surprising that a logical mind reared in such an environment should have espoused the principle of non-killing. In his western education Gandhi became acquainted with The Sermon on the Mount, and the writings of Tolstoy and Thoreau, but he tells us himself that he was attracted to these philosophies because they expressed ideas in which he already believed.[55]

In fact, the Hindese have long employed the non-violent methods of resistance which Gandhi has encouraged in our own day. In 1830, the population of the State of Mysore carried on a great movement of non-cooperation against the exploitation by the native despot, during which they refused to work or pay taxes, and retired into the forests. There was no disorder or use of arms. The official report of the British Government said:

[53]Shridharani, *War Without Violence*, 165-167.
[54]M. K. Gandhi, *The Story of My Experiments with Truth,* translated by Mahadev Desai and Pyrelal Nair (Ahmedabad: Navajivan Press, 1927-1929), the earlier portions of Vol. I.
[55]*Ibid.,* I, 322; Shridharani, 167.

"The natives understand very well the use of such measures to defend themselves against the abuse of authority. The method most in use, and that which gives the best results, is complete non-co-operation in all that concerns the Government, the administration and public life generally."[56]

In about 1900 there was a great movement of non-cooperation under the leadership of Aurobindo Ghose against the British Government in Bengal. Ghose wanted independence and freedom from foreign tribute. He called upon the people to demonstrate their fitness for self-government by establishing hygienic conditions, founding schools, building roads and developing agriculture. But Ghose had the experience Gandhi was to have later. The people became impatient and fell back on violence; and the British then employed counterviolence to crush the movement completely.[57]

The term "Satyagraha" itself was, however, a contribution of Gandhi. It was coined about 1906 in connection with the Indian movement of non-violent resistance in South Africa. Previously the English term "passive resistance" had been used, but Gandhi tells us that when he discovered that among Europeans, "it was supposed to be a weapon of the weak, that it could be characterized by hatred and that it could finally manifest itself as violence," he was forced to find a new word to carry his idea. The result was a combination of the Gujerati words *Sat*, meaning truth, and *Agraha*, meaning firmness —hence "truth force," or as it has been translated since, "soul force."[58]

The Process of Satyagraha

Shridharani, who considers himself a follower of Gandhi, has given us a comprehensive analysis of Satyagraha as a mass movement. He begins his discussion with this statement of the conditions under which it is possible:

"Satyagraha, as an organized mass action, presupposes that *the community concerned has a grievance which practically every member of that community feels*. This grievance should be of such large proportions that it could be transformed, in its positive side, into a 'Cause' rightfully claiming sacrifice and suffering from the community on its behalf."[59]

This necessity for community solidarity is often overlooked by followers of Gandhi who advocate reforms by means of non-violent direct action in our western society. Given the grievance of British

[56]Quoted by De Ligt, *Conquest of Violence*, 89.
[57]*Ibid.*, 89-90.
[58]Gandhi, *Experiments with Truth*, II, 153-154.
[59]Shridharani, 4. Italics mine.

rule, Shridharani believes that the Hindese were willing to accept Satyagraha first because, unarmed under British law, no other means were available to them, and then because they were predisposed to the method because of the Hindu philosophy of non-violence and the mystic belief that truth will triumph eventually since it is a force greater than the physical.[60]

The first step in Satyagraha is negotiation and arbitration with the adversary. Under these terms Shridharani includes the use of legislative channels, direct negotiations, and arbitration by third parties.[61] In reading his discussion one gets the impression that under the American system of government the later stages of Satyagraha would never be necessary, since the Satyagrahi must first exhaust all the avenues of political expression and legislative action which are open to him. If any sizeable group in American society displayed on any issue the solidarity required for successful use of this method, their political influence would undoubtedly be great enough to effect a change in the law, imperfect though American democracy may be.

The second step in Satyagraha is agitation, the purpose of which is to educate the public on the issues at stake, to create the solidarity that is needed in the later stages of the movement, and to win acceptance, by members of the movement, of the methods to be employed.[62] According to Fenner Brockway, the failure of Satyagraha to achieve its objectives is an indication that the people of India had not really caught and accepted Gandhi's spirit and principles.[63] This means that on several occasions the later stages of Satyagraha have been put into action before earlier stages of creating solidarity on both purpose and method have been fully completed. Despite Gandhi's tremendous influence in India, the movement for Indian independence has not yet fully succeeded. In view of the fact that so many of the people who have worked for independence have failed to espouse Gandhi's principles whole-heartedly, if independence be achieved in the future it will be difficult to tell whether or not it was achieved because the Indian people fully accepted these principles. Many seem to have done so only in the spirit in which the American colonists of the

[60]*Ibid.*, 192-209.
[61]*Ibid.*, 5-7.
[62]*Ibid.*, 7-12.
[63]A. Fenner Brockway, "Does Noncoöperation Work?" in Devere Allen (Ed.), *Pacifism in the Modern World* (Garden City, N. Y.: Doubleday, Doran, 1929), 126.

eighteenth century employed similar methods during the earlier stages of their own independence movement.[64]

Only after negotiation and arbitration have failed does Satyagraha make use of the techniques which are usually associated with it in the popular mind. As Shridharani puts it, "Moral suasion having proved ineffective the Satyagrahis do not hesitate to shift their technique to compulsive force."[65] He is pointing out that in practice Satyagraha is coercive in character, and that all the later steps from mass demonstrations through strikes, boycotts, non-cooperation, and civil disobedience to parallel government which divorces itself completely from the old are designed to *compel* rather than to *persuade* the oppressors to change their policy. In this respect it is very similar to the movements of non-violent resistance based on expediency which were considered in the preceding section.

The Philosophy of Satyagraha

It seems clear that Satyagraha cannot be equated with Christian pacifism. As Shridharani has said, "In India, the people are not stopping with mere good will, as the pacifists usually do, but, on the contrary, are engaged in direct action of a non-violent variety which they are confident will either mend or end the powers that be," and, "Satyagraha seems to have more in common with war than with Western pacifism."[66]

Gandhi's campaign to recruit Indians for the British army during the First World War distinguishes him also from most western paci-

[64]Nehru in his autobiography expresses strong differences of opinion with Gandhi at many points. In one place he says: "What a problem and a puzzle he has been not only to the British Government but to his own people and his closest associates! . . . How came we to associate ourselves with Gandhiji politically, and to become, in many instances, his devoted followers? . . . He attracted people, but it was ultimately intellectual conviction that brought them to him and kept them there. They did not agree with his philosophy of life, or even with many of his ideals. Often they did not understand him. But the action that he proposed was something tangible which could be understood and appreciated intellectually. Any action would be welcome after the long tradition of inaction which our spineless politics had nurtured; brave and effective action with an ethical halo about it had an irresistible appeal, both to the intellect and the emotions. Step by step he convinced us of the rightness of the action, and we went with him, although we did not accept his philosophy. To divorce action from the thought underlying it was not perhaps a proper procedure and was bound to lead to mental conflict and trouble later. Vaguely we hoped that Gandhiji, being essentially a man of action and very sensitive to changing conditions, would advance along the line that seemed to us to be right. And in any event the road he was following was the right one thus far; and, if the future meant a parting, it would be folly to anticipate it." Jawaharlal Nehru, *Toward Freedom* (New York: John Day, 1942), 190-191.

[65]Shridharani, 12. He lists and discusses 13 steps in the development of a campaign of Satyagraha, pp. 5-43.

[66]*Ibid.*, xxvii, xxx.

fists.[67] In an article entitled "The Doctrine of the Sword," written in 1920, Gandhi brought out clearly the fact that in his philosophy he places the ends above the means, so far as the mass of the people are concerned:

> "Where the only choice is between cowardice and violence I advise violence. I cultivate the quiet courage of dying without killing. But to him who has not this courage I advise killing and being killed rather than shameful flight from danger. I would risk violence a thousand times rather than the emasculation of the race. I would rather have India resort to arms to defend her honour than that she should in a cowardly manner remain a helpless victim of her own dishonour."[68]

Both pacifists and their opponents have noted this inconsistency in Gandhi's philosophy. Lewis calls Gandhi "a strange mixture of Machiavellian astuteness and personal sanctity, profound humanitarianism and paralysing conservatism."[69] Bishop McConnell has said of his non-violent coercion, "This coercion is less harmful socially than coercion by direct force, but it is coercion nevertheless."[70] And C. J. Cadoux has declared:

> "The well-known work of Mr. Gandhi, both in India today and earlier in Africa, exemplifies rather the power of non-co-operation than Christian love on the part of a group; but even so, it calls for mention . . . as another manifestation of the efficacy of non-violent methods of restraint."[71]

Gandhi's own analysis of his movement places much emphasis on the mystical Hindu idea of self-inflicted suffering. In 1920, he said, "Progress is to be measured by the amount of suffering undergone by the sufferer."[72] This idea recurs many times in Gandhi's writings. The acceptance of such suffering is not easy; hence his emphasis upon the need of self-purification, preparation, and discipline. Be-

---

[67]Speech at Gujarat political conference, Nov., 1917, quoted by Case, *Non-violent Coercion*, 374-375. See also Shridharani, 122, note.

[68]Quoted in Lewis, *Case Against Pacifism*, 107. A slightly different version is reprinted in Nehru, *Towards Freedom*, 81.

[69]Lewis, *Case Against Pacifism*, 99. He goes on to say, "He is anti-British more than he is anti-war. He adopts tactics of non-violence because that is the most effective way in which a disarmed and disorganized multitude can resist armed troops and police. He has never suggested that when India attains full independence it shall disband the Indian army. The Indian National Congress . . . never for one moment contemplated abandoning violence as the necessary instrument of the State they hoped one day to command." Pp. 99-100.

[70]Francis J. McConnell, *Christianity and Coercion* (Nashville: Cokesbury Press, 1933), 46.

[71]Cadoux, *Christian Pacifism*, 109.

[72]*Young India*, June 16, 1920, quoted by Shridharani, 169.

cause of the violence used by many of his followers during the first great campaign in India, Gandhi came to the conclusion that "before re-starting civil disobedience on a mass scale, it would be necessary to create a band of well-trained, pure-hearted volunteers who thoroughly understood the strict conditions of Satyagraha."[73]

The Empirical Origins of Gandhi's Method

Gandhi's autobiography brings out the origins of many of his ideas. We have already noted the importance of his Hindu training. He arrived empirically at many of his specific techniques. For instance, he describes in some detail a journey he made by coach in 1893 in South Africa, during which he was placed on the driver's seat, since Indians were not allowed to sit inside the coach. Later the coachman desired his seat and asked him to sit on the footboard. This Gandhi refused to do, whereupon the coachman began to box his ears. He describes the rest of the incident thus:

> "He was strong and I was weak. Some of the passengers were moved to pity and they exclaimed: 'Man, let him alone. Don't beat him. He is not to blame. He is right. If he can't stay there, let him come and sit with us.' 'No fear,' cried the man, but he seemed somewhat crestfallen and stopped beating me. He let go my arm, swore at me a little more, and asking the Hottenot servant who was sitting on the other side of the coachbox to sit on the footboard, took the seat so vacated."[74]

He had a similar experience in 1896 when his refusal to prosecute the leaders of a mob which had beaten him aroused a favorable reaction on the part of the public.[75] Gradually the principle developed that the acceptance of suffering was an effective method of winning the sympathy and support of disinterested parties in a dispute, and that their moral influence might go far in determining its outcome.

On his return to India after his successful campaign for Indian rights in South Africa, Gandhi led a strike of mill workers in Ahmedabad. He established a set of rules, forbidding resort to violence, the molestation of "blacklegs," and the taking of alms, and requiring the strikers to remain firm no matter how long the strike took—rules not too different from those that would be used in a strike by an occi-

---

[73]Gandhi, *Experiments*, II, 509-513.

[74]*Ibid.*, I, 268-269.

[75]Of the incident he says, "Thus the lynching ultimately proved to be a blessing for me, that is for the cause. It enhanced the prestige of the Indian community in South Africa, and made my work easier . . . The incident also added to my professional practice." *Ibid.*, I, 452-457.

dental labor union.[76] Speaking of a period during this strike when the laborers were growing restive and threatening violence, Gandhi says:

> "One morning—it was at a mill-hands' meeting—while I was still groping and unable to see my way clearly, the light came to me. Unbidden and all by themselves the words came to my lips: 'Unless the strikers rally,' I declared to the meeting, 'and continue the strike till a settlement is reached, or till they leave the mills altogether, I will not touch any food.' "

Gandhi insisted that the fast was not directed at the mill owners, but was for the purification of himself and the strikers. He told the owners that it should not influence their decision, and yet an arbitrator was now appointed, and as he says, "The strike was called off after I had fasted only for three days."[77] The efficacy of the fast was thus borne in on Gandhi.

In the Kheda Satyagraha against unjust taxation, which was the first big movement of the sort in India, Gandhi discovered that "When the fear of jail disappears, repression puts heart into people." The movement ended in a compromise rather than the complete success of Gandhi's program. He said of it, "Although, therefore, the termination was celebrated as a triumph of Satyagraha, I could not enthuse over it, as it lacked the essentials of a complete triumph."[78] But even though Gandhi was not satisfied with anything less than a complete triumph, he had learned that when a people no longer fears the punishments that an oppressor metes out, the power of the oppressor is gone.[79]

Non-Cooperation

It will be impossible for us here to consider in detail the great movements of non-cooperation on which Gandhi's followers have embarked in order to throw off British rule. In 1919 and again in the struggle of 1920-1922, Gandhi felt forced to call off the non-cooperation campaigns because the people, who were not sufficiently prepared, fell back upon violence.[80] In the struggle in 1930, Gandhi laid down more definite rules for Satyagrahis, forbidding them to harbor anger, or to offer any physical resistance or to insult their opponents, although they must refuse to do any act forbidden to them

[76]*Ibid.*, II, 411-413.
[77]*Ibid.*, II, 420-424.
[78]*Ibid.*, II, 428-440.
[79]See the quotation from Gandhi in Shridharani, 29.
[80]Gandhi, *Experiments*, II, 486-507; Shridharani, 126-129.

by the movement even at the cost of great suffering.[81] The movement ended in a compromise agreement with the British, but the terms of the agreement were never completely carried out. Repressive measures and the imprisonment of Gandhi checked the non-cooperation movement during the present war, at least temporarily.

Fasting

Gandhi also made use of the fast in 1919, 1924, 1932, 1933, 1939, and 1943 to obtain concessions, either from the British government or from groups of Hindese who did not accept his philosophy.[82] Of fasting Gandhi has said:

> "It does not mean coercion of anybody. It does, of course, exercise pressure on individuals, even as on the government; but it is nothing more than the natural and moral result of an act of sacrifice. It stirs up sluggish consciences and it fires loving hearts to action."[88]

Yet Gandhi believed that the fast of the Irish leader, MacSweeney, when he was imprisoned in Dublin, was an act of violence.[84]

In practice, Satyagraha is a mixture of expediency and principle. It is firmly based on the Hindu idea of *ahimsa,* and hence avoids physical violence. Despite Gandhi's insistence upon respect for and love for the opponent, however, his equal insistence upon winning the opponent completely to his point of view leads one to suspect that he is using the technique as a means to an end which he considers equally fundamental. He accepts suffering as an end in itself, yet he knows that it also is a means to other ends since it arouses the sympathy of public opinion. He regards non-cooperation as compatible with love for the opponent, yet we have already seen that under modern conditions it is coercive rather than persuasive in nature. Despite Gandhi's distinction between his own fasts and those of others, they too involve an element of psychological coercion. We are led to conclude that much of Gandhi's program is based upon expediency as well as upon the complete respect for every human personality which characterizes absolute pacifism.

---

[81]The rules, first published in *Young India,* Feb. 27, 1930, are given by Shridharani, 154-157.

[82]See the list given by Haridas T. Muzumdar, *Gandhi Triumphant! The Inside Story of the Historic Fast* (New York: Universal, 1939), vi-vii.

[83]*Ibid.,* 89.

[84]*Ibid.,* 90. Lewis quotes Gandhi thus: "You cannot fast against a tyrant, for it will be a species of violence done to him. Fasting can only be resorted to against a lover not to extort rights, but to reform him." *Case Against Pacifism,* 109.

The American Abolition Movement

The West also has had its movements of reform which have espoused non-violence as a principle. The most significant one in the United States has been the abolition crusade before the Civil War. Its most publicized faction was the group led by William Lloyd Garrison, who has had a reputation as an uncompromising extremist. Almost every school boy remembers the words with which he introduced the first issue of the *Liberator* in 1831:

> "I *will* be as harsh as truth, and as uncompromising as justice. . . . I am in earnest—I will not equivocate—I will not excuse—I will not retreat a single inch—AND I WILL BE HEARD."

He lived up to his promise during the years that followed, and it is no wonder that Parrington called him "the flintiest character amongst the New England militants."[85] In the South they regarded him as an inciter to violence, and barred his writings from the mails.

Garrison's belief in "non-resistance" is less often stressed, yet his espousal of this principle was stated in the same uncompromising terms as his opposition to slavery. In 1838 he induced the Boston Peace Convention to found the New England Non-Resistance Society. In the "Declaration of Sentiments" which he wrote and which the new Society adopted, he said:

> "The history of mankind is crowded with evidences proving that physical coercion is not adapted to moral regeneration; that the sinful dispositions of men can be subdued only by love; that evil can be exterminated from the earth only by goodness."[86]

Throughout his long struggle against slavery, Garrison remained true to his principles of non-resistance. But his denunciations of slavery made more impression on the popular mind, and aided in stirring up much of the violent sentiment in the North which expressed itself in a crescendo of denunciation of the slave owners. In the South, where anti-slavery sentiment had been strong before, a new defensive attitude began to develop. As Calhoun said of the northern criticism of slavery:

> "It has compelled us to the South to look into the nature and character of this great institution, and to correct many false impressions that even we had entertained in relation to it. Many in the South once believed that it was a moral and

---

[85]Vernon Louis Parrington, *Main Currents in American Thought* (New York: Harcourt Brace, 1930), II, 352.

[86]The "Declaration" is reprinted in Allen, *Fight for Peace*, 694-697.

political evil; that folly and delusion are gone; we see it now in its true light, and regard it as the most safe and stable basis for free institutions in the world."[87]

In the North the violent statements of the abolitionists aroused a physically violent response. Mobs attacked abolition meetings in many places, and on one occasion Garrison himself was rescued from an angry Boston mob. This violence in turn aroused many men like Salmon P. Chase and Wendell Phillips to espouse the anti-slavery cause because they could not condone the actions of the anti-abolitionists.[88] Garrison himself proceeded serenely through the storms that his vigorous writings precipitated.

Feelings rose on both sides, and many who heard and accepted the Garrisonian indictment of slavery knew nothing of his non-resistance principles.[89] Others, who did, came reluctantly to the conclusion that a civil war to rid the country of the evil would be preferable to its continuance. In time the struggle was transferred to the political arena, where men acted sometimes on the basis of interest and not always on the basis of moral principles. The gulf between the sections widened, and civil war approached.

As abolitionists themselves began to express the belief that the slavery issue could not be settled without bloodshed, Garrison disclaimed all responsibility for the growing propensity to espouse violence. In the *Liberator* in 1858 he said:

"When the anti-slavery cause was launched, it was baptized in the spirit of peace. We proclaimed to the country and to the world that the weapons of our warfare were not carnal but spiritual, and we believed them to be mighty through God to the pulling down even of the stronghold of slavery; and for several years great moral power accompanied our cause wherever presented. Alas! in the course of the fearful developments of the Slave Power, and its continued aggressions on the rights of the people of the North, in my judgment a sad change has come over the spirit of anti-slavery men, generally speaking. We are growing more and more warlike, more and more disposed to repudiate the principles of peace. . . . Just in proportion as this spirit prevails, I feel that our moral power is departing and will depart. . . . I will not trust the war-spirit anywhere in the

[87]Quoted in Avery Craven, *The Coming of the Civil War* (New York: Scribners, 1942), 161.

[88]Jesse Macy, *The Anti-Slavery Crusade* (New Haven: Yale University Press, 1919), 69-70.

[89]For the many elements in the abolition movement, see Gilbert Hobbs Barnes, *The Antislavery Impulse, 1830-1844* (New York: D. Appleton-Century, 1933).

universe of God, because the experience of six thousand years proves it not to be at all reliable in such a struggle as ours. . . .

"I pray you, abolitionists, still to adhere to that truth. Do not get impatient; do not become exasperated; do not attempt any new political organization; do not make yourselves familiar with the idea that blood must flow. Perhaps blood will flow—God knows, I do not; but it shall not flow through any counsel of mine. Much as I detest the oppression exercised by the Southern slaveholder, he is a man, sacred before me. He is a man, not to be harmed by my hand nor with my consent. . . . While I will not cease reprobating his horrible injustice, I will let him see that in my heart there is no desire to do him harm,—that I wish to bless him here, and bless him everlastingly,—and that I have no other weapon to wield against him but the simple truth of God, which is the great instrument for the overthrow of all iniquity, and the salvation of the world."[90]

Yet Garrison's fervor for the emancipation of the slaves was so great that when the Civil War came, he said of Lincoln and the Republicans:

"They are instruments in the hand of God to carry forward and help achieve the great object of emancipation for which we have so long been striving. . . . All our sympathies and wishes must be with the Government, as against the Southern desperadoes and buccaneers; yet of course without any compromise of principle on our part."[91]

Although Lincoln insisted that the purpose of the North was the preservation of the Union rather than emancipation, eventually he did free the slaves. It would seem that Garrison, for all his non-resistance declarations, bore some of the responsibility for the great conflict.

In this case, as in the case of Satyagraha, the demand for reform by non-violent means was translated into violence by followers who were more devoted to the cause of reform than they were to the non-violent methods which their leaders proclaimed.

VI. NON-RESISTANCE

The preceding section of this study dealt with those who rejected physical violence on principle, and who felt no hatred toward the persons who were responsible for evil, but who used methods of bringing about reform which involved the use of non-physical coercion, and in some cases what might be called psychological violence.

---

[90]Wendell Phillips Garrison, *William Lloyd Garrison* (New York: Century, 1889), III, 473-474.

[91]Letter to Oliver Johnson, quoted in Allen, *Fight for Peace*, 449-450.

These advocates of non-violent direct action not only resisted evil negatively; they also attempted to establish what they considered to be a better state of affairs.

This section will deal with true non-resistance. It is concerned with those who refuse to resist evil, even by non-violent means, for the most part basing their belief upon the injunction of Jesus to "resist not evil." For them, non-resistance becomes an end in itself, rather than a means for achieving other purposes. They are less concerned with reforming society than they are with maintaining the integrity of their own lives in this respect. If they have a social influence at all, it is only because by exhortation or, more especially by the force of example, they induce others to accept the same way of life. However, in their refusal to participate directly in such evil as war, even non-resistants do actually resist evil.

The Mennonites

The Mennonites are the largest and most significant group of non-resistants. For over four hundred years they have maintained their religious views, and applied them with remarkable consistency.[92] Their church grew out of the Anabaptist movement, which had its origins in Switzerland shortly after 1520. The Anabaptists believed in the literal acceptance of the teachings of the Bible, and their application as rules of conduct in daily life. Since they did not depend for their interpretations upon the authority of any priesthood or ministry, differences grew up among them at an early date. The more radical wing, from which the Mennonites came, accepting the Sermon on the Mount as the heart of the Gospel, early refused to offer any physical resistance to evil.[93] Felix Manz, who was executed for his beliefs in 1527, declared, "No Christian smites with the sword nor resists evil."[94] Hundreds of other Anabaptists followed Manz into martyrdom without surrendering their faith.

In a day before conscription had come into general use, the Anabaptists suffered more for their heresy and their political views than they did for their non-resistance principles. In their belief in rendering unto Caesar only those things which were Caesar's and unto God the things that were God's, they came into conflict with

---

[92] See the pamphlet by C. Henry Smith, *Christian Peace: Four Hundred Years of Mennonite Peace Principles and Practice* (Newton, Kansas: Mennonite Publication Office, 1938).

[93] C. Henry Smith, *The Story of the Mennonites* (Berne, Ind.: Mennonite Book Concern, 1941), 9-30.

[94] John Horsch, *Mennonites in Europe,* (Scottdale, Pa.: Mennonite Publishing House, 1942), 359.

the authorities of both church and state. The established church they refused to recognize at all, and they came to regard the state only as a necessary instrument to control those who had not become Christians. Far in advance of the times they adopted the principle of complete separation of church and state, which for them meant that no Christian might hold political office nor act as the agent of a coercive state, although he must obey its commands in matters which did not interefere with his duty toward God. On the basis of direct scriptural authority, they placed the payment of taxes in the latter category.[95]

The modern Mennonites are descended from the followers of Menno Simons, who was born in the Netherlands in 1496. In 1524 he was ordained as a Catholic priest, but he soon came to doubt the soundness of that religion, and found his way into Anabaptist ranks, where he became one of the leading expounders of the radical principles, placing great emphasis upon non-resistance. In his biblical language, he thus stated his belief on this point:

> "The regenerated do not go to war, nor engage in strife. They are the children of peace who have beaten their swords into plowshares and their spears into pruning hooks, and know of no war. They render unto Caesar the things that are Caesar's and unto God the things that are God's. Their sword is the sword of the Spirit which they wield with a good conscience through the Holy Ghost."[96]

In time the followers of Menno Simons gained in influence, while branches of the Anabaptist movement which did not follow the principle of non-resistance died out. Here and there other non-resistant groups such as the Hutterites and the Moravian Brethren continued.[97]

Ultimately the Mennonites found their way into several parts of Europe, from the North Sea to Russia, in their search for a home where they might be free from persecution. The founding of Germantown in the new Pennsylvania colony in 1683 marked the beginning of a migration which in the years that followed brought the more radical of them to America.[98] With the coming of conscription in Europe, those who held most strongly to their non-resistant principles came to the United States to escape military service. Those who remained in Europe gradually gave up their opposition to war, but those in America have largely maintained their original position.[99]

Today they still refrain from opposing evil, and believe in the separation of church and state, which to them means a refusal to

[95]Smith, *Story of the Mennonites*, 30-35.   [98]Smith, *Story of the Mennonites*, 536-539.
[96]Quoted by Horsch, 363.   [99]Smith, *Christian Peace*, 12-15.
[97]*Ibid.*, 365.

hold office and, in many cases, to vote or to have recourse to the courts. They pay their taxes and do what the state demands, as long as it is not inconsistent with their duty to God. In case of a conflict in duty, service to God is placed first. Since they do not believe that it is possible for the world as a whole to become free of sin, they maintain that the Christian must separate himself from it. They make no attempt to bring about reform in society by means of political action or other movements of the sort which we have considered under non-violent direct action.[100]

Since the term "pacifist" has come into general use to designate those opposed to war, the Mennonites have usually made a distinction between themselves as "non-resistants" and the pacifists, who, they claim, are more interested in creating a good society than they are in following completely the admonitions of the Bible. They also disclaim any relationship to such non-resistants as Garrison or Ballou, even though these men reached substantially the same conclusion about the nature of the state, or with Tolstoy who even refused to accept the support of the state for the institution of private property. The American non-resistants they regard primarily as reformers of human society, and Tolstoy as an anarchist who rejected the state altogether, rather than accepting it as a necessary evil.[101] In so far as the Mennonites have used social influence at all, it has been through the force of example, and in their missionary endeavors to win other individuals to the same high principles which they themselves follow.

The New England Non-Resistants

The Mennonites are undoubtedly right in making a distinction between their position and that of the relatively large group of "non-resistants" which arose in New England during the middle of the nineteenth century. We have already noted the "Declaration of Principles" written by Garrison and accepted by the New England Non-Resistance Society in 1838. Despite the fact that Garrison insisted that an individual ought not to participate in the government of a state which used coercion against its subjects, his life was devoted to a campaign against the evil of slavery. In the "Declaration" itself he said:

> "But, while we shall adhere to the doctrine of non-resistance and passive submission to enemies, we purpose, in a moral and spiritual sense, to speak and act boldly in the

---

[100]Edward Yoder, et al., Must Christians Fight: A Scriptural Inquiry (Akron, Pa.: Mennonite Central Committee, 1943), 31-32, 41-44, 59-61, 64-65.
[101]Ibid., 62-63; and for a full discussion of the attitude see Guy F. Hershberger, "Biblical Non-resistance and Modern Pacifism" in Mennonite Quarterly Rev., XVII (July, 1943), 115-135.

cause of GOD; to assail iniquity in high places, and in low places; to apply our principles to all existing civil, political, legal and ecclesiastical institutions; and to hasten the time, when the kingdoms of this world will have become the kingdoms of our LORD and of his CHRIST, and he shall reign forever."[102]

Garrison was essentially a man of action; the real philosopher of the non-resistance movement was Adin Ballou, a Universalist minister of New England who devoted his whole life to the advancement of its principles. In 1846 he published his *Christian Non-Resistance: In All Its Important Bearings,* in which he set forth his doctrine, supported it with full scriptural citations, and then presented a catalogue of incidents which to his own satisfaction proved its effectiveness, both in personal and in social relationships.

Although Ballou listed a long series of means which a Christian non-resistant might not use, he insisted that he had a duty to oppose evil, saying:

"I claim the right to offer the utmost moral resistance, not sinful, of which God has made me capable, to every manifestation of evil among mankind. Nay, I hold it my duty to offer such moral resistance. In this sense my very non-resistance becomes the highest kind of resistance to evil."[103]

Nor did Ballou condemn all use of "uninjurious, benevolent physical force" in restraining the insane or the man about to commit an injury to another. He finally defined non-resistance as "simply non-resistance of injury with injury—evil with evil." Rather, he believed in "the essential efficacy of good, as the counter-acting force with which to resist evil."[104]

In applying his principle rigorously, Ballou, like the Mennonites, came to the conclusion that the non-resistant could have nothing to do with government. If he so much as voted for its officials, he had to share the moral responsibility for the wars, capital punishment, and other personal injuries which were carried out in its name. He insisted:

"There is no escape from this terrible moral responsibility but by a conscientious withdrawal from such government, and an uncompromising protest against so much of its fundamental creed and constitutional law, as is decidedly

[102]Allen, *Fight for Peace,* 696.
[103]Ballou, *Christian Non-Resistance,* 3.
[104]*Ibid.,* 2-23.

anti-Christian. He must cease to be its pledged supporter, and approving dependent."[105]

Like the Mennonites, he saw that the reason that governments were unchristian was that the people themselves were not Christian; but unlike the Mennonites he maintained that they might eventually become so, and that it was the duty of the Christian to hasten the day of their complete conversion. "This," he said,

"is not to be done by voting at the polls, by seeking influential offices in the government and binding ourselves to anti-Christian political compacts. It is to be done by pure Christian precepts faithfully inculcated, and pure Christian examples on the part of those who have been favored to receive and embrace the highest truths."[106]

The Mennonites believed that man was essentially depraved; Ballou believed that he was perfectible.[107]

Tolstoy

Many people regard the writings of Count Leo Tolstoy as the epitome of the doctrine of non-resistance. Tolstoy arrived at his convictions after a long period of inner turmoil, and published them in *My Religion* in 1884. In the years that followed, his wide correspondence introduced him to many others who had held the same views. He was especially impressed with the 1838 statement of Garrison, and with the writings of Ballou, with whom he entered into correspondence directly.[108]

However, he went further than Ballou, and even further than the Mennonites in his theory, which he formulated fully in *The Kingdom of God is Within You,* published in 1893. He renounced the use of

---

[105]*Ibid.,* 18.

[106]*Ibid.,* 223-224.

[107]Perhaps this is the point at which to insert a footnote on Henry Thoreau, whose essay on "Civil Disobedience" is said to have influenced Gandhi. Although he lived in the same intellectual climate that produced Garrison and Ballou, he was not a non-resistant on principle. For instance, he supported the violent attack upon slave holders by John Brown just before the Civil War. He did come to substantially the same conclusions, however, on government. He refused even to pay a tax to a government which carried on activities which he considered immoral, such as supporting slavery, or carrying on war. On one occasion he said, "They are the lovers of law and order who observe the law when the government breaks it." Essentially, Thoreau was a philosophical anarchist, who placed his faith entirely in the individual, rather than in any sort of organized social action. See the essay on him in Parrington, II, 400-413; and his own essay on "Civil Disobedience" in *The Writings of Henry David Thoreau* (Boston: Houghton Mifflin, 1906), IV, 356-387.

[108]Aylmer Maude, *The Life of Tolstoy,* (New York: Dodd, Mead, 1910), II, 354-360, where the letters to and from Ballou are quoted at length. See also Count Leo N. Tolstoy, *The Kingdom of God is Within You,* translated by Leo Wiener (Boston: Dana Estes & Co., 1905), 6-22.

physical force completely even in dealing with the insane or with children.[109]. He severed all relations with government, and went on to insist that the true Christian might not own any property. He practiced his own doctrines strictly.

Tolstoy had quite a number of followers, and a few groups were established to carry out his teachings. These groups have continued to exist under the Soviet Union, but their present fate is obscure. His works greatly influenced Peter Verigin, leader of the Dukhobors, who shortly after 1900 left Russia and settled in Canada in order to find a more hospitable environment for their communistic community, and to escape the necessity for military service.[110]

However, Tolstoy's theory is so completely anarchistic that it does not lend itself to organization. Hence his chief influence has been intellectual, and upon individuals. We have already noted the great impact that his works made on Gandhi, while he was formulating the ideas which were to result in Satyagraha.

Neither in the case of Gandhi, nor of Peter Verigin, however, were Tolstoy's doctrines applied in completely undiluted form. The Mennonites also disclaim kinship with him on the grounds that he sought a regeneration of society as a whole in this world.[111]

For most men the doctrine of complete anarchism has seemed too extreme for practical consideration, but it would seem that Tolstoy arrived at the logical conclusion of a system of non-resistance based on the premise that man should not combat evil, nor have any relationship whatever with human institutions which attempt to restrain men by means other than reliance upon the force of example and goodwill.

[109]In a letter to L. G. Wilson, Tolstoy said: "I cannot agree with the concession he [Ballou] makes for employing violence against drunkards and insane people. The Master made no concessions, and we can make none. We must try, as Mr. Ballou puts it, to make impossible the existence of such people, but if they do exist, we must use all possible means, and sacrifice ourselves, but not employ violence. A true Christian will always prefer to be killed by a madman, than to deprive him of his liberty." Maude, *Tolstoy*, II, 355-356.

[110]J. F. C. Wright, *Slava Bohu: The Story of the Dukhobors* (New York: Farrar and Rinehart, 1940), 99.

[111]Hershberger says of him: "He identified the kingdom of God with human society after the manner of the social gospel. But since he believed in an absolute renunciation of violence for all men, Tolstoy was an anarchist, repudiating the state altogether. Biblical nonresistance declines to participate in the coercive activities of the state, but nevertheless regards those as necessary for the maintenance of order in a sinful society, and is not anarchistic. But Tolstoy found no place for the state in human society at all; and due to his faith in the goodness of man he believed that eventually all coercion, including domestic police, would be done away." *Mennonite Qu. Rev.*, XVII, 129-130.

VII. ACTIVE GOODWILL AND RECONCILIATION

The term "resistance" has occurred frequently in this study. As has been pointed out, this word has a negative quality, and implies opposition to the will of another, rather than an attempt to realize a positive policy. The preceding section dealt with its counterpart, "non-resistance," which has a neutral connotation, and implies that the non-resister is not involved in the immediate struggle, and that for him the refusal to inflict injury upon anyone is a higher value than the achievement of any policy of his own, either positive or negative.

Non-violent coercion, Satyagraha, and non-violent direct action, on the other hand, are definitely positive in their approach. Each seeks to effectuate a specified change in the policy of the person or group responsible for a situation which those who organize the non-violent action believe to be undesirable. However, even in such action the negative quality may appear. Satyagraha, for instance, insofar as it is a movement of opposition or "resistance" to British rule in India is negative, despite its positive objectives of establishing a certain type of government and economic system in that country.

The employment of active goodwill is another approach to the problem of bringing about desired social change. Its proponents seek to accomplish a positive alteration in the attitude and policy of the group or person responsible for some undesirable situation; but they refuse to use coercion—even non-violent coercion. Rather they endeavor to convince their opponent that it would be desirable to change his policy because the change would be in his own best interest, or would actually maintain his own real standard of values.

Many of those who would reject all coercion of an opponent practice such positive goodwill towards him, not because they are convinced that their action will accomplish the social purposes which they would like to achieve, but rather because they place such an attitude toward their fellowmen as their highest value. They insist that they would act in the same way regardless of the consequences of their action, either to the person towards whom they practice goodwill or to themselves. They act on the basis of principle rather than on the basis of expediency. In this regard they are like many of the practitioners of other methods of non-violence; but unlike them they place their emphasis on the positive action of goodwill which they *will* use, rather than upon a catalogue of violent actions which they will not use.

To those who practice the method of goodwill all types of education and persuasion are available. In the past they have used the printed and spoken word, and under favorable circumstances even political action. They hope to appeal to "that of God in every man," to bring about genuine repentance on the part of those who have been responsible for evil. If direct persuasion is not effective, they hope that their exhibition of love towards him whom others under the same circumstances would regard as an enemy may appeal to an aspect of his nature which is temporarily submerged, and result in a change of attitude on his part. If it does not, these advocates of goodwill are ready to suffer the consequences of their action, even to the point of death.

Action in the Face of Persecution

The practice of positive goodwill is open to the individual as well as to the group. Since he does what he believes to be right regardless of the consequences, he will act before there are enough who share his opinion to create any chance of victory over the well organized forces of the state or other institutions which are responsible for evil. The history of the martyrs of all ages presents us with innumerable examples of men who have acted in this way. Socrates is of their number, as well as the early Christians who insisted upon practicing their religion despite the edicts of the Roman empire. Jesus himself is the outstanding example of one who was willing to die rather than to surrender principle. It cannot be said of these martyrs that they acted in order to bring about reforms in society. They suffered because under the compulsion of their faith they could act in no other way, and at the time of their deaths it always looked as though they had been defeated. But in the end their sacrifices had unsought results. The proof of their effectiveness is declared in the old adage that "the blood of the martyrs is the seed of the church."

If we seek examples from relatively recent times, we may find them in the annals of many of the pacifist sects of our own day. Robert Barclay, the Quaker apologist of the late seventeenth century, stated the position which the members of the Society of Friends so often put to the test:

> "But the true, faithful and Christian suffering is for men to profess what they are persuaded is right, and so practise and perform their worship towards God, as being their true right so to do; and neither to do more than that, because

of outward encouragement from men; nor any whit less, because of the fear of their laws and acts against it."[112]

The early Quakers suffered severely under the laws of England
in a day when religious toleration was virtually unheard of. George
Fox himself had sixty encounters with magistrates and was imprisoned
on eight occasions; yet he was not diverted from his task of preaching
truth. It has been estimated that 15,000 Quakers "suffered" under
the various religious acts of the Restoration.[113] But they continued
to hold the principles which had been stated by twelve of their leaders,
including Fox, to King Charles shortly after his return to England:

> "Our principle is, and our practice always has been, to
> seek peace and ensue it; to follow after righteousness and
> the knowledge of God; seeking the good and welfare, and
> doing that which tends to the peace of all.
>
>   .   .   .   .
>
> "When we have been wronged, we have not sought to
> revenge ourselves; we have not made resistance against au-
> thority; but whenever we could not obey for conscience
> sake, we have suffered the most of any people in the na-
> tion . . . "[114]

These sufferings did not go unheeded. Even the wordly Samuel
Pepys wrote in his diary concerning Quakers on their way to prison:
"They go like lambs without any resistance I would to God they
would either conform or be more wise and not be catched."[115]

In Massachusetts, where the Puritans hoped to establish the true
garden of the Lord, the lot of the Quakers was even more severe.
Despite warnings and imprisonments, Friends kept encroaching upon
the Puritan preserve until the Massachusetts zealots, in their despera-
tion over the failure of the gentler means of quenching Quaker ardor,
condemned and executed three men and a woman. Even Charles II
was revolted by such extreme measures, and ordered the colony to
desist. After a long struggle the Quakers, along with other advocates
of liberty of conscience, won their struggle for religious liberty even
in Massachusetts. There can be little doubt that their sufferings played

[112]Robert Barclay, *An Apology for the True Christian Divinity; being an Explanation
and Vindication of the Principles and Doctrines of the People Called Quakers*
(Philadelphia: Friends' Book Store, 1908), Proposition XIV, Section VI, 480.

[113]A. Ruth Fry, *Quaker Ways: An Attempt to Explain Quaker Beliefs and Practices
and to Illustrate them by the Lives and Activities of Friends of Former Days*
(London: Cassell, 1933), 126, 131.

[114]Quoted by Margaret E. Hirst, *The Quakers in Peace and War: an Account of
Their Peace Principles and Practice* (New York: George H. Doran, 1923),
115-116.

[115]Quoted in Fry, *Quaker Ways*, 128-129.

an important part in the establishment of religious liberty as an American principle.[116]

In our own day the conscientious objector to military service, whatever his motivation and philosophy, faces a social situation very similar to that which confronted these early supporters of a new faith. For the moment there is little chance that his insistence upon following the highest values which his conscience recognizes will bring an end to war, because there are not enough others who share his convictions. He takes his individual stand without regard for outward consequences to himself, because his conviction leaves him no other alternative. But even though his "sufferings" do not at once make possible the universal practice of goodwill towards all men, they may in the end have the result of helping to banish war from the world.

Coercion or Persuasion?

A man who is willing to undergo imprisonment and even death itself rather than to cease doing what he believes is right knows in his own heart that coercion is not an effective means of persuasion. The early Quakers saw this clearly. Barclay stated his conviction in these words:

> "This forcing of men's consciences is contrary to sound reason, and the very law of nature. For man's understanding cannot be forced by all the bodily sufferings another man can inflict upon him, especially in matters spiritual and supernatural: 'Tis argument, and evident demonstration of reason, together with the power of God reaching the heart, that can change a man's mind from one opinion to another, and not knocks and blows, and such like things, which may well destroy the body, but never can inform the soul, which is a free agent, and must either accept or reject matters of opinion as they are borne in upon it by something proportioned to its own nature."[117]

And William Penn said more simply, "Gaols and gibbets are inadequate methods for conversion: this forbids all further light to come into the world."[118]

Other religious groups who went through experiences comparable to those of the Friends came to similar conclusions. The Church of the Brethren, founded in 1709 in Germany, took as one of its leading principles that "there shall be no force in religion," and carried it out so faithfully that they would not baptize children, on the

---

[116]Hirst, 327; Rufus M. Jones, *The Quakers in the American Colonies* (London: Macmillan, 1923), 3-135.

[117]Barclay, *Apology*, Prop. XIV, Sec. IV, 470.

[118]Fry, *Quaker Ways*, 59-60.

ground that this act would coerce them into membership in the church before they could decide to join of their own free will. The Brethren have refused to take part in war not only because it is contrary to the spirit of Christian love, and destroys sacred human life, but also because it is coercive and interferes with the free rights of others.[119]

For the person who believes in the practice of positive goodwill towards all men, the refusal to use coercion arises from its incompatibility with the spirit of positive regard for every member of the human family, rather than being a separate value in itself. In social situations this regard may express itself in various ways. It may have a desirable result from the point of view of the practitioner, but again we must emphasize that he does what he does on the basis of principle; the result is a secondary consideration.

Ministering to Groups in Conflict

One expression of this philosophy may be abstention from partisanship in conflicts between other groups, in order to administer impartially to the human need of both parties to the conflict.

In this connection much has been made of the story of the Irish Quakers during the rebellion in that country in 1798. Before the conflict broke into open violence the Quarterly Meetings and the General National Meeting recommended that all Friends destroy all firearms in their possession so that there could be no suspicion of their implication in the coming struggle. During the fighting in 1798 the Friends interceded with both sides in the interests of humanity, entertained the destitute from both parties and treated the wounds of any man who needed care. Both the Government forces and the rebels came to respect Quaker integrity, and in the midst of pillage and rapine the Quaker households escaped unscathed. But Thomas Hancock, who told the story a few years later, pointed out that in their course of conduct the Friends had not sought safety.

> "It is," he said, "to be presumed, that, even if outward preservation had not been experienced, they who conscientiously take the maxims of Peace for the rule of their conduct, would hold it not less their duty to conform to those princi-

---

[119]D. W. Kurtz, *Ideals of the Church of the Brethren,* leaflet (Elgin, Ill.: General Mission Board, 1934?); Martin G. Brumbaugh in *Studies in the Doctrine of Peace* (Elgin, Ill.: Board of Christian Education, Church of the Brethren, 1939), 56; the statement of the Goshen Conference of 1918 and other statements of the position of the church in L. W. Shultz (ed.), *Minutes of the Annual Conference of the Church of the Brethren on War and Peace,* mimeo (Elgin: Bd. of Chr. Ed., Church of the Brethren, 1935); and the pamphlet by Robert Henry Miller, *The Christian Philosophy of Peace* (Elgin: Bd. of Chr. Ed., Church of the Brethren, 1935).

ples; because the reward of such endeavor to act in obedience
to their Divine Master's will is not always to be looked for in
the present life. While, therefore, the fact of their outward
preservation would be no sufficient argument to themselves
that they had acted as they ought to act in such a crisis, it
affords a striking lesson to those who will take no principle,
that has not been verified by experience, for a rule of human
conduct, even if it should have the sanction of Divine
authority."[120]

It is in this same spirit that various pacifist groups undertook
the work of relief of suffering after the First World War in "friendly"
and "enemy" countries alike, ministering to human need without
distinction of party, race or creed. The stories of the work of the
American Friends Service Committee and the *Service Civil* founded
by Pierre Ceresole are too well known to need repeating here.[121]
It should not be overlooked that in this same spirit the Brethren and
the Mennonites also carried on large scale relief projects during the
interwar years.

The Power of Example

A social group that acts consistently in accordance with the
principles of active goodwill also exerts great influence through the
force of its example. A study of the Quaker activities in behalf of
social welfare was published in Germany just before the First World
War, by Auguste Jorns. She shows how, in relief of the poor, education, temperance, public health, the care of the insane, prison reform,
and the abolition of slavery, the Quakers set about to solve the problem within their own society, but never in an exclusive way, so that
others as well as members might receive the benefits of Quaker enterprises. Quaker methods became well known, and in time served as
models for similar undertakings by other philanthropic groups and

---

[120]Thomas Hancock, *The Principles of Peace Exemplified in the Conduct of the
Society of Friends in Ireland During the Rebellion of the year 1798, with
some Preliminary and Concluding Observations* (2nd ed., London, 1826),
28-29. All the important features of the story are summarized in Hirst, 216-224.

[121]Lester M. Jones, *Quakers in Action: Recent Humanitarian and Reform Activities
of the American Quakers* (New York: Macmillan, 1929); Rufus M. Jones,
A Service of Love in War Time (New York: Macmillan, 1920); Mary Hoxie
Jones, *Swords into Plowshares: An Account of the American Friends Service
Committee 1917-1937* (New York: Macmillan, 1937); Willis H. Hall, *Quaker
International Work in Europe Since 1914* (Chambery, Savoie, France: Impri-
meries Reunies, 1938). On *Service Civil*, see Lilian Stevenson, *Towards a
Christian International, The Story of the International Fellowship of Recon-
ciliation* (Vienna: International Fellowship of Reconciliation, 1929), 27-31,
and Alan A. Hunter, *White Corpuscles in Europe* (Chicago: Willett, Clark,
1939), 33-42.

public agencies. Many modern social work procedures thus had their origins in the work of the Friends in a relatively small circle.[122]

Work for Social Reform

The activity of Quakers in the abolition of slavery both in England and America, especially the life-long work of John Woolman in the colonies, is well known. Here too, the first "concerned" Friends attempted to bring to an end the practice of holding slaves within the Society itself. When they had succeeded in eliminating it from their own ranks, they could, with a clear conscience, suggest that their neighbors follow their example. When the time came, Quakers were willing to take part in political action to eradicate the evil. The compensated emancipation of the slaves in the British Empire in 1833 proved that the reform could be accomplished without the violent repercussions which followed in the United States.[123]

Horace G. Alexander has pointed out that the person who voluntarily surrenders privilege, as the American Quakers did in giving up their slaves, not only serves as a witness to the falsehood of privilege, but can never rest until reform is achieved.

> "The very fact," he says, "that he feels a loyalty to the oppressors as well as to the oppressed means that he can never rest until the oppressors have been converted. It is not their destruction that he wants, but a change in their hearts."[124]

Such an attitude is based upon a faith in the perfectibility of man and the possibility of the regeneration of society. It leads from a desire to live one's own life according to high principles to a desire to establish similar principles in human institutions. It rejects the thesis of Reinhold Niebuhr that social groups can never live according to the same moral codes as individuals, and also the belief of such groups as the Mennonites that, since the "world" is necessarily evil, the precepts of high religion apply only to those who have accepted the Christian way of life. Instead, the conviction of those who hold this ideal that it is social as well as individual in its application leads them into the pathways of social reform, and even into political action.

---

[122]Auguste Jorns, *The Quakers as Pioneers in Social Work,* trans. by Thomas Kite Brown (New York: Macmillan, 1931).

[123]Henry J. Cadbury, *Colonial Quaker Antecedents to British Abolition of Slavery,* An address to the Friends' Historical Society, March 1933 (London: Friends Committee on Slavery and Protection of Native Races, 1933), reprinted from *The Friends' Quarterly Examiner,* July, 1933; Jorns, 197-233.

[124]Horace G. Alexander in Heard, *et al., The New Pacifism, 93.*

Political Action and Compromise

The Quakers, for instance, have been noted for their participation in all sorts of reform movements. Since every reform in one sense involves opposition to some existing institution, Clarence Case has been led to call the Quakers "non-physical resistants;"[125] but since their real objective was usually the establishment of a new institution rather than the mere destruction of an old one, they might better be called "non-violent advocates." They were willing to advocate their reforms in the public forum and the political arena. Since, as Rufus Jones has pointed out, such action might yield to the temptation to compromise with men of lesser ideals, there has always been an element in the Society of Friends which insisted that the ideal must be served in its entirety, even to the extent of giving up public office and influence rather than to compromise.[126] In Pennsylvania the Quakers withdrew from the legislature when it became necessary in the existing political situation to vote support of the French and Indian war, but they did so not because they did not believe in political action, in which up to that moment they had taken part willingly enough, but rather because under the circumstances of the moment it was impossible to realize their ideals by that means.[127]

Ruth Fry, in discussing the uncompromising attitude of the Friends on the issue of slavery, has well described the process of Quaker reform:

> "One cannot help feeling that this strong stand for the ultimate right was far more responsible for success than the more timid one, and should encourage such action in other great causes. In fact, the ideal Quaker method would seem to be patient waiting for enlightenment on the underlying principle, which when seen is so absolutely clear and convincing that no outer difficulties or suffering can affect it: its full implications gradually appear, and its ultimate triumph can never be doubted. Any advance towards it, may be accepted as a stepping stone, although only methods consistent with Quaker ideals may be used to gain the desired end. Doing anything tinged with evil, that good may come, is entirely contrary to their ideas."[128]

She goes on to say, "As ever, the exact line of demarcation between methods aggressive enough to arouse the indolent and those beyond the bounds of Quaker propriety was indeed difficult to draw."[129]

[125]Case, *Non-Violent Coercion*, 92-93.
[126]Rufus M. Jones, *The Quakers in the American Colonies*, 175-176.
[127]Jones, *Quakers in the Colonies*, 459-494; Isaac Sharpless, *A Quaker Experiment in Government* (Philadelphia: Alfred J. Ferris, 1898), 226-276.
[128]Fry, *Quaker Ways*, 171-172.
[129]*Ibid.*, 177.

In such a statement we find a conception of compromise which is different from that usually encountered. In it the advocate of the ideal says that for the time being he will accept less than his ultimate goal, provided the change is in the direction in which he desires to move, but he will not accept the slightest compromise which would move away from his goal.

The Third Alternative

The logical pursuit of such a principle leads even further than the type of compromise which Ruth Fry has described, to the establishment of a new basis of understanding which may not include any of the principles for which the parties in conflict may have been striving, and yet which brings about reconciliation.

Eric Heyman, speaking in religious terms, has said of this process of discovering a new basis of understanding through the exercise of positive goodwill, even toward an oppressor:

"That is the way of God, and it is therefore the way of our discipleship as reconcilers; the way of non-resistance to evil, of the total acceptance of the consequences of evil in all their lurid destructiveness, in order that the evil doer may be reconciled to God. . . . The whole consequences of his presence, whether small or great must be accepted with the single realisation that the whole process of the world's redemption rests upon the relationship which the Christian is able to create between himself and his oppressor. This course has nothing in common with resistance; it is the opposite of surrender, for its whole purpose and motive is the triumphing over evil by acceptance of all that it brings. . . . The resistance of evil, whether by way of violence or 'non-violence' is the way of this world. Resignation to evil is the way of weak surrender, and yields only a powerless resentment; at its best it is non-moral, at the worst sheerly immoral. Acceptance of evil is the triumphant answer of the redeemer. In the moment of his acceptance he knows of a certainty that he has overcome the world."[130]

This process of finding a new basis of relationship has been called "a third alternative, which produces no majority rule and no defeated minority."[131] The Quakers have long used this method in arriving at decisions within their own meetings. They refuse to make motions and take votes which produce clearcut divisions within the group, but insist that no action shall be taken until all divergent points of view have been expressed, and a statement drawn up which

---

[130]Eric Heyman, *The Pacifist Dilemma* (Banbury, England: Friends' Peace Committee, 1941), 11-12.
[131]Carl Heath, "The Third Alternative" in Heard, *et al.*, *The New Pacifism*, 102.

embodies "the sense of the meeting" and is acceptable to all. As Elton Trueblood has said, "The overpowering of a minority by calling for a vote is a kind of force, and breeds the resentment which keeps the method of force from achieving ultimate success with persons."[132] Douglas Steere has described the process in these words:

> "This unshakable faith in the way of vital, mutual inter-action by conciliatory conference is held to be applicable to international and interracial conflict as it is to that between workers and employer, or between man and wife. But it is not content to stop there. It would defy all fears and bring into the tense process of arriving at this joint decision a kind of patience and a quiet confidence which believes, not that there is no other way, but that there is a 'third-alternative' which will annihilate neither party."[133]

M. P. Follett, twenty years ago, wrote a book entitled *Creative Experience,* in which she supported this same conclusion on the basis of scientific knowledge about the nature of man, society and politics. Speaking of the democratic process she said:

> "We have the will of the people ideally when all desires are satisfied. . . . The aim of democracy should be integrating-desires. I have said that truth emerges from difference. In the ballot-box there is no confronting of difference, hence no possibility of integrating, hence no creating; self-govern-ment is a creative process and nothing else. . . . Democracy does not register various opinions; it is an attempt to create unity."[134]

It might be said that in so far as democracy has succeeded, it has done so because of its adherence to this principle. The division of a society into groups which are unremittingly committed to struggle against each other, whether by violent or non-violent means, until one or the other has been annihilated or forced to yield outwardly to its oppressors for the time being, will inevitably destroy the loyalty to a common purpose through which alone democracy can exist.

The contrast between the British and American attitudes toward the abolition of slavery presents us with a case in point. In Great Britain, the Emancipation Act contained provisions for the compen-sation of the slave owners, so that it became acceptable to them. In the United States the advocates of abolition insisted that since slavery was sin there could be no recognition of the rights of the owners. Elihu Burritt and his League of Universal Brotherhood were as much

---

[132]D. Elton Trueblood, "The Quaker Method of Reaching Decisions" in Laughlin, *Beyond Dilemmas,* 119.

[133]Douglas V. Steere, "Introduction" to Laughlin, *Beyond Dilemmas,* 18.

[134]M. P. Follett, *Creative Experience* (New York: Longmans, Green, 1924), 209.

opposed to slavery as the most ardent abolitionists, yet of the League Burritt declared: "It will not only aim at the mutual pacification of enemies, but at their conversion into brethren."[135] Burritt became the chief advocate of compensated emancipation in the United States. Finally the idea was suggested in the Senate and hearings had been arranged on the measure.

> "But," Burritt said, "just as it had reached that stage at which Congressional action was about to recognize it as a legitimate proposition, 'John Brown's raid' suddenly closed the door against all overtures or efforts for the peaceful extinction of slavery. Its extinction by compensated emancipation would have recognized the moral complicity of the whole nation in planting and perpetuating it on this continent. It would have been an act of repentance, and the meetest work for repentance the nation could perform."[136]

The country was already too divided to strive for this "third alternative," and, whether or not slavery was one of the prime causes of the Civil War, it made its contribution to creating the feeling which brought on the conflict. In the light of the present intensity of racial feeling in the United States, it can hardly be said that the enforced settlement of the war gave the Negro an equal place in American society or eliminated conflict between the races.

One of the virtues of the method of reconciliation of views in seeking the "third alternative" is that it can be practiced by the individual or a very small group as well as on the national or international scale. James Myers has described its use within the local community in the "informal conference." In such a conference, the person or group desiring to create better understanding or to eliminate conflict between elements of the community calls together, without any publicity, representatives of various interests for a discussion of points of view, with the understanding that there will be no attempt to reach' conclusions or arrive at any official decisions. James Myers' experience has indicated that the conferences create an appreciation of the reasons for former divergence of opinion, and a realization of the possibilities of new bases of relationship which have often resulted in easing tensions within the community and in the solution of racial, economic and social conflicts.[137]

Even on the international level, individuals may make some contribution toward the elimination of conflicts, although, in the face

---

[135]Quoted in Allen, *Fight for Peace*, 428.

[136]Quoted in *Ibid.*, 437.

[137]James Myers, *"Informal Conferences"* a *New Technique In Social Education*, Leaflet (New York: Federal Council of Churches of Christ in America, 1943).

of the present emphasis upon nationalism, and the lack of common
international values to which appeal may be made, their labors are
not apt to be crowned with success. As in all the cases which we
have been considering, however, concerned individuals and groups
may act in this field because they feel a compulsion to do so, regardless of whether or not their actions are likely to be successful in pro-
ducing the desired result of reconciliation, and the discovery of the
third alternative.[138]

VIII. CONCLUSIONS

Those who do not share the pacifist philosophy are prone to
insist that the pacifists place far too much emphasis upon the refusal
to employ physical force. These critics maintain that force is non-
moral in character, and that the only moral question involved in its
use is whether or not the purposes for which it is employed are "good"
or "bad." They fail to realize that these concepts themselves arise
from a subjective set of values, different for every social group on the
basis of its own tradition and for every individual on the basis of his
own experience and training.

The "absolute" pacifist places at the very apex of his scale of
values respect for every human personality so great that he cannot
inflict injury on any human being regardless of the circumstances in
which he finds himself. He would rather himself suffer what he considers to be injustice, or even see other innocent people suffer it,
than to arrogate to himself the right of sitting in judgment on his
fellow men and deciding that they must be destroyed through his
action. For him to inflict injury or death upon any human being
would be to commit the greatest iniquity of which he can conceive,
and would create within his own soul a sense of guilt so great that
acceptance of any other evil would be preferable to it.

The person who acts on the basis of such a scale of values is
not primarily concerned with the outward expediency of his action
in turning the evil-doer into new ways, although he is happy if his
action does have incidental desirable results. He acts as he does
because of a deep conviction about the nature of the universe in which
all men are brothers, and in which every personality is sacred. No
logical argument to act otherwise can appeal to him unless it is based
upon assumptions arising out of this conviction.

---

[138]See George Lansbury, *My Pilgrimage for Peace* (New York: Holt, 1938); Bertram
Pickard, *Pacifist Diplomacy in Conflict Situations: Illustrated by the Quaker
International Centers* (Philadelphia: Pacifist Research Bureau, 1943).

Those who place their primary moral emphasis upon respect for human personality are led to hold many other values as well as their supreme value of refusing to use violence against their fellow men. Except in time of war, when governments insist that their citizens take part in mass violence, the absolute pacifist is apt to serve these other values, which he shares with many non-pacifists, without attracting the attention which distinguishes him from other men of goodwill. He insists only that in serving these subsidiary values he must not act in any way inconsistent with his highest value.

Many pacifists, and all non-pacifists, differ from the absolutists in that they place other values before this supreme respect for every human personality. The pacifists who do so, refuse to inflict injury on their fellows not because this is itself their highest value, but because they believe other less objectionable methods are more effective for achieving their highest purposes, or because they accept the argument that the means they use must be consistent with the ends they seek. They would say that it is impossible to achieve universal human brotherhood by methods which destroy the basis for such brotherhood.

Such persons assess non-violence as a *tactic,* rather than accepting it as a value in itself. John Lewis comes to the conclusion that under certain circumstances violence is a more effective method. Gandhi believes in non-violence both as a principle and as the most effective means of achieving his purposes. Every individual who looks upon non-violence as only a means, rather than as an end in itself, will accept or reject it on the basis of his estimate of the expediency of non-violent methods. Some come to the conclusion that violence can never be effective and therefore refuse to use it under any circumstances; others decide on each new occasion whether violence or non-violence will best serve their ends in that particular situation. In such cases the question is one of fact; the decision must be based upon the available evidence.

From the diversity of opinions that exist at the present time it is obvious that the social sciences are not yet ready to give an unequivocal answer to this question of fact. Since the values that men hold subjectively are themselves social facts which the scientist must take into account, and since they vary from age to age, community to community, and individual to individual, it may never be possible to find the final answer. Meanwhile the individual facing the necessity for action must answer the question for himself on the basis of the best information available to him. Even if he refuses to face the issue for himself and accepts the prevalent idea of our own day that violence is an effective means of achieving desirable purposes, he has actually answered the question without giving thought to it.

The potential tragedy of our generation is that the whole world has been plunged into war on the basis of the prevalent assumption that violence is an effective means of achieving high social purposes. Even that part of the planning for peace that is based upon maintaining international order by force rests upon this same assumption. If the assumption be false, mankind has paid a terrible price for its mistake.

Another assumption on which the advocates of violence act is that the use of physical force in a noble cause inevitably brings about the triumph of that cause. History gives us no basis for such an assumption. There is much evidence that force sometimes fails, even when it is used on the "right" side. Although the sense of fighting in a righteous cause may improve the morale and thus increase the effectiveness of an army, actually wars are won by the *stronger* side. It is a curious fact that on occasion both opposing armies may feel that they are fighting on the side of righteousness. Napoleon summarized the soldier's point of view when he said that God was on the side of the largest battalions. During the uncertain process of violent conflict, the destruction of human life—innocent and guilty alike—goes on.

Just as there is evidence that violence used in a righteous cause is not always successful, there is evidence that non-violent methods sometimes succeed. Without attempting to give the final answer to the question whether violence creates so much destruction of human values that its apparent successes are only illusory, we can say that the success or failure of both violence and non-violence is determined by the conditions under which both are used, and attempt to discover the circumstances under which they have been effective.

(1) No great social movement can arise unless the grievance against the existing order is great and continuous, or the demand for a new order is so deeply ingrained in the minds of the people in the movement that they are willing to expend great effort and undergo great sacrifices in order to bring about the desired change.

(2) The group devoted to the idea of change must be large enough to have an impact on the situation. This is true whether the group desires to use violent or non-violent methods. In any case there will be a balancing of forces between those desiring change and those who oppose it. All of the non-violent techniques we have considered

require sufficient numbers so that either their refusal of cooperation, their participation in politics, or their practice of positive goodwill has a significant effect upon the whole community.

(3) The group that has a strong desire to bring about social change may be augmented in strength by the support of other elements in the population who do not feel so strongly on the issue. The less vigorous support of such neutrals may be the element that swings the balance in favor of the group desiring change. This "third party" group may also remain indifferent to the conflict. In that case the result will be determined solely by the relative strength of the direct participants. In any case, the group desiring change will be defeated if it alienates the members of the third party so that they join the other side. This latter consideration gives a great advantage to the practitioners of non-violence, since in our own day people generally are disposed to oppose violence, or at least "unlawful" violence, and to sympathize with the victims of violence, especially if they do not fight back. A definite commitment on the part of the reformers not to use violence may go far toward winning the initial support of the group neutral in the conflict.

(4) These conditions of success must be created through the use of education and persuasion prior to taking action. The sense of grievance or the desire for social change must be developed in this way if it does not already exist. Even such a violent movement as the French Revolution grew out of a change in the intellectual climate of France created by the writers of the preceding century. Only when a large enough group has been won over to the cause of reform by such an educational campaign can the second requisite for success be obtained. Finally, much educational work must be done among the less interested third parties in order to predispose them to favor the changes advocated and to sympathize with the group taking part in the movement of reform.

The final result of any social conflict is determined by the balancing of forces involved. Violence itself can never succeed against a stronger adversary, so those who desire to bring about social change or revolution by violence have to begin with the process of education to build a group large enough to overcome the violent forces which are likely to be arrayed against them. Even a violent revolution must be preceded by much non-violent educational preparation. But even when the group using violence has become large enough to overcome the physical force arrayed against it, its victory rests upon the coercion of its opponents rather than upon their conversion. Though defeated, the opponents still entertain their old concepts and look forward to the day of retribution, or to the counter-revolution. A social order so established rests upon a very unstable foundation. Revolutionaries have attempted in such circumstances to "liquidate" all the opposition, but it is doubtful that they have ever been completely successful in doing so. The ruthless use of violence in the process of liquidation has usually alienated third parties against the regime that uses it, and thus augmented the group that might support the counter-revolution.

Advocates of non-violence must start in the same way as the violent revolutionaries to build their forces through persuasion and education. They must assess properly the attitude of the third party and carry on educational work with this group until it is certain that it will not go over to the other side at the moment of action.

By the time a revolutionary or reforming group was large enough to use violence successfully, and to weather the storm of the counter-revolution or reaction, it would already have won to its side so large a portion of the community that it could probably succeed without the use of violence. This would certainly be true in a country like the United States. We must ask the question as to whether the energy consumed in the use of violence might not bring better results if it were expended upon additional education and persuasion, without involving the destruction of human life, human values, and property which violence inevitably entails.

Even most of the ardent advocates of war and violent revolution admit that violence is only an undesirable necessity for the achievement of desirable ends. Non-violent methods pursued with the same commitment and vigor would be just as likely to succeed in the immediate situation as violence, without bringing in their train the tremendous human suffering attendant upon violence. More important is the fact that a social order based upon consent is more stable than one based upon coercion. If we are interested in the long range results of action, non-violence is much more likely to bring about the new society than is violence, because it fosters rather than destroys the sense of community upon which any new social order must be founded.

Pacifist Living Today and Tomorrow

"There Ought to Be a World Like..."

"It may take many years more of experience and suffering before the Christian World awakes universally to the truth that war and all its methods are absolutely incompatible with the teaching, the spirit, the kingdom and the way of the life of our Lord and Master Jesus Christ. . . . It may well be said that the world is not yet ready for this advanced idealism . . . But, in any case, there ought to be a world like the one for which Christ lived and died. And that kind of a world will never actually come unless some of us take the vision and hope seriously and set to work to make it real here on this very earth. It will be said again that these dreams and hopes are visionary and impractical—even Christ himself, with all His spiritual power and divine authority, failed to 'change human nature,' came up against the thick bossed shield of fixed habit and ancient custom and ended His beautiful life in dark defeat and ignominious death. The answer is that He has been changing human nature ever since, that His Cross has become the most decisive factor in human history, and that it appears to be a better venture to die for love and truth and an ideal world than to live along the grooves of fixed habit and ancient custom and the old stupid compromise. The world will at least be better off if there is a Christian group, even a small one . . . resolved to live for these hopes, for this way of life, to bear their clear testimony for peace and love at any cost, and at any price, and ready, if the last supreme sacrifice is demanded, to die for that faith and for that vision.'

by RUFUS M. JONES.
—From *The Faith and Practice of the Quakers*

Commander-in-chief of the British Forces in Libya, General Sir Archibald Percy Wavell asked his troops, "Have you ever thought what a world we could make if we put into peace endeavors the energy, self-sacrifice and cooperation we use in the wastefulness of war?"

—Quoted in *Life Magazine*, February 17, 1941.

Pacifist Living — Today and Tomorrow

•

A BRIEF EXPLORATION OF PACIFISM

Under Conscription, In Time of War, and in Post-War Reconstruction

•

First Printing

March, 1941.

•

15 cents each

$12.00 per hundred

Postpaid

•

Published Jointly by

THE PEACE SECTION, AMERICAN FRIENDS SERVICE COMMITTEE

20 South 12th Street, Philadelphia, Pennsylvania

and

PENDLE HILL

A Center for Religious and Social Study Maintained by Members of the Society of Friends

Wallingford, Pennsylvania

Introduction

The material in this pamphlet grew out of a three-weeks seminar at Pendle Hill, January 14 to February 7, 1941, which considered the general subject of "Pacifism under Conscription, in Time of War, and in Time of Post-War Reconstruction." This was the second annual seminar initiated by the Peace Section of the American Friends Service Committee, the first one having dealt mainly with the problems of the conscientious objector. The thirty-nine people who participated represented areas as widely separated as Vermont, Canada, and California. Some twenty-five men and women gave addresses or led discussions.

In order to share more widely the values of the conference, a committee composed of Barbara Allee, John W. Copithorne, Ernest Lefever, Margaret B. Robinson, Jeannette F. Stetson, Alice Way, and E. Raymond Wilson, was asked to present in accessible form the implications of the group thinking on some fundamental issues confronting pacifists. This pamphlet results from two weeks' editing of the Seminar sub-committee reports.

It is not published as the official findings of the Seminar, which adopted no formal resolutions, nor as a creed or final formulation for pacifists. It does not necessarily represent the point of view of the Boards of Directors of the American Friends Service Committee nor of Pendle Hill. Because of limited time and experience, important areas, such as propaganda, the economic bases of a possible world community, and the rapidly shifting scene of national legislation, have not been treated. This pamphlet is submitted as a basis for study, discussion and action. It is our hope that it may suggest constructive and effective patterns of thinking and living at this critical time in the world's history when facism, communism, militarism, and war make totalitarian claims which can only be countered by total pacifism. This booklet is predicated upon the belief that pacifism today calls for dynamic and sacrificial living on the frontier of man's search for a peaceful world community. The present crisis asks nothing less than life or death in non-violent resistance to war here and abroad and dedication to rebuilding the shattered fabric of a world society.

E. RAYMOND WILSON,
Pendle Hill, Wallingford, Pennsylvania.
February 21, 1941.

Pacifist Living—Today and Tomorrow

A Brief Exploration of Pacifism Under Conscription, in Time of War and Post-War Reconstruction

PART ONE—STRATEGY FOR PACIFISTS TODAY

Part One — Strategy for Pacifists Today

I. ACROSS BORDER LINES—SOME AREAS FOR POSITIVE ACTION NOW

1. Why Starve Europe?

a. Salient Facts

Today the world is bent on large-scale destruction and death, and is creating wholesale bitterness, hate, suffering and despair. In a large area in Europe actual hostilities have practically ceased, but death goes on by the more subtle process of starvation. Why should America not put its resources into feeding Europe instead of supplying the weapons for mutual destruction?

At the time when millions are starving in Europe and Asia, the United States has a surplus of wheat which on July 1, 1940, amounted to 376,000,000 bushels, with an anticipated year's export of 25 million bushels in normal trade, according to the U. S. Department of Agriculture.* "The corn carry-over as of October 1, 1940," states a press release of the U. S. Department of Agriculture dated September 12, 1940, "is estimated at 600,000,000 bushels. This is the largest carryover on record," and the release goes on to estimate that because of the dislocation of the war the regular export trade probably will not absorb more than 20,000,000 bushels. This means nearly *one billion bushels* of wheat and corn surplus in the United States, plus nearly 300 million bushels in Canada which might be used in feeding a hungry world without taking a single slice of bread out of the mouths of people in the United States and Canada. Can we expect a moral blessing when we in the Western Hemisphere sit astride the greatest concentration of surplus food the world has ever seen in its history?

On the other hand, even under normal conditions Belgium imports 49 per cent of its food, Holland 33 per cent, Norway 57 per cent, Finland 22 per cent and so on. The need is particularly acute in occupied and unoccupied France, Belgium and Spain.

We should press for arrangements by which food and clothing could pass through the British blockade. The distribution should be administered

---

* "Wheat and the A A A," Agricultural Adjustment Administration, U. S. Department of Agriculture, October, 1940, page 32.

5

under the supervision of authorized Americans or other neutrals. This means agreement that such shipments will not be bombed, torpedoed or seized by either belligerent, and that food sent to the continent will not be diverted by the Germans for military use, and that shipments will cease if misappropriated by Germany or any one else.

b. Arguments Against Feeding

One argument brought forward against this plan is that it would influence the outcome of the war by enabling Germany to take more out of the conquered countries and so reduce the effect of the blockade on itself. This is based on the assumption that the blockade is successful. But Germany is open to the East and has the food resources of the Balkans, Russia and the Ukraine to fall back upon. The amount of food which Germany has taken from conquered nations is still a matter of dispute. Germany will be one of the last nations to suffer starvation this time, because, remembering the effects of the blockade in the First World War, she has spent years working to make herself self-sufficient by *ersatz* and other methods. The result therefore is that so far as food is concerned the blockade is primarily hurting England's friends and not her enemy.

The second argument is that since Germany has conquered this territory, it is now up to her to take care of its population. Do we want the people of liberal France, Holland, Belgium and Norway to think that for help, security and the necessities of life, they can look only to the German military machine, meaning as it does the relinquishing of their liberal, democratic tendencies and beliefs? Should we willingly put this powerful instrument of persuasion, control and propaganda in the hands of the Nazis? This is assuming that Germany would undertake such a relief program were it left to her. At present there is little indication that she would. Every country at war, measures its supplies by the necessities of war. Since Germany does not know how long the present war will last, she is not likely to feed these countries at the risk of depleting supplies which she thinks may be needed for the German army and people.

From the point of view of the democracies such a relief program would keep alive a link with the conquered nations now represented only by their bombing planes over Amsterdam, Antwerp, Calais, Bordeaux and Oslo. It would show these people that they had not been abandoned in their suffering It is hard to stand up courageously for human rights when you see your children dying of starvation and feel in yourself the constant pain of hunger with no end or relief in sight.

6

A third argument frequently heard is that the people in the occupied countries would rather submit to starvation than see the blockade modified. Reports from American Friends Service Committee workers in both unoccupied and occupied territory do not support this contention. Perhaps it is significant that the advocates of starvation are not those who are dying from starvation, and are often very well fed Americans.

c. What Can We Do?

The American Friends Service Committee, aided by the Brethren Service Committee, the Mennonite Central Committee and other bodies is now giving supplementary feeding to some 40,000 children a day in unoccupied France. The food is bought on the European continent, which becomes increasingly difficult of course, and meets only a fraction of the need.

The Service Committee has undertaken to send at least $10,000 a month to England beginning with February, 1941, to be distributed by English Quakers for relief purposes. But the aim of the Service Committee is to be impartial and give relief to both sides. It stands ready to assist in further extension of relief on the continent if the way can be opened.

On February 16, 1941, Herbert Hoover broadcast a plan which he said had been submitted to the British and German governments, proposing that an initial experiment be made in Belgium to test whether the people there could be fed without military advantage to either side; that such feeding should be done in soup kitchens to prevent any diversion, that at the start 1,000,000 women and 2,000,000 children should be cared for with 50,000 tons of food a month. He proposed further that the German governments give free passage to relief ships and that the whole operation be supervised by some neutral body.

The British have given permission for a limited supply of milk, medicines, and children's clothing to go to unoccupied France. One ship a month is getting into Finland now, on condition that the cargo be used in that country only.

Since conditions change rapidly, readers of this pamphlet are encouraged to write to the Relief Section of the American Friends Service Committee, and to the National Committee on Food for the Small Democracies, 420 Lexington Avenue, New York City, for up-to-date information and suggestions indicating how individuals and groups may be helpful.

7

The Service Committee invites contributions toward the work now being done in France under the supervision of more than fifty workers, and toward the aid being sent to England.

2. Peace—Negotiated or Dictated?

In spite of enormous difficulties we believe that we should press for a negotiated peace, and that the best interests of mankind and of the United States will be served by asking for a statement of the peace aims of the belligerents, and a search for a formula by which the war may be terminated.

Many American people desire above all things that the war shall stop, shall stop without victory for either side, and that it shall be stopped by reason and hope, not by exhaustion in a military stalemate.

A negotiated peace means agreement by both sides to a minimum set of terms upon which both sides are willing to cease fighting, and a determination to collaborate in reconstruction instead of mutual destruction. A negotiated peace does not mean unilateral surrender, nor "appeasement", as the word is commonly used now.

At the very outset of the war the National Peace Conference proposed that the United States should join with other neutrals to set up a permanent commission to work continuously for mediation and a negotiated peace. The National Study Conference in February, 1940, convened by the Federal Council of Churches which represented some twenty-eight communions, was almost unanimous in favor of a negotiated peace.

a. Why Negotiate?

The following considerations, among others, might be advanced in favor of pressing for a negotiated peace:

1. Can victory necessarily assure peace? After the last war peace and freedom were associated with an Allied victory and German defeat. Woodrow Wilson's idea of peace without victory was more sound in terms of its probable psychological and political effects.
2. If the wars in Europe and Asia last much longer there is every probability that they will spread involving still more countries.
3. The longer the wars go on, the greater the likelihood that the United States will enter the military phase with convoys, an expeditionary force and a large number of troops.

4. Stalin and revolutionary communism, instead of democracy, are more likely to be the winners in a war of exhaustion in Europe.

5. The continuance of the war means the starvation of untold numbers of women and children in countries like France, Belgium and Holland which are caught in the vise of British and German blockades and the British and German war machines.

6. The longer the war, the greater the destruction and loss of life, the more intense the hatred engendered and the more difficult the psychological basis of peace.

7. The longer the war goes on the more inevitable it is that the United States will have to finance not only its own enlarged military program, but the British war effort as well.

8. Unfortunately the war is not going to solve the problems which created it—in fact the war will undoubtedly intensify many of them.

b. Difficulties Involved

Among the major difficulties in securing a negotiated peace are the following:

1. Can the United States serve as an effective influence toward a negotiated peace since we have given up all pretense of neutrality and have become "the arsenal of the democracies"? If we do not press for a negotiated peace, it will not be realized. In wartime it is embarrassing for either side to initiate peace moves, because such a step would be interpreted as a sign of weakness. Both sides will want our help when war is over. The South American republics might be willing to join the United States in seeking a truce.

2. Can any peace be negotiated with Hitler and the present German Government? Can a military victory be achieved over the Germans without the possibility of sacrificing many lives, in an attempted military invasion of the continent by the British? While the military situation may change overnight, the most likely prospect at this writing, is for a continued military stalemate with no clear-cut decision either way in the near future. The bulk of the German people did not want this war and would probably welcome peace. This is certainly true of the British. Europe may have a better chance of returning to sanity and democracy if the efforts towards reconstruction can be

9

started now rather than after the greater destruction and increased hatreds of a prolonged war. The longer the war goes on the more difficult it will be to develop a formula that will be acceptable to both sides. In war both sides are confronted with the problem of saving face. It is easier to save face if the war has not gone on too long, and if there is neutral encouragement for the war to stop.

Anne O'Hare McCormick writes in the New York Times of February 15, 1941, "Whatever the end of the war, even now it is clearly written across the face of Europe that Hitler has won only enemies. He is still what he was in the beginning—the thwarted architect, eaten by a passion for an order he can never achieve because a disorganizing force cannot organize, and because he has to build his new edifice with the cooperation of nations whose very existence depends on pulling it down and pulling him down."

3. Can a just peace be negotiated with the Tory interests of the British Empire? Quite likely the effect of a negotiated peace would be to strengthen the elements of the government in Great Britain which are closest to the common people, such as the British Labor Party. During the war there has been an active element in Great Britain supporting the idea of a negotiated peace and carrying on an educational program towards this end. There is no assurance that a completely just peace can be secured by negotiation, but provisions should be incorporated for its review and modification before many years. The peace *dictated* by the Allies in 1919 was neither just nor durable.

For Further Reading:

"Where Are We Going?" by A. J. Muste, Fellowship of Reconciliation, 2929 Broadway, New York City, 1941. 10 cents.

3. Refugees—Our New Americans

a. A Friendly Service in Which All Can Join

Aid to refugees supplies an urgent human need at this time, renders a distinct patriotic service in forwarding the assimilation and Americanization of future citizens, and at the same time expresses in practical terms the pacifist philosophy of brotherhood. Learning to know refugees is an enriching experience. Through their eyes we see our own country afresh, its beauties and its blemishes, and through their suffering we learn what values are important to man uprooted from the material and spiritual soil which has sustained him.

Temporary hospitality for the newly arrived refugee is an important service that almost any citizen can give. The newcomer needs time to rest, to relax, to learn a new language and new customs. Even more he needs tenderness, sympathy, understanding and wise guidance.

Then, if he is to adjust himself satisfactorily to his new life, he must have a job. To help the refugee prepare himself to become self-supporting in this country, to arrange a period of apprenticeship, to help him in making the necessary contacts, so that his native ability and his former experience and training will contribute most in his new country is a difficult task, but one that is essential to the eventual adjustment of the refugee.

First of all, before he can enter the United States, the refugee must have a guarantee of financial support from an American citizen. Although emigration from Europe has been retarded because of transportation difficulties, there are many young German refugees who have been interned in Canada, and who are now free to enter the United States, if they can get affidavits of support and visas. Europeans who are here on visitors' visas, and who dare not return to their own countries, also need affidavits in order to get visas for permanent residence. Free movement from one country to another is becoming increasingly difficult, but as long as immigration is at all possible for refugees, it is vitally important to keep the doors open and to make it possible for them to come.

Finally, there is the need for continuing friendship, encouragement and guidance. Europeans are not used to the swift tempo of American life and are often disillusioned when their new friends seem to drop them because they are too busy for the courtesies which Europeans are accustomed to regard as precious expressions of true friendship.

b. How Many Refugees Have Come In?

Just as it is important to interpret American ways to the refugee, so there is a constant need to correct the many erroneous beliefs and false fears about the recent influx of refugees. A few facts will help to correct false impressions:

Under our present law restricting immigration to a yearly quota from each country, it was possible for 1,230,192 immigrants to have entered this country during the past eight years. The actual number of those who came was less than one-third that number, or 395,716. The number from Germany and Austria was 100,987—less than half of the number that could have come under the quota. On the other hand, during the same period, roughly 25,000 Germans left the United States, so that *the total increase in German population has been only about 75,000 persons in eight years.*

Of the total number of refugees who have come to the United States to settle, about 25% are of the Christian faith. The percentage might be higher, if the Christian groups had organized as efficiently and whole-heartedly as did the Jewish groups.

According to the Immigration and Naturalization Service figures of 1939, 55% of the refugees are women and children with no occupation, or unemployable men. This means that more than half of the newcomers will not immediately compete in the labor market, but will be consumers of American-made goods and services. To consider the other 45%,

8% are professional men and women

18% are in commercial occupations

12% are skilled workers

1% are farmers

4% are servants

1% are in occupations which do not fall into any of the above classifications

1% are unskilled workers.

The fear that the refugees will merely swell the relief rolls and become objects of charity has no more foundations than the fear that they will take jobs away from Americans. Every immigrant to this country must have an affidavit of support, to insure that he will not become a public charge. The affidavit must come from an American citizen who must prove to the satisfaction of our consuls abroad that he has sufficient means to provide for the refugee and that he is sincerely concerned so that there will be no question that he will fulfill his obligation, if that should be necessary.

Two years ago it was still possible to measure the European refugee problem. The numbers ran into hundreds of thousands who were being forced out of Germany and Austria. Today, countless hordes of homeless people shift back and forth across Europe, and the number of them increases every day that the war continues. In China, millions more have been driven from their homes. The refugee is a war victim for whom pacifists should feel a deep responsibility.

National agencies for aiding refugees include:

American Committee for Christian German Refugees, 287 Fourth Avenue, New York City

American Friends Service Committee, 20 South 12th Street, Philadelphia

Catholic Committee for German Refugees, 259 West 14th Street, New York City

Council of Jewish Women, 1819 Broadway, New York City

Friends of Refugee Teachers, 178 Coolidge Hill, Cambridge, Massachusetts

International Student Service, 8 West 40th Street, New York City

Jewish Joint Distribution Committee, 100 East 42nd Street, New York City

National Refugee Service, 165 West 46th Street, New York City

For Further Reading:

"The Social and Economic Consequences of Exclusionary Immigration Laws," American Committee for Protection of Foreign Born, 79 Fifth Avenue, New York, N. Y., 1939.

"Meet the Refugees," Woman's Press, 600 Lexington Avenue, New York, N. Y., 1940, free on request.

Norman Angell and Dorothy Buxton, "You and the Refugee," Penguin Series, 1939, 25c.

"The Plight of Refugees in a Preoccupied World," Woman's Press, 1940, free on request.

"Refugee," Prentice-Hall, 1940, $2.50. The personal account of two "Aryan" Germans. May be ordered through the American Friends Service Committee.

4. Looking Southward

One field of international relations in which much work can be done in spite of the war conditions, is that of Latin America. The United States has until recently put very little constructive effort into her relations with her southern neighbors and the results of her blind, selfish policies there, both on the part of the government and in the commercial, economic and individual contacts, have created a feeling of ill-will and distrust that will take much time and intelligent, unselfish action to replace.

The government more recently has made an effort in this direction, with its much publicized "good neighbor" policy, its reciprocal trade agreements, and the cooperative spirit its delegates showed at the Lima and Havana conferences, but it has still a long way to go. A few treaties based on mutual expediency are not enough to break down antagonisms created by a century of exploitation, arrogance, and imperialism. This is perhaps an especially good time for work in this field, for the American people as a whole, feeling isolated from Europe and Asia by war, are turning their attention southward. We should use this interest to achieve a permanent improvement in our relations with Latin America.

a. A Suggested Program

The needed work might be said to fall into six sections.

1. We should educate our people in the history, culture, customs and present trends of the various Latin American countries. We should urge more schools to include Spanish in their curriculum. We should, in our education, stress not only our differences, but our similarities with the people and life of these countries and try to develop not only knowledge and interest in them, but a respect for their achievements and culture. There is so apt to be condescension in our thinking about them. Special emphasis should be placed on being hospitable and friendly to Latin Americans who visit this country. We should invite exchange students into our homes and seek to know them better.

2. We should encourage Americans to visit Latin America, but not with a feeling of superiority or that they are going to see the "quaint" nations. We should go prepared to appreciate the beauties of their landscape and their colorful culture and to make friends with a unique and delightful people. Tourists, students, commercial salesmen or independent business men should be impressed with the fact that they go as unofficial ambassadors of the United States and that not they but their whole country is judged by their attitudes and behavior.

3. We should keep a close watch on our government's relations with Latin America. We should encourage it not only to continue its more enlightened policies, but to go even further in cooperating politically and economically on a basis of equality and mutual interest, rather than seeking to further the interests of the United States even at the expense of the weaker nations. We should urge also that our government be prepared to offer her good services in mediating any dispute between other nations of this hemisphere, and that we in

turn promise to submit any disputes with them to arbitration or mediation by a third power or an international authority.

4. We should work toward some sort of a code which would limit the power of American business interests to exploit the markets, labor, land and raw materials of the Latin American countries and people. We should attempt to have our government give the people of Latin America some assurance that it is not solely interested in protecting our big business and industrial corporations in their often ruthless monopolistic and exploitative enterprises there, but that it is also concerned for the protection of individual rights and interests, as being more in keeping with our democratic principles.

5. We should resist the present military imperialism which is going on under the guise of hemispheric defense. The trading of destroyers for the leasing of naval bases means that inhabitants are transferred like pawns on imperial chessboards without consultation. If military expediency dictates, the United States will take over the islands and colonies of European nations situated in the Western hemisphere. We should look forward to the internationalization and demilitarization of the Panama Canal along with Gibraltar and Singapore as one of the goals in the development of world government.

6. We can expand what is already being done in interchange. For two years the Peace Section of the American Friends Service Committee has had a work camp peace seminar in Mexico. This should not only be continued, but other similar projects extended to other Latin American countries. At least one camp should be established in Puerto Rico by the Civilian Public Service.

We can encourage study groups to use more extensively the excellent material published by the Pan American Union, Washington, D. C. The Maryland Women's International League provides monthly lessons on Latin America to 500 homemakers' clubs in rural Maryland. For years the Institute of International Education has been administering exchange fellowships to and from Latin America which should be increased in number. This winter the University of North Carolina set up special courses and programs for leading representatives of Latin America who came for a period of intensive study in the United States under arrangements worked out by the Grace Line.

15

Our government has made a notable beginning in setting up the Division on Cultural Relations now under the direction of Nelson Rockefeller. The Lima Conference provided for an interchange of a limited number of students and professors between all countries in Latin America. This interchange ought to be vastly enlarged.

For Further Reading:

Pan-American News, Bi-Weekly Information Service, Washington Bureau, Foreign Policy Association, 1200 National Press Building, Washington, D. C. $3.00 per year.

The Hemisphere, Confidential Weekly Report, The Hemisphere Corporation, 154 Nassau Street, New York City. $5.00 per year.

Lewis Hanke, "Plain Speaking about Latin America," *Harper's Magazine,* October, 1940.

Samuel Guy Inman, "Latin America, Its Place in World Life," Willett Clark, 1940, $3.75.

John T. Whitaker, "Americans to the South," Macmillan, 1939, $2.50.

Duncan Aikman, "The All-American Front," Doubleday, 1940, $3.00.

"Look at Latin America," Foreign Policy Association, 1940, 25c.

5. Puerto Rico—Slave or Free?

In Puerto Rico we see an example of the economic, social and political evils which result from imperialism. Here is an American colonial problem. We are now responsible for the welfare of the people of the island over which we gained control by the Spanish-American war. Puerto Rico is grievously over-populated; unemployment is high and the wages very low —9 cents a day for some workers in the embroidery industry. Embroidery and the production of sugar are the chief industries of the island. As a natural result, physical health and the morale of the population has suffered; living conditions are wretched; it is reported that one out of every three persons has a venereal disease.

Puerto Rico's problems are those of colonial economy. Absentee ownerships of land and industry and restricted trade policies drain wealth away from the island. Political corruption has been flagrant. It has been very easy for Puerto Rico to be forgotten by the rest of the United States. Our legislators are chiefly concerned about their own constituents, and Puerto Rico is not represented by a voting member of Congress.

In addition to studying and publicizing our colonial problem in Puerto Rico, pacifists will be concerned for the maintenance of freedom of speech and the right of assembly there, both of which have been scandously sup-

16

pressed in the past. Political parties advocating statehood or complete independence should be allowed to continue their activities without the charge of treason. Increased militarization of Puerto Rico as a strategic military outpost to defend the Panama Canal will add to the social problems of the island.

For Further Reading:
Article on Puerto Rico in the *Fortune Magazine*, February, 1941.

6. Why Fight Japan?

As this pamphlet is being published the tension between Japan and the United States grows more ominous every day. Japan, still unsuccessful in actually conquering China, is turning her attention toward the South, where she comes into conflict with American, British, French and Dutch interests. The linking of Japan with the Axis powers has also complicated the relations in the Far East.

After three and one-half years of conflict between Japan and China, there is still no end of hostilities in sight, although both countries are economically exhausted.

The following recommendations are made as possible lines of action at this time:

1. That we urge our government to investigate the possibility of setting up a commission composed of representatives from Japan, China, Russia and other nations bordering upon the Pacific to work out minimum requirements for a negotiated peace. The attempt should be made to work out a fundamental peace settlement in the Orient and not merely a truce between Japan and China.

2. The United States should be willing to contribute toward a fundamental settlement along the following lines:

   a. New commercial treaty with Japan.

   b. Revise Exclusion Act and place Japan, China and other nations on quota basis.

   c. Relinquish extra-territoriality, and withdraw our naval and military forces from China.

   d. Try to help Japan get assured access to raw materials including oil.

17

For Further Reading:

"The Churches and the International Situation," Federal Council of Churches, 1940, 15c.

T. A. Bisson, "American Policy in the Far East: 1931-1940," Institute of Pacific Relations, 1940, $1.25.

"Our Far Eastern Record," William Lockwood, Institute of Pacific Relations, 1940, 25c.

"America Holds the Balance in the Far East," Institute of Pacific Relations, 1940, 25c.

Westel W. Willoughby, "Japan's Case Examined," Johns Hopkins Press, 1940, $2.50.

7. Bridges of Understanding

Doors Are Closing

Today, in spite of the marvelous advances we have achieved in the fields of communication and transportation, these channels are gradually being closed in the international world, largely because of the war. Travel between the United States and Europe now is limited to the few persons who can get passports to ride the trans-Atlantic airways, and the news is censored or colored for propaganda purposes. Future cooperation and understanding depends on keeping these channels open just as far and just as long as we can, and seeing that they are used as much as possible for constructive ends and positive information.

It is encouraging that the Friends centers in Vienna, Paris, Amsterdam and Copenhagen have kept on functioning every day in spite of military invasion and are something of a symbol of the possibilities of service in a divided, war-torn world. The Y. M. C. A. is still active in prison camps and other work over the continent in Europe. All organizations of an international character should make every effort to keep in touch with their leaders and members abroad primarily to relieve the feeling of isolation which those abroad have and to reaffirm the international fellowship.

We Can Build Understanding

Individuals should constantly reassert their understanding and goodwill for their personal friends in other countries by letters and messages. Wherever possible actual visits should be made abroad by representatives of religious and humanitarian organizations whose only motive is that of re-establishing contacts in order to supplement the slim knowledge of facts upon which we have to base our understanding, and to learn in what ways and in what fields constructive action might be undertaken. The people sent over by the American Friends Service Committee attempt to be such emissaries of goodwill.

18

At the time of writing this report the situation between the United States and Japan is critical and here again there should be a two-way exchange of friendly visitors to help clarify the misunderstandings and to seek solutions that are constructive.

Other doors are apt to be closing now, too. As differences grow more sharply defined and questions lose their academic character and become immediate and demanding of decisive action, we are conscious of a desire to avoid the people with whom we disagree and to cling more and more to those with whom we feel in accord. We are prone to allow those subjects in which we disagree to overshadow and even blot out those fields in which we agree and have a common interest. Though this is perhaps a natural and human tendency, we should do everything we can to overcome it, for as groups or individuals grow further apart, and become more isolated from each other, the basis for understanding shrinks and even the ability to communicate our ideas disintegrates and becomes less effective.

This is just the opposite result from the one for which we should be working. We should make every effort therefore to keep these channels open, to stress our agreements and any constructive projects we can undertake together and when possible attempt to discuss objectively and in a friendly spirit our areas of difference, not for the purpose of convincing the other side, but in order to gain a better understanding of their point of view and of our relative positions.

II. WITHIN THE UNITED STATES

1. Keep America Out of War

Although many groups are interested in keeping America out of war, for the pacifist it is a primary concern. Going into war means the unavoidable acceptance of totalitarianism within the country, making more widespread the destruction of life and culture, the intensification of hatred and bitterness, submission to censorship and propaganda and the identification of patriotism with the slaughter of human life. Going to war means also that the rights of labor, civil liberties, social legislation and other hard fought gains may be surrendered almost over night.

The question is not why should we keep our country out of war, but how. It should be clear that pacifists take this attitude not as nationalistic isolationists primarily interested in saving their own skins, but as world citizens working for a world-wide cooperative society and the betterment of all mankind.

A large part of all pacifist activity is directly or indirectly helping to keep the United States out of war and consequently an intensification of the total program will accomplish much toward this end.

At the present rate of involvement if the war continues we may soon be in war despite all contrary efforts. A substantial part of *our* effort should be for goals that will not be lost entirely even if war is declared.

War feeds upon itself—its totalitarianism becomes more demanding, violence more widespread, destruction breeds counter destruction, hatred stultifies the moral nature of man.

During the last war, according to Defense Papers No. 2 published by the American Association for Adult Education, the following were deemed criminal enough for conviction:

Advocating heavier taxation instead of huge bond issues.

Urging a law for a referendum on war.

Declaring that war was contrary to the teaching of Christ.

Criticizing the Red Cross.

Among the things which can be done to aid in the struggle to keep America out of war are the following:

1. Point out that war is morally and spiritually wrong, that good ends cannot be achieved by immoral methods, that settlements brought about by violence will probably have to be maintained by violence.

2. Resist proposed legislation which grants "all aid short of war," and which gives to the President dictatorial powers at home. If we become the arsenal of the war, can we avoid being a target as well?

3. Press for a negotiated peace, not to save America from war, but to save mankind from mutual destruction.

4. Encourage the United States to tackle vigorously world reconstruction when the wars in Europe and Asia are brought to a close. If the United States were to spend on world reconstruction a fraction of its present armament expenditures, the result might be revolutionary. In twenty years, the entire world spent on the processes of international cooperation through the League of Nations, the In-

ternational Labor Organization and the World Court less than one hundred and thirty-five million dollars, or about what the United States is now spending every week for armaments.

5. Urge that the belligerents state clearly their war and peace aims. The German Nazis have been fairly frank about their growing designs for a Europe under Nazi domination if they are victorious. What would Great Britain do with a victory if she achieved it with American aid or even with American participation in the war? Do we have any reason to believe that the victors, if any, in this war will be more just than they were at Versailles?

6. Defeat any move to make peacetime military conscription a permanent policy such as is being advocated by various groups in the United States.

7. Share the huge surplus of wheat and corn with the starving at home and abroad.

8. Support the principle of world cooperation and world federation and help prepare the citizens of the United States to be ready to make substantial sacrifices toward that end.

9. Work for the right of the people themselves to vote before entering war.

2. Constructive Defense

Today the general watchword of the nation is defense. The militarists call for conscription and greater production in armaments; the patriots call for the showing of greater respect for the flag, more singing of "God Bless America," and more stringent measures against aliens and Americans of uncertain sympathies; the politicians call for more emergency measures to grant more power—all in the name of defense.

We are concerned, as are many others who are not pacifists, not only with an external danger, but with an internal danger as well, a danger that we see developing in our very defense program itself. We believe that the strong Democracy is the working, moving Democracy going forward, and not barricading itself behind material defenses. Today we see tendencies to limit our democratic practices, rather than to extend and deepen them. We find communities in which individuals and groups have set themselves up to control free speech and action in their town. We find schools being forced to substitute military drill for their regular physical education program, under

21

pressure from defense-conscious parents. We find appropriations for slum clearance, conservation, public works, education and housing being cut, while billions are spent for the military defense of these human and material resources.

Educators have sensed this tendency and in many communities defense councils are being organized which have as one of their objectives the mobilizing of education to "defend democratic culture." With this in mind a constructive program of adult education is being planned which emphasizes the democratic values of free discussion. There will be a tendency for this program to degenerate, but all efforts should be made to see that when it is carried through it retains its democratic and constructive character.

Internal Defense

Suggestions circulated in *Community Councils in Action*, December, 1940, for defense education give major consideration to such items as the following:

1. *Civic Responsibility*. In this time of crisis, preparation for assuming ever-increasing civic responsibility is the duty and privilege of every individual in a democracy. Schools should provide widespread opportunities for thoughtful study and discussion of American institutions and ideals, the philosophy and history of democracy, and the present threats to its survival in the world.

2. *Leadership*. Any defense program must depend for its success upon the quality of its leadership. Educators therefore should accept responsibility for the organization of a program of leader-finding and leader-training.

3. *Propaganda*. Adult education should stand for education rather than for propaganda, for reason rather than for emotion, in the consideration of the issues of the day. A study of war propaganda methods is therefore important.

4. *Tolerance*. Adult educators should seek not merely to safeguard minority differences from attack; more positively, they should seek to develop such understanding cooperation with minority groups as will enrich our cultural life.

5. *Civil Liberties*. Adult education should help the population to understand what civil rights and liberties are guaranteed by law; why it is im-

portant that these rights be safeguarded; and what the threats to civil liberties are. *Fear of Hitler must not Hitlerize America.*

6. *Social Program.* There is need for an aggressive program of adult education concerned with those aspects of social life in which democracy has not yet been largely achieved. Gains in social legislation on security, housing, etc., must not be pushed aside under the guise of "emergency," and it must be widely recognized that unsolved human problems—like those of unemployment, migrant labor, and farm tenancy undermine democratic morale. The man in the street must enjoy the fruits of democracy if its values are not to remain mere words. A responsible part in determining his own fate, must become part of his first-hand experience. Democracy ill-achieved leads to its own undoing. It inspires no unstinted efforts, calls for no large sacrifices.

7. *Morale.* Morale and character for democratic living are not to be developed through the use of badges, buttons, flags, and songs, whatever value these devices may have as symbols of democratic ideals. The character and morale necessary for the advance of democracy must grow out of an appreciation of the values of the democratic way of life. Adult education, therefore, must develop a genuine respect for personality and other attitudes basic to democracy.

8. *Play.* Help to keep alive the spirit of play and recreation as an antidote for tension, uncertainty, and hysteria, and capitalize the emerging interest in physical fitness for a constructive program of healthful living.

9. *Public Affairs.* Provide for frank and impartial consideration of national issues. It has never been more important that the attitudes and will of the people be formed on the basis of the best available facts.

Such an outline indeed, provides "opportunity for adults to grow in the stature of humanity."

A subject of great possibilities is the study of war and peace aims, involving the history of the causes, and the current development of the war through dictatorships with their brutality and their ultimate stagnation, and finally the goals toward which we are striving. Although such courses of study are apt to raise issues of national self-righteousness they delve deeply into the cause and cure of war. In such a course it should be obvious that bitterness and injustice can sow only the seeds of future strife. These are elements in the "defense of democratic culture," which enlist our whole-hearted and patriotic support.

We may be timid, particularly in time of war, about joining an educational council in which militarists and super-nationalistic groups seem to be of predominant influence. Many a trivial point might be sacrificed, however, for the privilege of insisting, in such a council, that labor and minority groups be recognized, and that education for democracy should really educate people to understand and prize the heritage of freedom, tolerance and equality which our constitution guaranteed.

The publications of the American Association for Adult Education give helpful suggestions for conducting adult groups. In most communities there is a forum, Y. M. C. A., W. P. A., service club, or teacher group which is already conducting work in adult education in which we can participate and exert a kindly influence upon the thought processes of others.

Our efforts should be to relate the idea of defense to human values, to an appreciation and conservation of the vast human and material resources of this country, to the preservation of the fundamental democratic beliefs upon which this nation was founded, and to their extension into all areas of our national life. Since the world is larger and more complex than our own nation, can we as a nation feel that we have an answer for the world's difficulties, until we have proved that we can put our own house in order?

For Further Reading:

"Community Councils in Action," American Association for Adult Education, 60 East 42nd Street, New York, N. Y., December, 1940.

"Education and National Defense," Progressive Education Association, November, 1940.

3. Protect Civil Liberties

As religious people our ultimate goal is a universal cooperative common-wealth in which every individual has certain rights that guarantee him maximum personal and social development. Although this is far in the future, we must now address ourselves to the task of preserving and extending human rights wherever possible.

In America our job is not to maintain the status quo, for we see on every hand the violation of civil liberties. There are probably millions of Americans among the Negroes, sharecroppers, and migrant laborers, who are denied the right to vote. After the last election there were mass arrests in certain areas of Philadelphia where the Negro citizens did not support the machine. Already legislation has been passed curtailing aliens' opportunities for employment. Further basic rights are likely to be relinquished as laws are being modified "for the duration of the emergency."

As war hysteria increases certain individuals and groups will fall victims of "fifth-column" propaganda. We can combat emotionally charged phrases and develop understanding by bringing facts to bear on situations where people are unjustly accused. In a number of instances peace-loving citizens have averted conflict by interpreting the position of Jehovah's Witnesses to the flag-conscious or Legion-controlled community. We should encourage legislation which increases the right of individuals and minorities to participate freely in society.

Especially should we seek to maintain the provisions for the conscientious objector to military conscription. In many cases our efforts might be strengthened by cooperating with others who are working for freedom of speech, of assembly, of the press, and of conscience.*

Even though we are attempting to protect all minorities from unjust attack, we feel that we have a right to know certain facts about any organization operating in America. The list of officers, a statement of purpose or aims and the source of funds are some of the facts that should be available to the public about all groups from the German-American Bund to the Fellowship of Reconciliation and the National Association of Manufacturers.

For Further Reading:
"Safeguarding Civil Liberties," by Robert Cushman, Public Affairs Pamphlet, 1940, 10c.

4. Promote Racial Understanding

One of the largest opportunities for constructive pacifist action in the United States lies in improving the conditions under which our Negro population lives and works. This is a chance for the pacifist to demonstrate his fundamental belief in universal brotherhood and basic human rights. Though there is probably no simple and immediate solution for the discrimination which eleven million Negroes suffer, there is a long term job of education and constructive action to be undertaken, until the walls of prejudice and misunderstanding are broken down.

---

* For twenty years the American Civil Liberties Union, 31 Union Square West, has been organized to protect freedom of speech and assembly under the Bill of Rights of the U. S. Constitution as essential for peaceful progress in a democracy.

Appropriations for educational equipment for Negroes in this country is pitifully inadequate compared with those received by our white population. Here is a challenge to democratic opportunity which ought to be faced squarely in an effort to bring the standards of Negro education up to that of the rest of the country.

The idea that standards or ratings of intelligence or ability can be made on a basis of race or color must be abolished. There are shiftless and ignorant Negroes, of course, but there are also shiftless and ignorant white people. Most of us do not know in detail the contributions to society made by outstanding Negroes in the United States. Men and women should be appraised on their ability and accomplishments and contributions to the general welfare, irrespective of their racial background or the color of their skin.

The task calls for skill, patience and tact, particularly in the South, for one is not dealing with a point of reason logically taken, but with a deep and subtly acquired emotional pattern. If one is hasty or lacking in sensitiveness to slight changes in public opinion, he will create not a better, but a worse situation, by frightening and uniting the forces of intolerance and conservatism into a reactionary movement, often with grave consequences.

Pacifists can work on this problem in a number of ways. Often pacifist groups or organizations can unite with other concerned individuals or groups in making a survey of the situation in their own community. This could include educational, health and recreational facilities as well as conditions of housing, employment and relief. Special interest should be given to the extension of public services to Negroes, for example, in caring for their delinquents, insane and feeble minded, aged and chronically ill. Sometimes by working with the local Urban League or the National Association for the Advancement of Colored People, one can discover specific instances of discrimination which can be attacked or of immediate legislation needing the additional political pressure of an outside group to carry it through the state or city government.

For those who are establishing work camps, the Negro slum area offers special opportunities for service. Here, by getting to know their neighbors personally and talking over their problems as well as by working with them on a common task, a new understanding can be gained and a new sense of fellowship developed. Negroes should be encouraged to join such groups and to share the work, play, and worship experiences.

26

Other racial minorities in the United States offer similar opportunities for friendly cooperation in improving their life and status. Discrimination against the Japanese and the Mexicans is acute in various sections of the country. Prejudice is often expressed against people of German extraction, many of whom may even have fled from Germany to escape persecution or militarism.

The Service Bureau for Inter-Cultural Education, 300 Fourth Avenue, New York City, under the direction of Rachel Davis DuBois, has done notable work in preparing material and projects for increasing appreciation of the various racial and cultural groups which make up and enrich our American democracy. Their material has been widely used in schools and churches.

For Further Material Consult:

> The Urban League, 1140 Broadway, New York City. Their magazine, *Opportunity*, $1.50 per year.
>
> The National Association for the Advancement of Colored People, 69 Fifth Avenue, New York City, publishes *The Crisis*, membership and subscription, $2.50 per year.
>
> Friends Committee on Race Relations, Alberta Morris, Secretary, 20 South 12th Street, Philadelphia, Pa.
>
> *We Americans*, The Atlantic Monthly, 1939, paper, 25 cents.

5. Combat Anti-Semitism

Effects of Anti-Semitism

Anti-Semitism has greatly increased in the United States during the past decade. Its chief effects are as follows:

1. Discrimination against Jews in employment; in admission into preparatory schools, colleges and professional schools, in summer hotels, clubs, residential neighborhoods, etc.

2. Tendency of Jews to feel that they are universally disliked and cold-shouldered.

3. Tendency of some Jews to become over-aggressive or servile.

4. Tendency of Jews to concentrate in large cities and in a few professions and industries.

Non-Jews have become more susceptible to the widespread propaganda against Jews. People are prone to regard faults of some Jews as characteristic of Jews as a whole—such as unscrupulousness in business or professional life or the lack of cleanliness or good manners. Three of the

numerous misconceptions often attributed to the Jews are that they monop-
olize economic opportunities, that they do not wish to associate with non-
Jews, that they are engaged in an international conspiracy to overthrow
Christian civilization or to extend the war.

Anti-Semitism has been taken up by several hundred national organizations who directly or indirectly blame the Jews, along with other minority
groups, for the evils of American life. Jews are thus among those maliciously
used as scapegoats. Anti-Semitism is an instrument in the hands of reac-
tionaries, fascists, and Christian religious fanatics. In some of these organizations it is a device of unscrupulous, self-seeking adventurers.

How to Overcome Anti-Semitism

1. Find out the facts about (a) discrimination against Jews; (b) the
   Jews and Judaism.

2. Spread the knowledge of these facts in the religious, educational,
   occupational, political, and social organizations with which you are
   associated.

3. Get to know more Jews and work with them in projects of mutual
   concern.

4. Develop a sense of fellowship, understanding and justice toward
   them.

5. Help remove the injustices and inefficiences in our economic order
   which are the primary causes for the increase in Anti-Semitism.

For help in securing literature and in carrying out the suggestions listed
above, the National Conference of Christians and Jews, 300 4th Avenue, New
York City, will be useful.

For Further Reading:

"Jews in America," by the editors of *Fortune*, Random House, New York, 1936, $1.00.

"The Attack on Democracy," *Propaganda Analysis*, January 1, 1939, 25c.

"Some Facts About Jews," by Philip S. Bernstein, *Harper's Magazine*, April, 1939.

Mrs. Abel J. Gregg, "New Relationships with Jews and Catholics," Association Press,
New York, 1934, 25c.

Hugo M. Valentin, "Anti-Semitism, Historically and Critically Examined," Viking
Press, New York, 1936, $3.00.

"The Rising Tide of Anti-Semitism," by Alvin Johnson, *Survey Graphic*, February,
1939.

James W. Parkes, "The Jew and His Neighbor," London, 1930.

6. Creative Homes

Even in time of stress the religious pacifist home can be a force of incalcuable influence in the creation of active pacifist ideals. Such a home should have an atmosphere of universality, and of "taken-for-granted" hospitality to both intimates and strangers. Conversation in any home reveals how faithfully children reflect their parents' social attitudes. They become either critical or sympathetic towards other nationalities and races, they learn either to laugh at foreigners or to aim at understanding cultural differences, they use derogatory or respectful terms in referring to others. Practices such as the following may be drawn upon to help create desirable attitudes.

1. Close connection and frequent contacts with persons from other countries and races.

2. Familiarity with foreign customs, language peculiarities, and food.

3. An alert interest on the part of the parents in social and international problems.

4. Choice of books, magazines, newspapers, radio programs, etc., on the basis of their breadth, tolerance, and sympathetic portrayal of life among many different racial or class groups.

5. Cultivation of an appreciation for the beautiful, as portrayed by the culture of all nations.

6. To develop democracy within the home, children should be taught to take their share of housework and should be encouraged in this no matter how inefficient they may seem at first. They should be given an important place in conversation, they should share in the responsibility of entertaining guests.

7. The child should learn to be equally at home in all levels of society, neither overawed by wealth nor embarrassed by poverty.

8. Economic discipline within the family is important. Sacrifice and hardship should be linked with a concern to help relieving suffering throughout the world.

9. Parents and children should discipline themselves to overcome the temptation to nag when they are impatient and tired. Habitual respect for others, if developed in the home, will prove indispensable in the successful meeting of opposition in the outside world.

10. Especially in times of crisis, the expression of liberal attitudes by either parents or children outside the home may bring discrimination and persecution upon children by other children. If the home atmosphere is strong and affectionate, it will help provide security for its members at such times.

In a democratic family every member contributes according to his ability and receives according to his need. As pacifists we are striving to make this fundamental law of the family, the law of the community, the law of the nation, and the law of the world.

7. Pacifists in a Democracy

The Pacifist and His Government

There are two views we may take of government. One that it is "our enemy," that it is organized for violence or potential violence and that the pacifist cannot cooperate with it. The other view holds that the pacifist is not against government as such but against certain of its practices. In organizing conduct for an increasing area of life, government by the majority usually means a lag in moral conscience and, therefore, the minority has a responsibility for influencing government to take more advanced steps. This latter view would encourage the pacifist to take an active part in political action and refuse cooperation only when conscience or judgment forbade.

Pacifist groups ought to maintain normal contacts with government officials without wasting their time or making a nuisance of themselves. Representatives of churches or organizations might interview the governor and the director of Selective Service in their state, expressing their concern that war hysteria be kept down, that the United States should not enter the war, that civil liberties be maintained, that the rights of the conscientious objectors be respected, and offer their cooperation along these lines. They could ask that the way be left open for them to call attention to violation of these principles. This helps officials see that pacifists are human beings with a sense of responsibility for good government.

Pacifists might well widen their relations to members of Congress. On important issues Congressmen should be seen either in Washington, or preferably in their home communities. Representatives and Senators should be encouraged by a letter when their vote is favorable to peace principles. Too often correspondence is limited to opposition or censure, or is directed to

Congressmen in the last 72 hours before a vote is taken. The tone of letters should be courteous and direct.

Procedure with Draft Boards

Pacifists should familiarize themselves with the regulations regarding conscientious objectors under the Selective Service Act by actually reading this material themselves.* Where it seems feasible a delegation drawn from the community which the draft board covers should interview the draft board, explain their interest in fair and proper treatment for conscientious objectors, and offer their cooperation to help the draft board in seeing that justice is done. In cases of irregularity, such as refusal to furnish Form 47, or other arbitrary action by the board, it is better to confer with the board first. If that is ineffective, then get in touch with the state director of Selective Service, or with Paul Comly French, National Service Board for Religious Objectors, 996 National Press Building, Washington, D. C., who can take the matter up with the proper officials in the headquarters of the Selective Service Administration in Washington. The name and address of the state director of Selective Service can be secured from the local draft board.

A simple and brief statement entitled *Why They Cannot Go to War* was prepared by a joint committee of the Women's International League for Peace and Freedom and the Peace Section of the American Friends Service Committee especially for use with local draft boards and non-pacifists.

In case of questions of law or questions of procedure where legal experience or advice might be useful, pacifists may write to the Lawyers Committee of the American Friends Service Committee for such information. They are prepared also to give helpful suggestions to local lawyers who may be handling cases for conscientious objectors.

The Conscientious Objector Under Conscription

There has been no attempt in this pamphlet to go into any detail regarding the problems of the conscientious objector under conscription, or the Civilian Public Service, organized by the three historic peace churches in cooperation with other religious bodies, which has been set up to administer the year's work of national importance under civilian direction required

---

*Volume Three, Selective Service Regulations. *Classification and Selection.* U. S. Government Printing Office, 1940. 10 cents. (Do not send stamps.)
The Conscientious Objector Under the Selective Training and Service Act of 1940. American Friends Service Committee, 1940. 5 cents. (Contains full text of the law.)

by the Selective Service Act. A brief pamphlet regarding Civilian Public Service is now under preparation. Material on these questions is already available in pamphlet form from the American Friends Service Committee; the General Boards of the Church of the Brethren, 22 South State Street, Elgin, Illinois; the Fellowship of Reconciliation, 2929 Broadway, New York City; or the War Resisters League, 2 Stone Street, New York City.

For Further Reading:
"What About the Conscientious Objector?" American Friends Service Committee and the Women's International League, 1940, 15 cents.
"Help Wanted," American Friends Service Committee and Pendle Hill, 1940, 15 cents.
"The London Tribunal Questions the C. O.," American Friends Service Committee, 1940, 5 cents.
"Christian Conscience and the State," Calhoun and Bainton, Congregational Council for Social Action, 1940, 15 cents.
Norman Thomas, "Is Conscience a Crime?" 1928, 75 cents. (Can be ordered from the American Friends Service Committee.)
Harold Gray, "Character Bad," Harper Brothers, 1934, $1.00. (Can be ordered from the American Friends Service Committee.)
Paul Comly French, "We Won't Murder," Hastings House, 1940, $1.50.

III. PACIFISM IF CONSCRIPTION IS EXTENDED

1. Permanent Military Service

The four major proposals for extending conscription are: (1) reducing the age limit to 18, (2) raising the limit from 900,000 individuals per year to 2,000,000, (3) making conscription a permanent policy, and (4) extending the idea of conscription to require a year's service for every young man and woman.

Pacifists will naturally oppose any extension of military conscription and will work actively for the repeal of the Selective Service and Training Act which now requires military service of some 900,000 men per year. It is extremely important to work against the militarization of our nation, the propagandizing of men's minds through the press, radio, and movies, and to be active war resisters at the places where the military machine affects and touches us or our community.

2. Universal Civilian Service

If, as now seems possible, Congress is asked to pass a law requiring a year's compulsory civilian or military service of every young man and possibly every young woman, more complex issues are raised.

Pacifists are not necessarily opposed in theory to a certain amount of compulsion by the state—compulsory education and compulsory vaccination, for example. It should be pointed out, however, that compulsory education is directed toward the benefit of each individual, not toward servile obedience to the state, and full opportunity is given for private schools with varying emphases.

Naturally the pacifist tries to keep an open mind about new movements and he is very deeply concerned in finding more positive and adequate solutions for the problems of unemployment, discipline, and participation in democracy. If he is opposed to proposals for compulsory civilian service, he will need to be even more dedicated to the search for a better social and political order.

Objections to Compulsory Service

The following reasons, however, embody some of our main objections to compulsory civilian service:

a. Such a proposal at this time is indirectly, if not directly, a part of the general tendency toward war and totalitarianism.

b. The aim of the compulsion is not directly for the benefit of the individual as in education and traffic regulations, but for the benefit of the state.

c. This is very much the same means of coping with unemployment and a skeptical youth as was adopted by Hitler and which similarly avoids dealing with the real issues behind both situations, by creating, as in Germany, possibly new and more serious situations.

Oswald Garrison Villard says in his article, "No Compulsory Work Camps," in the February, 1941, *Fellowship:*
"Finally, it is interesting to note that just as we hear this demand for compulsory work service in this country, Dr. Robert Ley, the head of Hitler's 'Workers' Front' has declared in a speech to the German workers that as soon as Hitler has won his victory, both compulsory work camps and enforced military service will be abandoned in Germany. Yes, of course, I am aware that the Nazis are the worst liars on earth and the most confirmed falsifiers and tricksters, and I do not overlook Ley's qualifying phrase. None the less, that Dr. Ley felt himself compelled, whether sincerely or insincerely, to promise the abolition of

33

the work camps and military conscription, is proof positive that they are both unpopular with the German masses and that the unrest and unhappiness among them is serious enough now to make him hold out a future without these two institutions which Hitler proclaimed to be permanent feature of the Nazi 'reborn' Germany."

d. The problem could be much better solved by enlarging the framework of the existing educational system. Some contend that we need compulsory civilian service camps because too many young people are poorly trained in the simple rudiments of first aid, home nursing, personal hygiene, community service, and so on, but education is the predominant need to be met. Many of our school buildings are not used in the late afternoon or evening. Extension courses, correspondence courses and other educational means could be vastly increased without undue cost. The authorizations for military expenditures made by Congress in the calendar year 1940 totaled approximately 17 billion dollars which is four times the total value of the buildings, endowment, equipment and libraries of all our technical and professional schools, colleges and universities. So if only a portion of our military expenditures were diverted to the more enduring investment in educational facilities, the opportunities could be increased enormously. Specialized voluntary training would be infinitely preferable to the results of a militarized, regimented, compulsory system.

e. The government does not have a sufficiently able and experienced corps of men and women to administer and train millions of young people in civilian pursuits, and to put them in military camps would be to violate every tradition of American democracy.

Ways of Meeting the Situation

If compulsory service is enacted into law, pacifists probably will meet the situation in different ways, just as they are now doing under the Selective Service Act, such as:

a. Get jobs of a sacrificial nature, not allowing the government to move them to activities which contribute less to human betterment and accepting whatever penalty may be exacted.

b. Refuse to register for compulsory service and go to jail, taking a chance on whether they may be paroled or not.

c. Set up alternative work camps for pacifist training which should be on a voluntary sacrificial basis, paid for by the pacifists and their families.

The Voorhis Bill

It is too early to predict in what final form the proposal for compulsory civilian service may come before Congress. However, an analysis of the Voorhis Bill, H. R. 162, already introduced into the House of Representatives, indicates the broad outlines of possible legislation which the administration may begin pushing before long.

This bill was introduced by Congressman Jerry Voorhis, of California, on the first day of the 77th Congress, January the 3rd, 1941, "to provide a balanced program of national defense, to offer opportunity for constructive service to the nation by its citizens, and to create a national service and training program in the United States."

The bill states that in order for the United States to preserve its integrity and institutions, there must be a broadening of opportunities for the American youth in constructive lines; a preservation of the national wealth by the conservation of our "human and natural" resources; also the maintenance of a defense system including an adequate armed force. This policy would be upheld by the required services of all males residing in the United States or its possessions between the ages of 18 and 24 for a period of 12 months.

All males between 18 and 24 are required to register for this service upon a day designated by the President; and any other males who feel so obligated may register on this day in order to volunteer their services.

Starting with the calendar year of 1941, any males who have reached the age of 18 during the past year are required to register on the day set aside by the President and in the place and manner prescribed by this bill.

All men who register under this act will be subject to call sometime while they are between the ages of 18 and 24 for the assigned period of time to the work for which the commission feels that they are best suited after studying their first, second and third preferences.

The President will have the power to appoint an American Service Commission consisting of from between 7 and 15 members. The Commission shall have the authority to select the registrants as nearly as possible in accordance with their preference of service and the year they choose to serve, and when the various national service agencies can constructively use them. This board would include representatives of religious, educational, labor, agricultural, industrial, and youth organizations.

In this act is provided the complete exemption from military service of persons who are, either because of conscientious or religious convictions, opposed to military service; but they must perform some service as called for in this bill for the required period of time. However, men in the armed forces will receive $30 a month while those in civilian activities will receive $25 a month. To this pay is added the necessary traveling expenses from their homes to their respective camps. In the event that a person is engaged in a course of study, a training course, or an industry that is essential to the defense and welfare of the country, the Commission will have the authority to declare these as essential and thereby exempt the person from further service.

The Commission as prescribed in this act has the authority to set up service camps in South or Central America, where such camps might possibly help in the promotion of friendship and goodwill in the neighboring nations. However, before this could be accomplished, a civilian agency— experienced in the field—would have to carry on the proper negotiations with the nations involved.

The following list is that set up by the act as those services a man might perform:

1. Work in the Civilian Conservation Corps.
2. Work in the Civil Aeronautics Authority.
3. Work in the National Youth Administration.
4. Agent in the Public Health Service Branch.
5. Recruit in the Army, Navy, or the Marine Corps of the United States.
6. Member of the Forestry or Soil Conservation Branch.
7. Engineer in the United States Army.
8. Member of the Coast Guard or of the Coast and Geodetic Survey Branch.

To this list may be added other agencies which the Commission deems necessary to our national defense system.

For Further Reading:
   Tobin and Bidwell, "Mobilizing Civilian America," Council of Foreign Relations, 1940, $2.75.
   Petersen and Stewart, "Conscription Manual," Bender and Company, 1940.

IV. PACIFISM PREPARING FOR THE POST-WAR WORLD

1. Planning for Larger Service in Europe

No matter what the outcome of the war, there must be an attempt to build a new world from the ruins of the old. One of the difficulties then is going to be the very different ideologies that have developed and been fostered in the various countries. Peoples of the totalitarian nations will have to be reintroduced to the ideas of universal fellowship and human rights. They will have to be refamiliarized with the language and thinking of liberal democracy and to have its terms redefined.

How will this difficult task be accomplished? Dr. Hans Simons, of the New School of Social Research in New York City, has suggested that it be combined with the relief work which must surely be carried on. If relief workers undertake this delicate and important job, they will need an extensive preparation, not only in language and in sociology and psychology, but in the history and philosophy of the ideology they are trying to supplant, seeking to discover why it worked as it did, and what constructive elements it contained. They will also have to acquire the more intangible techniques of fellowship, tact, patience, understanding and personal discipline.

Here is a concrete job for pacifists and educators to undertake right now to work out a plan and curriculum for training such builders and interpreters of the future. They must have thought through their ideas and the problems involved, and have the ability to express themselves clearly and persuasively. They must have the clear vision of a creator, the executive ability needed to administer the relief work and the personal qualities necessary to insure confidence and to make the message of universal fellowship become a reality. We should begin now to set up training centers to develop such people in sufficient number to do the job effectively and broadly when the way opens.

The Civilian Public Service Camps may be able to select some of the ablest and most mature conscientious objectors and give them an intensive preparation in language, first aid, methods and problems of relief work, and modern European history with special emphasis on recent developments in Central Europe, including the achievements and defects of the Nazi regime, and a careful consideration of plans for post-war political development. Some of these emissaries might become the civil servants of the new World State or European Union if either is established after the war.

2. Training for Political Responsibility

Are the pacifists in any real way prepared for the kinds of political tasks and responsibilities which they may be asked to assume upon the close of hostilities? A. J. Muste pointed out in the Seminar that in Europe after the last war many of the men entrusted with power were those who had opposed the war and foretold its consequences. They were for the most part moderates who opposed international war, but did not renounce the use of violence in civil war or within nations. These leaders and groups for the most part were engulfed by the aftermath of the violence, hatred and economic dislocation which followed four years of the First World War.

After this war it is not inconceivable that the task of reorganization and political responsibility may be entrusted by war-weary people to those who have renounced both internal and external violence. Once the idea is discarded that war can ever solve problems even temporarily, and if pacifists were to take a strong lead, other people of brains and experience and ability would join with them to organize the world on another basis. If we are to be prepared to accept this opportunity, if it is given to us, we must build up confidence by the clarity of our thinking and analysis, the depth of our conviction and integrity and the stability and vision of our service and cooperation. Our success or failure, in positions of political responsibility, will depend upon whether we put our trust completely on the spiritual side and refuse to compromise with violence. The people who base their power completely on the spirit, and have nothing else to lose, cannot be finally crushed or destroyed.

We would record our hope that in the near future a group might devote some sustained thinking to the pattern of the kind of a world the pacifist would like to build. If agreement could be reached on the nature of a world society we want, perhaps an agreement could be reached on means to that end. With the exception of establishing criteria for judging proposals for world government, and a brief session on the cooperative movement as it relates to peace, the Seminar did not explore in detail the nature and structure of a widespread pacifist society.

38

3. The Church and the New World Order

Introductory Note

The far-reaching report of the recent Malvern Conference is a source of great encouragement to Americans. It is heartening to know that there is a group in England looking beyond the present conflagration toward the building of a new social and economic order in Europe as well as in the rest of the world. Even more significant is the fact that this group was made up of more than two hundred leaders of the Church of England. The conference met under the chairmanship of the Archbishop of York who presented the resolution below which was adopted unanimously. The amendment, introduced by Sir Richard Acland, was accepted by a very large majority.

Can those who have supported the war (and that includes the majority of those attending the Malvern Conference) reverse the forces of destruction any better when this war is over than after the first World War? Will the challenge issued in this epoch-making conference be accepted when the job of rebuilding the post-war world is undertaken, or is it destined to be just another resolution? How much will the answer depend on those who are working non-violently for a cooperative society rather than for a restless armistice?

Resolution of the Malvern Conference*

We, being members of the Church of England assembled in conference at Malvern from January 7 to 10, 1941, after seeking the guidance of the Holy Spirit, and having given the best consideration that we could to the present crisis of civilization, are generally agreed upon the following propositions:

1. The war is not to be regarded as an isolated evil detached from the general condition of Western civilization during the last period. Rather it is to be seen as one symptom of a widespread disease and maladjustment resulting from loss of conviction concerning the reality and character of God, and the true nature and destiny of man.

2. Because the church is not an association of men gathered together by the act of their own wills but is a creation of God in Jesus Christ, through which as his body Christ carries on his work for men, it has the duty and

---

* Reprinted by permission from *The Christian Century*, February 19, 1941.

the right to speak not only to its members but to the world concerning the true principles of human life.

3. The first, and if fully understood the whole, duty of the church is to be in very deed the church—the community of the Spirit drawing men and nations into itself, that they may become sharers in its God-given life and so fulfill their several destinies according to God's purpose.

4. The church as we know it does not manifest this life of true community. We therefore urge that enterprises be initiated whereby that life can be made manifest: for example, (a) where possible, the whole congregation habitually worshiping together should regularly meet to plan and carry out some common enterprise, however simple, for the general good; if there are social evils in the locality, such as bad housing or malnutrition, let them consider how the evil can be remedied, either by securing the enforcement of existing laws or in other ways; (b) in other places let "cells" be formed upon the basis of common prayer, study and service; (c) besides such cells there should be groups of people not ready as yet to join in Christian devotion, but who come together to study and discuss what is the Christian way of life for them and for society. Many have been led by this to ask for instruction in doctrine and prayer.

In all such schemes, the Christian people of a district should combine to show true neighborliness, as this is illuminated by the parable of the Good Samaritan.

5. It is of great importance that Christian people should take the fullest possible share in public life, both in Parliament, in municipal councils, in trade unions and all other bodies affecting the public welfare, and constantly seek such ways of expressing Christian principles through those channels.

6. In addition to what the church can do locally through its several congregations, there is urgent need that it bring order into the chaos of its own financial system, and so reconstruct this as to make it an expression of unity of purpose and especially of brotherhood in the ministry. Until it does this, its testimony to the world will be blunted. We fully endorse the following declaration of the Madras Conference:

> It is not enough to say that if we change the individual we will of necessity change the social order. That is a half-truth. For the social order is not entirely made up of individuals now living. It is made up of inherited attitudes which have come down from generation to generation through customs, laws, institutions, and these

40

exist in large measure independently of individuals now living. Change those individuals and you do not necessarily change the social order unless you organize those changed individuals into collective action in a wide-scale frontal attack upon those corporate evils.

It should not be necessary to say that such a view as this does not in any way minimize the crucial significance of personal religion. This must always be the spring of Christian life.

7. For it has a testimony to the world. The Christian doctrine of man as created and redeemed by God for eternal fellowship with himself supplies on the one side the only sure foundation of freedom and of justice, and also on the other hand requires that men shall have an opportunity to become the best of which they are capable and shall find in the prosecution of their daily tasks fulfillment and not frustration of their human nature. Conversely the Christian doctrine of man as a child of God carries with it the sacredness of human personality, and a civilization or social order must be adjudged by the extent to which it recognizes this in practice.

8. Because we have neglected the true end of man we have lost the controlling principle which allots to human activities their proper sphere and due relations to one another. Consequently in the last period the economic activity of man, which is entirely concerned with means, has become predominant, as though to produce material wealth were man's true end. We have here an example of the pervasive influence of human sin which the church must always keep before the minds and consciences of men. This is as relevant to schemes of reform to be operated by sinful men as to our judgment of the situation in which we find ourselves.

9. The proper purpose of work is the satisfaction of human needs; hence Christian doctrine has insisted that production exists for consumption—though it must always be remembered that the producer is also human and must find in production itself a sphere of truly human activity.

10. The industrial world as we know it offends against these principles. To a large extent production is carried on not to supply the consumer with goods but to bring profits to the producer, and the producer in turn is often subordinated to the purely financial ends of those who own the capital plant or supply the credit to erect or work it.

11. This method of ordering industry, which tends to treat human work and human satisfaction alike as means to a false end—namely, monetary gain

—becomes a source of unemployment at home and dangerous competition for markets abroad. We have seen the unemployment of Germany cured by an armament program, whether adopted primarily for this purpose or not, and have cured our own, though (even so) not completely, by the same means. The system under which we have lived has been a predisposing cause of war even though those who direct and profit by it have desired peace.

12. This system also tends to recklessness and sacrilege in the treatment of natural resources. It has led to the impoverishment of the agricultural community and is largely responsible for the problem of the "mass man," who is conscious of no status spiritual or social, who is a mere item in the machinery of production, and who easily develops the herd psychology which is automatically responsive to skillful propaganda.

13. Accordingly we believe that the most vital demands to be made by the church with a view to social reconstruction are two: The restoration of man's economic activity to its proper place as the servant of his whole personal life, and the expression of his status in the natural world as a child of God for whom Christ died.

To this end we urge:

(a) That the monetary system be so administered that what the community can produce is made available to the members of the community, the satisfaction of human needs being accepted as the only true end of production.

(b) Inasmuch as human status ought not to depend upon the changing demands of the economic process, no one should be deprived of the support necessary for "the good life" by the fact that there is at some time no demand for his labor.

(c) This status of man as man, independently of the economic process, must find expression in the managerial framework of industry; the rights of labor must be recognized as in principle equal to those of capital in the control of industry whatever the means by which this transformation is effected.

(d) In international trade a genuine interchange of materially needed commodities must take the place of a struggle for a so-called favorable balance.

(e) The church should strive to keep alive in all men and in all functional groups a sense of vocation by constantly calling upon them to consider what is the purpose of their various activities, and to keep this true to the purpose of God for his people.

(f) In all that is planned regard must be paid to the family as by God's appointment the basic social unit on whose stability and welfare all other social welfare in large measure depends.

(g) In like manner we must recover reverence for the earth and its resources, treating it no longer as a reservoir of potential wealth to be exploited, but as a storehouse of divine bounty on which we utterly depend. This will carry with it a deliberate revival of agriculture by securing to the agricultural laborer good wages and to the farmer a secure and just price. We regard this as indispensable to the true balance of the national life.

(h) The question having been propounded upon moral grounds whether a just order of society can be established so long as ownership alone is a source of income or so long as the resources necessary to our common life are privately owned, we urge that Christian people should face this question with open minds and alert consciences.

(i) Whatever may be the necessities of the period immediately following the war, our aim must be the unification of Europe as a cooperative commonwealth, first in common effort for the satisfaction of general need and secondly in such political institutions as express the common purpose and facilitate its development.

(j) We endorse the ten points put forward as foundations of peace by the two Anglican archbishops, the Cardinal Archbishop of Westminster, and the moderator of the Evangelical Free Church Council; we urge all Christian people to study those points and to support only such policies in the spheres concerned as tend to give effect to them.

(k) We urge that use be made of the opportunity provided by the presence of so many citizens of other countries in our own to make personal friendships with them and to learn more fully to understand the outlook of those nations.

(l) We regard as of primary importance the securing to all children and adolescents the educational opportunities best suited to develop their faculties and to enable them to take their full share as Christian citizens in the life of the community—economic, cultural and spiritual.

(m) Particularly we urge that the neglect of the adolescent population should cease. The primary need here is not necessarily to be met by schooling as now understood, though the raising of the school age to 15 as promised by the president of the Board of Education is greatly to be desired; but the primary need is that young people should be members of a community wider than the family of such a character that they appreciate their membership of it, and are conscious of responsibility for its honor and welfare.

Inasmuch as all these matters are such as should be the concern of the whole Christian community, we urge that all Christians unite in the furtherance of these aims.

At the heart of all the life and witness of the church is its worship. This must be so directed and conducted that its relevance to life and to men's actual needs is evident. For this purpose our traditional forms of matins and evensong, presupposing as they do acceptance of the tradition of the church and unfailing regularity of use, are largely unsuitable. They must in most places be supplemented by services of another type, whether liturgical or not, designed to bring before uninstructed people the truth concerning God as Creator, Redeemer and Sanctifier, his claim upon our lives, our need of his grace and our hope in his love and power.

The eucharist must be appreciated as the offering of ourselves and all we are—the bread and wine which are the product of man's labor expended upon the gifts of God—in order that Christ may present us with himself in his perfect self-offering, and that we may receive again from him the very gifts which we have offered now charged with the divine power, to be shared by us in perfect fellowship: so in our worship we express the ideal of our common life and receive strength to make it more real.

The Acland Amendment

God himself is the sovereign of all human life; all men are his children, and ought to be brothers of one another; through Christ they can become what they ought to be.

There can be no advance towards a more Christian way of life except through a wider and fuller acceptance of this faith, and through the adoption by individuals, of the way of living which it implies.

There is no structural organization of society which can guarantee the coming of the Kingdom of God on earth, since all systems can be perverted by the selfishness of man. Therefore, the church as such can never commit itself to any proposed change in the structure of society as being in itself a sure means of salvation.

44

But the church can point to those features of our existing order which, while they do not prevent individual men and women from becoming Christians, do act as stumbling blocks making it harder for the generality of men to live Christian lives.

In the present situation we believe the church should declare that the maintenance of that part of the structure of our society by which the ownership of the great resources of our community can be vested in the hands of private individuals, is such a stumbling block. As long as these resources can be so owned, men will strive for their ownership. Those who are most successful in this struggle will have sought this ownership for themselves as individuals and will be regarded as the leaders of our economic life. They will thereby set the tone of our whole society. As a consequence, it will remain impossible to abandon a way of life founded on the supremacy of the economic motive, or to advance nearer to a form of society founded upon a belief in the authority of God's plan for mankind.

The time has come, therefore, for Christians to proclaim the need for seeking some form of society in which this stumbling block will be removed. Those of us who support this resolution pledge ourselves to do so.

Christians, clergy and laity alike, cannot take part in this work unless they are prepared to advocate and bring about a complete reorganization of the internal financial life of the church. *(End of Malvern statement.)*

V. TOWARD WORLD GOVERNMENT

We recognize that no permanent peace is possible without law and order, and that war as a means of settling disputes has not only failed to bring order within the nations of the world, and harmony among them, but is a means of increasing strife and disharmony. In the past, many have not taken their full share in recognizing that law and justice are necessary, and that lack of them has brought us to the chaos we are in today. The development of world government is a major responsibility that pacifists ought to work on immediately.

This chapter is extremely brief and does not begin to do justice to the importance nor the complexity of the task of achieving world government. However, we started by setting up criteria by which various proposals might be evaluated, hoping that such suggestions would encourage the reader to utilize more intelligently the growing literature in this field, and that other pacifist writers might treat some of these questions at much more length.

We have as a begining, tried to draw up (1) a Bill of Rights for mankind; (2) a list of the fundamental principles which should underlie an effective International Authority; (3) a list of the minimum powers which should, in our opinion, be delegated to the International Authority, and (4) a brief analysis of the various plans now proposed in this field. We recognize that this formulation is *not complete or final*, but present it for the consideration of thoughtful people everywhere for use as a basis of further discussion and study.

It has become imperative to adjust man's life to increasingly dangerous conditions which have developed, in part, at least, from a lack of cooperation between nations, and in part from a too great concentration of control and aggressive power within nations. It is important that nations come into a closer union with mutual respect, and that they develop a code of laws which will be as just and fair to all as it is possible to achieve. This code of laws should recognize the individual rights of man without distinction of sex, race, color, creed or condition.

During the formulation of the Bill of Rights the various proposals made in England and in France have been closely studied. We are grateful to these groups for their work in this field, and wish to pay special tribute to Mr. H. G. Wells from whose book, *The Rights of Man*, we have adapted a number of these ideas. It must be borne in mind, however, that the chief aim has been to prepare a Bill of Rights and Powers to which pacifists might subscribe, and which may be used by them as criteria by which they can judge proposed plans for world government, and to serve as goals toward which we ought to be working.

1. A Proposed Bill of Rights for Mankind

1. *Social Heritage.* It is the right of every man to enjoy, for his lifetime, and without discrimination a fair share of the social benefits derived from scientific and cultural progress.

2. *Education.* Every man shall have the right to free public education in accordance with his capacity and gifts.

3. *Right and Opportunity to Work.* Every man shall have the right and opportunity to work under conditions which safeguard health and to earn enough to meet his needs including a minimum standard of leisure and cultural activity.

4. *The Right to Buy and Sell.* Every man shall have the right to buy or sell, without discriminatory restrictions, anything which is compatible with the common welfare.

5. *Private Property.* Every man shall have the right to hold property and shall be entitled to police and legal protection. But no man shall exploit others through the ownership or administration of property.

6. *Freedom of Movement.* Every man shall have the right to travel freely about the world.

7. *Privacy of the Home.* Every man's home and property shall be protected against the entry of others without his permission, except as prescribed by law.

8. *Right of Public Trial.* Every man accused of a breach of the law shall have the right of a public trial by his peers within a reasonably brief period of time after his arrest.

9. *Punishment.* No man shall be subject to mutilation, to bodily assault or to imprisonment under unhealthy or insanitary conditions, or to the death penalty. He shall not be forced to take drugs, nor shall they be administered to him without his knowledge or consent, except for medical reasons, and then only under competent medical authority. Any punishment administered shall attempt to be redemptive rather than retributive, and shall endeavor to reinstate the individual as a useful member of society.

10. *Freedom of Thought, Speech, Worship and Assembly.* Every man shall have full freedom of thought, speech, worship and assembly. No political opinion shall be considered a crime. He shall have adequate protection from any lying or misrepresentation that might injure his reputation or character. There shall be no secret dossier kept on any individual that is not subject to his challenge concerning the information contained therein.

11. *Right of Conscience.* No man shall be conscripted for any service to which he has conscientious objections.

We recognize that the above Bill of Rights does not cover the cooperative processes which we believe should characterize man's development in the near future, nor do they state the individual's obligations to society for the enjoyment of such rights. This Bill is primarily a list of rights which the tyranny of government has tended to take away from him.

2. Some Fundamental Principles Underlying an International Authority

In addition to the foregoing Rights of Man, and to the powers which should be delegated to the International Authority, there are certain fundamental principles that should underlie this Authority, if it is to be successful and satisfactory. Among these are:

1. The ultimate aim of such an International Authority shall be to include all nations of the world in its membership as soon as may be practicable.

2. Some provision should be made for voting and representation not only by governments but by individuals or functional groups.

3. Colonial possessions and dependencies shall be developed as rapidly as possible, to a point where they are qualified to enter as members on a basis of equality with existing members.

4. All legislation shall be public and definite. No secret treaties or laws shall be binding on individuals, organizations, communities or nations.

5. To insure free exchange and the flow of information and ideas between nations the International Authority should be able to regulate such world-wide services as the radio, news-gathering facilities, communications, and postal services.

6. The aim of the International Authority shall be the prevention of disputes by peaceful change or the settlement of all disputes by peaceful means, the abolition of war for any purpose and complete world disarmament.*

7. There shall be complete separation between Church and State.

---

*Footnote: Most pacifists are in favor of some kind of world government. They are not united on whether they could support such an authority if it included methods or ideas which they believe at variance with their ideals—for example, some kind of an international armed police force. Primarily because they did not believe in the use of military force to maintain law and order, the Quakers in America withdrew from political life for at least a century; likewise the Mennonites have largely refrained from political action and participation in government.

Some would resolve the dilemma by refusing political cooperation. In this case they beg the question and leave the solution for others to work out. Others would support world government, in general, even if it did involve some compromise with their principles, on the ground that only by such procedure could international anarchy and violence be overcome and only through some such evolution could a non-violent world be achieved. Still others would support the major ideas of world government, but refuse personal support or participation in specific areas, such as any military service. The Seminar did not discuss these problems in detail.

For an illuminating discussion from the pacifist point of view see the chapter *Is an International Police Force Needed?* in *Must We Go to War?* by Kirby Page, Farrar and Rinehart, 1937.

48

3. Proposed Minimum Powers

To be effective the International Authority should have the following minimum powers:

1. The power to settle disputes between its members. This would include provision for submitting justiciable disputes to an appropriate system of courts, and non-justiciable cases to inquiry, conciliation or arbitration.

2. The power to investigate conditions likely to lead to international disputes and to take all necessary legal action to settle them.

3. The power to control colonies and strategic points such as the Panama Canal, the Suez Canal, Gibraltar, Singapore, and the Dardanelles.

4. The power to regulate distribution of essential raw materials.

5. The power to regulate migration and to regulate and propose movements of population so that unhealthy and unjust conditions shall be abolished.

6. The power to tax people directly.

7. The power to regulate currencies, as for example, to prevent unfair practices such as varying the exchange rates through currency devaluation and outright inflation.

8. The power to remove hindrances to the free movement of capital.

9. The power to regulate commerce between members and non-members. The existing tariffs between the members to be gradually abolished.

10. The power to take the steps necessary to bring about a minimum but increasing standard of living for the entire world.

11. The power to pass laws in accordance with the above principles, powers, and proposed Bill of Rights.

12. The power to amend its constitution. The power to set up means to study and make recommendations for legislation on particular problems as they arise.

4. Brief Analysis of Proposed Plans for World Organization

I. Revivified League of Nations

A. PRESENT LEAGUE SET-UP.

1. *Basis of membership*—Any nation may be admitted by a two-thirds vote of the assembly. A member may also be expelled by the assembly.

2. *Assembly*—The larger body composed of representatives of all member governments.
   a. Each member state one vote.
   b. Made up of representatives of governments—not peoples.
   c. Decisions must be unanimous.
   d. Admits states to membership, and elects non-permanent members to the Council.
   e. Serves as appeal board from Council.

3. *Council*—Meeting frequently as an executive committee.
   a. The "Great Powers" have permanent seats (4-6) and nine others have non-permanent seats.
   b. Supervises mandates.

4. Assembly and Council independent in all important items—not like bi-cameral legislature.

5. *Secretariat*—Permanent administrative body, no separate power.

6. *Other coordinated bodies.*
   a. World Court.
   b. International Labor Organization.

7. *Committees:* Health, Disarmament, Communications, Mandates and many others.

8. Virtually no power—Nations retain sovereignty—League can only advise courses of action, not enforce them.

B. PROPOSED REFORMS.

1. *Bruce Report* would divide League into
   a. Social, economic and humanitarian Section.

b. Political Section.

2. *Swiss Committee of the International Peace Campaign.*
   a. League to have new spirit and more authority.
   b. Police force and general disarmament.
   c. Justice and reorganization of economic life.

3. *British League of Nations Union.*
   a. Limitation of national sovereignties.
   b. Mandatory judication.
   c. Limitation of armaments and some international police.
   d. Some economic and social control.
   e. Protection of minorities.

II. Regional Pacts

A. PAN-EUROPA—Count Coudenhove-Kalegri—1922—Pan Europe and four other regional groups using the United States as its economic model and Pan American Union as its political model. Therefore no political power.
   a. Pan-America.
   b. British Commonwealth.
   c. Soviet Union.
   d. Asiatic.

B. EUROPEAN FEDERAL UNION—Aristide Briand—1929.

A United States of Europe in which the member states retained their sovereignty.

C. UNITED STATES OF EUROPE—Alfred Bingham.

1. Regional groups—5 or 6, consisting of
   a. United States of Europe.
   b. British Empire (England would belong to both *a* and *b*).
   c. The Western Hemisphere (Canada belongs to *b* and *c*).
   d. Asia.
   e. Soviet Union.

2. United States of Europe.
   a. Council of States—legislative.
   b. Council of Nationalities (mainly cultural matters).
   c. Assembly elected according to population.

3. Development of Federal Army and Navy with gradual disarmament of national armies and immediate abolition of national navies.
4. World Organization in economics—immediately.
5. Colonies to be mandated or brought to self-government.

D. NEW REPUBLIC—1940.
  1. European Federation with sub-units, such as Scandinavian or Danubian federation.
  2. Authority over tariffs, mandates, labor, etc.
  3. Federal Police Force.

III. World Government

Lloyd and Schwimmer—All inclusive, non-military, democratic.

A. *Parliament*—10 delegates from each state to vote individually.

B. *Commissions* to plan economic, political, social, educational changes.

IV. Federal Union—Union Now

A. *Voluntary union of Democracies*, anticipating growth to world union.

B. *Bi-cameral system* elected by citizens of each member unit according to population.
  1. Executive Board, consisting of five members, three elected directly by all citizens, one member elected by the Senate and one by the House.
  2. Premier and Cabinet dependent upon vote of confidence of both houses.
  3. Judiciary, including a supreme Court for the Union with no interstate questions excluded from its jurisdiction.

C. *Fields in which the Union will have authority*.
  1. Citizenship.
  2. Defense.
  3. Customs, free trade within Union.
  4. International currency.
  5. Postal and communication system.
  6. Direct taxation.
  7. Police and military forces.

For Further Reading:

"World Organization," Olive Reddick, Women's International League, Philadelphia, 1941, 25 cents (from which the above brief analysis of proposed plans for world organization has been adapted).

Harold Laski, "Where Do We Go from Here?" Viking, New York, 1940, $1.75.

"Essential Facts about the League," Columbia University Press, New York, 1939, 25 cents.

H. G. Wells, "The Rights of Man," Penguin Books, New York, 1940, 25 cents.

H. G. Wells, "A New World Order," Knopf, New York, 1940, $1.00.

Luman J. Shafer, "The Christian Alternative to World Chaos," Round Table Press, 1940, $2.00.

"European Plans for World Order," William Maddox, Academy for Political and Social Science, Philadelphia, 1940, 25 cents.

Clarence Streit, "Union Now with Britain," Harpers, 1941, $1.75.

"The Essence of Union Now," Federal Union, Inc., New York, 25 cents.

W. B. Curry, "The Case for Federal Union," Penguin Books, New York, 25 cents.

H. R. G. Greaves, "Federal Union in Practice," Allen & Unwin, London, 1940, $1.50.

"Pros and Cons for a Federation of Nations," Foreign Policy Association, New York, 5 cents.

Eduard Benes, "Democracy Today and Tomorrow," Macmillan, 1939, $3.00.

Mrs. H. G. Swanwick, "Collective Insecurity," Jonathan Cape, London, 1937, $2.00.

"Chaos, War or a New World Order," Lola Maverick Lloyd, Campaign for World Government, 1938, 166 West Jackson Blvd., Chicago, Ill.

"Common Questions About the Future United States of the World," Campaign for World Government, 1940, 166 West Jackson Blvd., Chicago, Ill.

Part Two — Pacifist Living in a War-Making Society

VI. PACIFISM IF THE UNITED STATES ENTERS THE WAR

1. General Pacifist Philosophy

War is the time of testing for a pacifist. He is opposed to his nation's war policy and cannot participate in it actively, nor further it directly. He must bear witness to the way of love and non-violence and bear it positively in a manner that will be effective. Each individual must find and draw his own line. For one, it may mean going to prison; for another, refusal to do military service and, instead, taking Civilian Public Service; for a third, it may mean giving up a job; for a fourth, the expressing of an opinion or the opposing of a plan which results in his dismissal from a job; for a fifth, the refusal to participate in community activities directly concerned with the general war effort. Each must remember that his testimony is concerned with the creation of a new world, not only with opposition to the old. Each bears witness to a way of life; the strength of his testimony will be his ability to live it in war time and his refusal to compromise with opposing standards and methods.

It is natural in time of war for pacifists to become increasingly conscious of their segregation from the main thought and movement of their community and nation. As the war progresses, their position becomes more and more isolated and set apart from the general point of view, being thrown into relief by the growing hysteria. They are apt to feel then, that the social and emotional tension under which they are living is the result of being a small and unpopular minority. The danger is that this will develop into a feeling of self-righteousness and self-pity and that they will think of themselves as misunderstood martyrs. For this reason it is important to remember that during a war pacifists are not the only ones who are living in a constant state of taut nerves and heightened emotions. Few people are in a frame of mind to give fair consideration to points of view other than their own, even if in ordinary times they are just, reasonable, and tolerant. Pacifists should, therefore, avoid needless arguments or endless discussions, which can only result in making enemies rather than winning converts to the pacifist stand.

Since one cannot make a full and complete explanation for every move he makes, it is usually wise to err on the side of showing sympathy for the ideas of others rather than emphasizing objections, which are likely to be misinterpreted. One should be more interested in living out his ideal of brotherhood than in maintaining the pacifist label. To the average person the term "pacifist" means "draft-dodger," "appeaser," "fifth columnist," and nearly everything else which we all oppose. It is helpful to practice stating one's position more explicitly than is possible in a single word. (See Richard Gregg's pamphlet, *Pacifist Program*.)

In this statement it should be made clear that pacifists are in sympathy with the aim of preserving freedom and democracy and that their opposition to the war is not to achieve victory for the other side but because they are opposed to war as a method, which is incompatible with their humanitarian and religious beliefs. Pacifists are not "fifth columnists."

Scrupulous care should be taken to obey and cooperate with the law in every way possible. Pacifists base their belief in law and order, devoid of violence or the threat of violence, on the assumption that voluntary cooperation under law will bring better results. It is for them to prove by their own example that such a theory works. Laws should be disobeyed only when they are felt to be in conflict with the higher laws of God or clearly violate one's conscience.

Pacifists should continue to perform their usual functions and play their normal roles in the community as long as possible. If there is any "setting apart," they must accept it with good grace and without bitterness toward those who fail to understand their position, but they should never seek to withdraw themselves. The realization that understanding and tolerance are often casualties of war, will help them to keep their perspective and spiritual fellowship.

It is well to remember that the sense of dedication and willingness to sacrifice is not limited to pacifists. The mother watching her sons go off to war, the idealistic young soldier preparing for his first baptism of fire, are not figures to belittle. They are making far greater sacrifices for their belief than most pacifists are asked to make for theirs. We should never lose our humbleness of spirit and our sense of fellowship with those who, though they do not agree with us, are undergoing great emotional and spiritual strain and showing a devotion as great, if not greater, than our own.

After all, we are all seeking the truth and we should do everything we can to help others find it, rather than trying to put them in the wrong in order to vindicate our position.

2. The Individual Pacifist in a War Making Society

The role of the individual pacifist in time of war is a difficult, but extremely important one, especially if he is more or less isolated from an organized group. As a pacifist he is opposed to war, yet much of the thinking, talking and activity in his community is directed toward the war effort. For a man of military age the pattern is rather well-defined. He may decide not to register and go to jail; or he may register and ask for non-combatant service in the army, or alternative service under civilian direction; or he may register and refuse to accept alternative service, and go to jail. His choice, though demanding a clearly thought-out position, is relatively simple and the decision is clear-cut.

For many pacifists, however, the question is not so clear, nor so easily settled. Many are living and working in the midst of a war-making society and must, in most cases, continue to do so. They are faced with almost daily decisions of lesser or greater importance, many of which they will be unable to foresee and think through ahead of time. Sometimes the question involves only a slight act or minor question of principle, such as the question of buying products which include in their price taxes for military defense. Other decisions to be made may include the question of income from investments in companies which have been converted to war uses; the question of giving donations to partisan or semi-military relief organizations; the question of using defense stamps or of paying taxes and supporting government loans designed to finance the war.

But there are more difficult decisions facing some individuals. Since pacifists will not kill, they do not like to make instruments of death for others to use. Indifference at this point has been considered an evidence of weak conviction by both draft boards and friends. They need, therefore, to be willing to give or accept help in cases of unemployment for conscience sake, and should be willing to face starvation or death in giving the testimony which their individual situation thrusts upon them. Such situations develop when machinists find themselves given a new assignment which involves work on military equipment; when teachers find they are forced to compromise with truth and convert their teaching into propaganda for war; when ministers are asked to refrain from preaching pacifist sermons; when federal workers, civil servants, or those dependent on federal or state assistance, realize that a frank expression of their opinion on the war would result in their dismissal. There can be no final rule set down for the individual facing these situations. Each must seek to make up his own mind, on the basis of his belief and his sense of values, and after he has thought through and faced the consequences both to himself and his family.

Women, too, have deeper problems as war progresses. Office workers sense increasing resentment among their associates; teachers in schools and colleges find their position more and more difficult to maintain under the pressure of public opinion, and often from the school authorities themselves. Others are constantly urged to join the women's auxiliary units of the army or to participate more actively in civilian war work; some are offered or even conscripted for jobs in industry and public and civil service in order to release men for the army.

All who can, are advised to talk over their individual problems with a person or group who have had more experience and background in pacifism than they. Such a conference may result not only in good advice to the individual but a chance to clarify his own thinking.

If it is a question of a man who is married, he should also consult his wife and his children in order that the decision may be made with the full understanding of the entire family. There is no perfect answer, no completely consistent stand which fits every pacifist. Many occupations and investments help feed and service the war machine. Even watches may be used to time bombs and potatoes to feed soldiers. The ultimate decision always lies with the individual.

If some people are not to be forced by necessity and their responsibility to others, to remain in their jobs in spite of their conscience, pacifists must assume group responsibility, either to find them other positions, or to keep them and their families from utter starvation during the period of the war.

An individual often finds difficulties arising with one particular person, a neighbor or some person of authority under which he works. It is wise in such cases for him to go directly to the person and attempt to explain, quietly and fully, the position he holds. Though it may not be completely successful, a greater degree of mutual respect usually results, if this is done humbly and without rancor. This would be true in the case of a teacher who feels that certain aspects of her job compromise her position. She should point out to the principal that the conscientious objector is recognized by law and, in the case of military service, is given the choice of alternatives. Perhaps she would be allowed to substitute some other constructive school job or activity for that with which she does not feel in sympathy. If a satisfactory answer cannot be worked out by this method some other way must be tried, or the teacher may be forced to resign.

The individual should seek through his community relations to curtail and counteract the growth of intolerance and hate engendered by the war. Though he may not be acceptable as the leader of a discussion group, forum, or class, he can, by asking questions or participating as a member of the group, seek to direct the thinking into constructive lines. He should also volunteer for any public services where he can be of value, such as citizens' councils, or committees on housing, slum clearance, public welfare, educational surveys, or in groups designed to better relations between people of different races, faiths, nationalities, or economic levels. He should cooperate with city or state officials or with groups of citizens in carrying out such constructive projects.

It is important that each individual pacifist should work out a program of personal discipline. His role is an increasingly difficult one if his nation goes to war, and he must be trained in body and spirit to withstand strain and hardship. Simplicity, routine and controlled living should be the basis for such a disciplined life. Emphasis should be put on keeping in good health, and getting enough sleep, rest, exercise and recreation to be really an effective person. Time should be set aside each day for quiet meditation and reading which will result in renewed direction, clarity and strength and a sense of belonging to a large united company, even if one does not know any other pacifists personally. A regular work program is important to complete the discipline.

For those who spend all day behind a desk some form of simple handwork is advisable. The work should be useful and directed to the benefit of some one else. For women, sewing, knitting, weaving, or mending clothes for war victims or for home relief is possible. For men the making, mending or upholstering of furniture is useful, also weaving blankets or mending shoes for war victims. Those who use their hands in their regular activities should undertake more intellectual projects such as writing, studying or doing some simple research. Such a work routine gives calm, stability and purpose to the individual pacifist and by its disciplinary action trains him for greater activity in non-violent fields. (See Richard Gregg's *Discipline for Non-Violence*, Pendle Hill Pamphlet, 1941, 15 cents.)

If it is possible for the individual to find within his community or nearby some people who share his belief in the pacifist way of life, he would do well to join with them in the formation of a small pacifist group. At first it might meet informally to discuss peace topics or mutual problems, but the chances are that it would develop into a much more closely knit unit. Such a group should meet at least once a week and develop not only discussions but periods of group worship, based possibly on silent meditation, and group work projects. This working and worshiping together can develop a sense of fellowship achieved in no other way. Further discussion of such local groups will be found in the last section of this pamphlet.

Lastly, no individual pacifist can be really effective unless he belongs to one of the national organizations working in the peace field. Membership in the Foreign Policy Association, which publishes excellent factual reports, should also be urged.

3. Pacifist Action in Case of War

Besides meeting their individual and personal problems pacifists should undertake by group effort or through existing organizations, to carry out a program of positive action in case the United States actually enters the war.

The pacifists' program in war time should be to extend, clarify, intensify and adapt the work they have been carrying on in peace time. Their purpose and goals remain the same, and their methods, though subject to modification, remain within the non-violent pattern. The general public, on the other hand, finds itself adopting new sets of values and new habits of thought. Its dress, manners, even its code of morals, are subject to alteration and change. War stresses the short view, and makes tomorrow seem uncertain and far away, and the future to extend only as far as victory or defeat.

Into this framework the pacifist can exert a steadying influence. He sees the war with greater perspective, as a tragic and costly episode, and beyond it the involved and important questions of peace. He realizes that beyond everyday expediency there are basic rights and eternal values to be guarded, and he works out his program accordingly.

Whether or not this program can be carried out will depend to a large extent on the ability, imagination and persistence of the pacifists, and on the degree to which the nation's democratic freedom is preserved. The treatment of minorities is a good yardstick by which to measure the extent of this preservation, for their rights are the first to be curtailed. Sometimes civil liberties may be preserved by taking into court cases involving the infringement of specific rights, such as freedom of speech or assembly. Oftentimes a courageous stand in a community will achieve this end.

The Two Types of Activity

There are two main lines of action. One is to stress relief, projects of reconciliation, the releasing of goodwill and helpfulness, keeping contacts open and alive between groups and countries, if possible, and expressing the positive dynamic character of an active testimony at a time when most people are distressed and irritable. This makes pacifism on the whole a healing influence in a distraught society.

59

The other line of action is outright opposition to the war effort, a direct attack on situations contrary to the pacifist view. Much of pacifist action before the outbreak of war is of such a nature since the pacifists are resisting step by step the militarization and regimentation of their fellow citizens. The pacifist should not flinch from standing his ground where necessary, nor compromise his fundamental position. We feel, however, that the first type, that of quiet, creative action, is particularly needed and useful in a country at war. The true pacifist will never engage in actual physical sabotage.

Suggestions for Positive Action During Wartime

1. Pacifists should persistently ask the government to define the goals toward which it is directing the nation's efforts, what sort of world it is attempting to preserve or create; and what peace terms it would be willing to consider or offer. They should study any proposals made in the light of a durable, intelligent and constructive peace settlement and should work out and present proposals of their own.

2. The question of stopping the war is one on which at first few but pacifists may be concerned, but as the war progresses the issue will grow in importance until, before it ends, it may well become the most important issue in the country. The pacifists should raise the question continuously, always pointing out that a negotiated rather than a dictated, vindictive peace, holds the best hope of a successful and lasting settlement.

3. Groups of specially selected, trained and equipped young people should be formed into units to do rescue and relief work under civilian direction in places of particular need and danger, either in the United States or in other countries. There are such units in England today, working under the Friends' War Victims Relief Committee, which go into heavily bombed areas at a moment's notice to fight fires and do rescue and relief work.

4. Groups should also be formed for more general relief projects of feeding, rehabilitation, caring for homeless refugees and in reconstructing devastated areas. These workers, like all peace workers, should be particularly trained and disciplined people in order to express through their work the attitude and spirit of their belief. They should be prepared not only to carry on while war is in progress but to continue afterwards and to extend their work as far as possible into the areas made accessible upon the cessation of hostilities. People should be trained in languages now with this in mind and all pacifists should be trained in first-aid.

5. Those who cannot be members of foreign service groups should realize that there is a big job to be done at home in the "enemy" internment and prison camps which are set up in any country in time of war. Usually the work in these camps is carried on by neutrals, so that pacifists could do very little direct relief work there, but they could try to see that an adequate number of enlightened and trained neutrals were secured to care for the needs of the prisoners. They could also busy themselves collecting books, musical instruments, and any other small amenities which might bolster up morale and make the life of enforced idleness and segregation more creative.

6. Pacifists should also be prepared to undertake special work or relief projects at home in case of emergencies, such as floods, storms, accidents, fires or sickness. The influenza epidemic during the last war is such an example. Often regular relief agencies are dislocated or made short handed by the war.

7. The Civilian Public Service Camps for conscientious objectors should be maintained by the pacifists and their constituency as a continued witness to the government and public of their willingness to sacrifice and their ability to train the pacifists of military age for effective and constructive service to society.

8. Groups should also feel responsible for their members who have lost or given up their jobs because of their pacifist stand. Often this demands great economic hardship, not only for the individual, but for his family. To meet this need, it has been suggested that groups set up some sort of cooperative enterprise to which some could contribute time and work, and others, money, equipment or other physical resources. Sometimes mutual liability can be carried even further, to the point of complete or partial sharing of all resources of the group, and the setting up of an arrangement for cooperative living, on or near subsistence level. Some people feel that the benefits of such an arrangement far exceed the mere meeting of economic need, and that it contributes enormously to the group's fellowship, dedication and spiritual power. (See the next section of this pamphlet on "Building a Local Pacifist Group.")

9. In time of war special attention should be paid to the preservation of civil liberties. As the general tension increases, and emotions arise, minority groups often suffer and their rights are overlooked or discarded. This is particularly true of groups who oppose or are thought to oppose the war. Continuous effort should be made to protect the lives, property and rights of

61

aliens and to see that the war is not used as an excuse to repeal all the social legislation that has been passed and to rob labor of its hard won rights. Pacifists must strongly and persistently oppose the tendency to regimentation and to sacrifice long term good merely for short term expediency.

10. Regardless of how long the war lasts, it will end some time, and some arrangements for peace are inevitable. The character of the future world will depend largely on the nature of this peace. One must labor vigorously during the war to prepare for that peace, by studying ways to increase understanding and eliminate bitterness and by training people to go into other countries to bring hope, new ideas, and a sense of fellowship, as well as material relief. Every effort should be made to prepare public opinion to accept as an alternative to war some sort of world government or international authority. Groups should be set up to discuss the national sacrifices necessary to bring this about.

For Further Reading:

"Pacifist Program in Time of War, Threatened War or Fascism," Richard R. Gregg, Pendle Hill, Wallingford, Pa., 10 cents.

"If America Enters the War—What Should I Do?" Christian Century, 440 South Dearborn Street, Chicago, 1941, 15 cents.

"A Message from the National Study Conference on Churches in the International Situation," Walter Van Kirk, 297 Fourth Avenue, New York City, February, 1940, 15 cents.

"Discipline for Non-Violence," Richard R. Gregg, Pendle Hill, Wallingford, Pa., 15 cents.

VII. BUILDING A LOCAL PACIFIST GROUP

The success of pacifism, whether in terms of an individual philosophy or in terms of a social program is dependent on the development of pacifist personnel, whole-heartedly committed to the way of love. War is only an incident in a history of continual strife. If we were adequately meeting the "war on our waterfront and the fascism within our agricultural valleys," we would not find a strong tendency to differentiate between a pacifist program in war and in peace. Certainly there is a difference in degree, but essentially the problem of the pacifist group is to build a new way of life, adequate to meet any type of social strain. By adequate, we do not mean the avoidance of suffering or death, but we do mean the avoidance of spiritual breakdown or a feeling of isolation on the part of the individual.

1. The Need for a Group

A group is a necessity for pacifist action and survival in either war or peace. Ease or isolation is more apt to dissipate and waste energy than persecution. There should be no such thing as an isolated pacifist, even though our groups must at times be made up of individuals necessarily residing in more than one vicinity.

Purpose is the corollary of need; we have purposes in order to meet needs. We are writing this section of our report in terms of needs, because the degree of pacifist group development is such that needs are felt, but purposes are not yet matured.

Material Needs for a Group

1. Economic sharing within a group is necessary for actual physical survival of the individual and his family, when outer circumstances, such as military conscription and the shift of industry to munition making, removes the conscientious individual from his job.

2. A gradual growth toward sharing economic problems within a group gives practice in later development of responsibility toward the economic problem of other groups, the general community, and the world at large.

3. During times of persecution, it is important that a group feeling of absolute trust and confidence shall have been built up so strongly that it cannot be shaken. It may be very difficult to build this trust after a severe persecution has started without greater spiritual resources than are yet developed in any pacifist groups within our immediate knowledge.

4. By psychologically freeing us from the pressure toward an artificial standard of living, and by achieving tangible economies in supplying ourselves with the necessities of life, group action offers a medium for saving time and money in order to release these resources for socially constructive purposes.

Spiritual and Social Needs for a Group

1. Group morale aids the individual in carrying out a program of personal discipline. A group supplies a sense of oneness required to strengthen our infant loyalties, not yet developed enough to remain steady.

2. A small, intimate group makes possible a form of worship experience that is different from individual worship or from worship in larger groups, though probably functioning only in a pattern which includes the other two.

3. We need intimate group contact in order to bear the spiritual and psychological burden of actual and vicarious suffering.

4. By increasing the strength of the relationships between individuals, a group may rebuild the foundation pattern of social cohesion that our violent civilization has "burned out of the clay."

5. Group discussion, thinking, action, and living offers a medium through which practice and experience can be gained in functioning as a part of a social organism. (See Howard Brinton's *Creative Worship*.)

6. Group living aids in the development of psychological insight and creative personality. The type of individual we are seeking to create is described by Fritz Kunkel as "objective," and by Aldous Huxley as "non-attached." As medicine was at first concerned only with the dangerously ill, then much later with preventing illness, and only recently with the development of vigorous health, psychology is going through similar stages. The goal of psychology becomes the development of a vibrant personality, rather than one which is merely not sick. The joy, the freedom from strain and worry, and the freedom from pre-occupation with our own physical or social difficulties, that comes when we are working as part of an integrated group is testimony to the value that the group may contribute to this new field. To be lost in a cause greater than oneself leads to the creation of a poised, stable and dynamic personality.

7. The spiritual fortitude to stand firm against entrenched wrong, to follow our conscience in spite of physical hardship, to do the unpleasant tasks that will be a part of any non-violent action program is a need we all feel. The moral support of a group is valuable not only in helping us to do this, but in helping to do it in a spirit of love and understanding.

The Intellectual Need for a Group

By dividing ourselves on the strength of individual concerns to study and understand various aspects of life, we can function more adequately, and each individual can through the group have more intimate knowledge of all these aspects. A group can, when it sees the need, utilize all the resources of the group for a more complete testimony or action than any individual can give if acting alone.

2. Starting a Pacifist Group

Every pacifist should function as a part of an intimate group. If there are only three or four individuals in a community, they will find strength in close association with each other. The pattern of that association will vary for reasons of geography and personality, but little success has been achieved unless the group is willing to meet at least once a week. If there is a single person or couple who is isolated in any community, they should function as a part of a group in another locality, although unable to attend the weekly meetings. By writing to each weekly meeting and receiving a report of it by letter they will not lose complete contact. It may be considered a wise and necessary item in a pacifist budget under such circumstances for members to include a larger transportation item than would ordinarily be advisable for their standard of living.

Suggestions have been made that groups may be started by calling together persons listed on the rolls of the Fellowship of Reconciliation, the Wider Quaker Fellowship, and similar groups. While this may be a useful preliminary procedure to get persons of like mind acquainted with each other, no person from outside the community can start a pacifist group. He can with value testify regarding the help he personally has derived from participation in such a group in his own locality, but with this stimulus, the group must evolve from the felt need of the members themselves. The group process in essence is but the extension of intimate, personal friendship. In starting in a new community, these personal friendships may need to be cultivated intensively and consciously.

There are many reasons why individuals seek the association of the group, yet some common denominator is necessary for the group's functioning. Humility, a feeling of personal inadequacy, dissatisfaction with our present mode of living, desire to restrain our habits for more effective living, a desire for more adequate expression of our ideals in terms of needs around us, may all be elements in the "hunger and thirst" for a new way of living which is the basic motive of the group.

Much of the energy of the group is dissipated unless the membership of the group can be kept constant to a large degree, because of the necessity of continually explaining the idea to a new person, and because an intimate knowledge of each other is necessary to the complete functioning of the group. Any exceptions should be made with the common consent of the whole group. This is particularly necessary at that "adolescent" stage in which the group 'may be said to have developed a "group ego." This stage should be passed through as quickly as possible, but may be necessary, just as a period of living alone is often essential to a newly married couple. After the group has found its own unity and has learned to do thinking and worship which is more than the sum of the individuals within the group, it can then function as an outward-turned group in a fashion quite impossible at first. In order to keep from being stranded at the point of adolescence, the group needs always to strive to live and work as a part of the larger community.

Religious history would seem to indicate that the *size* of the group should vary from five to twelve. Where married couples already unified in purpose within the marriage unit are members of the group, a larger group might be equally successful.

Unless indicated by the economic needs of the moment as under times of economic stress, or when concerned with a cooperative living group for students, plans for communal living may well be kept from crystallizing until the group has begun to feel a sense of unity. No pattern for such living should be made a matter of rule, but experimentation can be very fruitful. Communal living grows out of "the driving urge to work out together the full implications of the Christian community." Distrust of historical precedent for communal living should not be made a reason for neglecting the values of group thought and action.

3. Development of the Pacifist Group

1. Mutual Liability

Unless indicated by the economic needs of the moment as under times of economic stress, or when concerned with a cooperative living group for students, plans for shared living in a group may well be kept from crystallizing until the group has begun to feel a sense of unity. No pattern for such living should be made a matter of rule, but experimentation can be very fruitful. Shared living grows out of the "driving urge to work out together the full implications of the Christian community". Distrust of historical precedents should not be made a reason for neglecting the values of group thought and action.

The next step in the development of a feeling of responsibility comes in realizing that the real need of the small group, the things which the small group cannot handle, becomes the real need of the larger pacifist community, as church, meeting, yearly meeting, local peace council, Fellowship of Reconciliation, or similar group; and conversely, that the growth of the larger fellowship becomes an imperative need of the small group. We can learn through this expanding horizon that all need is mutual need—what one needs to have someone else needs to give, or to create. The program of small group development does not purpose to drain energy from the larger religious program, but to give it impetus and continuity.

The final step in expanding our horizon is to realize our unlimited liability, to the extent of our total economic and spiritual resources and of our skills, toward the needs of every individual in the world, but this greater realization comes only as a climax to expanding series of closer loyalties.

The following program is not intended to be dogmatic in any sense, but is a suggestion of what has happened, or is contemplated, in groups we know. These points are not suggested as something to do immediately upon starting a new group, but are what might or could happen, approximately listed in the order in which they might occur. This program is not suggested as an alternative to the ashram as suggested by Muriel Lester, but could function either inside or outside that pattern. If any group sincerely follows the insight that is given them in their search for a way to express their feeling of mutual liability, they will see new ways to apply it to community patterns, which may well vary with the group. These are some methods in learning to share.

1. Cooperative enterprise, including home canning and baking, care of children, to give mothers time for recreation and outside interests, cooperative buying groups, and similar projects, can help us in learning how to work together, in saving money and energy, and in helping to build a non-violent economic order.

2. Time-sharing can often precede economic sharing. By helping each other with such everyday things as child care, ironing, gardening, repairing cars and machinery, persons can be released for outside tasks, such as serving on a refugee committee, and calling on the sick.

3. A significant step is taken when the group decides to have a uniform bookkeeping system or open accounts, thus comparing standards of living within the group. Muriel Lester used this in her first small group, "The

Brethren of the Common Table" (See her autobiography, *It Occurred to Me*). Making an inventory of the financial assets and debts, and of the skills of the group in order to know the resources of the group when planning pacifist action is a part of having open accounts.

4. Practice in group action and wise spending can result from group decision regarding the spending of individual surpluses to advance the cause of world brotherhood.

5. Greater spiritual growth may well result from leaving matters of personal expenditures up to the individual conscience, with consultation by the group when requested. This also contributes to efficiency, as there is better use of the group's time than the discussion of minute details of individual living, unless such details should be discussed under discipline when some item of expenditure is a barrier to the free flowing of the spirit.

6. A little-used method of pacifist action has been the plan of releasing members of the small group from the necessities of personal livelihood in order to carry out a concern. The choice of such member may be made on the basis of the strength of the individual concern or of the need of the individual for direct expression. The small group action in this manner is different from a group organized to carry out an action program for its own sake, in that it considers needs of the outer community and the needs of its own members for action as a part of an integrated whole. We must recognize the need of all individuals in the group to have the spiritual satisfaction of work directly pointed toward our larger goals, as well as the need of each of us for the spiritual discipline of doing routine work, or of earning money, so that others may be released. The whole group, by projecting itself, can share in the psychological and physical needs of the individual going out to do some difficult piece of action, so that there is not a great discrepancy in the comfort level of the home members or mobile members of the group. This is a method by which "householders" may secure the "mobility" of which Gerald Heard speaks.

Although not essential to this pattern, shared living or the joint use of equipment increases the ease with which a member may be released for carrying out a concern.

Where groups may desire to fit this program of mutual liability and pacifist action into an already existing religious unit, such as a Sunday School class, or young people's group, care should be taken to keep the group sufficiently constant, not too large, not hampered by time limits and restrictions, and above all to realize that the unique contribution of the small group is in creating channels for the best use of each individual's ability.

7. The sharing of a group is necessary in enabling the individual to live up to his conscience when there is a conflict regarding military service, or when vocational shifts are necessary due to encroaching munitions-making industry. This burden will need to be borne by the larger group rather than the small pacifist group in instances where large sections of a community or church are affected. In some Brethren congregations, for example, one-tenth to one-third of their membership is affected. But the small group can take the initiative in promoting this larger sharing. The principle to be used here is that suggested by Gibran in *The Prophet,* while it is good to give when asked, it is much better to give unasked, because you understand the need. The small group can make its approaches toward other groups in the desire to learn the needs of others and to share them, rather than in seeking help to meet its own needs.

The first step will need to be an inventory of the needs of the community. An excellent example of this was the proposal for a Service Exchange of the Baltimore Branch of the Fellowship of Reconciliation. In a two-page questionnaire they sought to find out what each of their members had to offer in meeting the needs of conscientious objectors to military activities of whatever sort, and also how many of their members were affected by this need for changing their occupation.

After needs are known, local groups must plan toward special measures to meet needs which cannot be matched between individuals. City groups may look toward the establishment of a farm base, or farm groups may look toward establishment of home industry in order to supply cash needs.

A clearing house for spreading the knowledge of these needs to a wide group must be set up. We recommend, that the local meeting or church revive or reconstitute a committee to (1) have oversight of the needs of families, and (2) to take care of their own members who are conscientious objectors in civilian camps, or other members of the community who have no local group. Such a committee might volunteer to carry the administration of a plan whereby all conscientious objectors, both men and women of all ages, put in a certain amount per month to a fund. Those who must go to Civilian Public Service camps could have their expenses paid from this fund to the extent that they themselves, or their families, could not handle those expenses. It has also been suggested that if each conscientious objector who withdraws money from the fund should attempt to pay back into it after his year of service, not only could the proposed Civilian Public Service camps be adequately financed, but we should have a fund of sizeable proportions available for constructive peace work after the crisis.

In order to take care of matters which become too large in any local group, the larger church units such as quarterly meetings, districts, and synods, should strive to become aware of the total and potential need, so that when difficulties arise, we will not need to waste time in setting up organization or in studying the problem.

Pacifist women can also prepare themselves to take up the burden of vocational shifts. (See article on *The Pacifist Family* in *Fellowship* for October, 1939.) The cooperative care of children can release some women to earn or supplement the family income by housework, nursing, bookkeeping, teaching, farm work, or more specialized skills within the group.

8. Finally, we can find opportunities to include other persons in the economic benefits and life of our group by sharing our homes with students, refugees, or unemployed. In groups of low income, the whole group may need to unite on one project, such as five persons signing affidavits for one refugee, whereas each alone would not be accepted by the government as adequate. We can plan to use our own community center, homes, or meeting house for rehabilitation or educational work. For further discussion of these possibilities, see the section on "Building Beyond the Group."

2. Study and Observation

The small pacifist group will find that its own education, the development of creative skills, the learning of useful facts, and the building of socially constructive attitudes is essential to its development.

Under a program of constant study should be included the methods and implications of a program of non-violence, the causes of war and of social chaos, and the interpretation of propaganda techniques, so that we do the kind of reading that will balance the propaganda we will inevitably meet. We need to develop an intimate understanding of the solutions proposed by other groups, such as labor unions, political groups, other religious groups, and the cooperative movement, so that we may become a constructive part of other movements, where possible, or a restraining influence where necessary, always seeking to trust the sincerity of other individuals and to open for them ways in which to express their real seeking.

The group needs to be well grounded in a knowledge of areas of social conflict. No one individual can know all these fields adequately, but every pacifist should know at least one field in detail. The group can help the individual in choosing this field, with some attempt toward balancing this study program within the group. If different persons make a special study of inter-racial conflicts, labor difficulties, both industrial and agricultural, refugee needs, etc., this can be of great help in developing concerns and more intelligent ways of meeting those concerns. War will never be abolished until we develop a more widespread understanding of the relation of economic, political and social patterns to the conflicts between nations. The problems of post-war reconstruction must be foreseen and solutions planned, so that when proposals for world government are suggested we will not only have criteria by which to judge them, but we will be prepared to take the lead in their evolution.

We should familiarize ourselves with other attempts at community building, stimulating our imaginations by seeing the effects of their experimentation. We should learn by observation and the interchange of experience, as well as by reading. We should plan personal contact with persons of different attitudes, experience, environment, and a racial or national background, and learn to know intimately the places where they live, the kind of books they read, and their cultural aspirations and expressions. By asking them to educate us, instead of continually telling them of our aspirations and solutions, we become more humble, wise, and understanding.

It is of great help in the total development of our pacifist group if we become familiar with as complete a range of biographical and devotional reading as possible. The process of social contagion can span time and distance if the lives and meditations of great souls are read with receptive imagination.

By proper attitudes, the actual work of trying to meet our own and others' needs in an intelligent manner can be our greatest education. A more systematic and concentrated program of study built around these needs may save us from wasteful or harmful action.

3. Worship

Worship is the way in which we contact the source of strength and fortitude necessary to mold our individual and group habits so that we may even attempt to live up to our ideals. Some of us hesitate to consider worship as a form of discipline, but rather as a basic need, as basic as food, shelter, and clothing. Regardless of interpretation on this point, a pacifist group will find it very fruitful to consider its worship needs seriously. There is an observable difference in the quality of group discussion which follows a vital worship period to one which grows immediately out of our pre-occupation with daily problems, showing the relation between worship and creative thinking. During worship we have a heightened sense of our own inadequacy, a more poignant feeling of suffering and the burden of the world's need; we learn to feel a sense of unity with people striving toward the same ends, a sense of unity with all people, and finally, a sense of joy and of power and of being a part of a universal Creative Activity. Unless the values of worship are implemented in one's life, one has not really worshipped. No program is well-rounded that is based on action alone. The spirit undergirding the action is an integral part of the action itself.

While individual worship, by whatever method the individual finds most fruitful, and participation in the worship of his church are both parts of a well-rounded spiritual life, they cannot take the place of worship within a small group. The group should feel free to experiment with different forms of worship, watching always for that form which seems most to knit the group into a unity, and which provides experiences not gained in individual or large group worship. Devotional reading and silence have been found helpful. For groups which have not had experience in worship through silence, it might prove useful to try first problem-solving silence or silence for an appreciation of the group, that is, thinking of each member of the group in turn, trying to imagine his needs, aspirations, and personality. Sometimes a sudden appreciation of hitherto unrecognized beauty of character in the individual about which one is thinking comes from these appreciation silences. The possibilities realized in this way may give the group a motivation for trying a worship silence. For a more complete description of the possibilities in silent worship see L. Violet Hodgkin, *Silent Worship, the Way of Wonder*, and Rufus Jones, *The Faith and Practice of the Quakers*.

4. Discipline

The purpose of discipline is to train both our conscious and unconscious reactions so that we may release energies to produce the light and power necessary for creative living. No set of rules, however admirable, can in themselves release energies and channel them into constructive thought and action. Each individual will need to accept voluntarlly, a physical and mental discipline which denies himself a thing that seems to block the spirit of love from flowing through him. Sometimes this may lead to eccentricity and a seeming hardness, an over-compensation for our weaknesses and temptations. When such concentration of energy has cleared the channel, the individual may find himself able to respond again to the average method of living and social amenities for the sake of efficiency or kindliness, or for seeming not to judge others for their manner of living. Having once proved our courage to ourselves, we may then decide on policy. Some individuals need to have a retreat, others to take special care to be sociable. The person who habitually over-eats may need to fast for a period; he who has used fasting to prove his superiority in righteousness may need to take care to eat three meals a day. The purpose of discipline is to be flexible and able to endure what is necessary to live in obedience to the will of God, or the over-Spirit.

Out of the mutual, self-criticism of the group we may see our weakness and plan a discipline specifically to meet those needs, either as an individual or a group. If some individual has difficulty in carrying out a discipline the entire group may need to impose that discipline on themselves in order to give him strength to follow through. The purpose of discipline is not to "be good" or to propitiate a watch-dog God, but to be free and clear. This freedom may be attained by submitting ourselves to the group process as has been suggested, rather than by setting up a code of conduct.

Interchanging disciplines between groups may serve the same function for the small group itself as mutual self-criticism within the group serves for the individual. Out of this program of inter-group criticism and stimulus it may be possible to develop a universal pacifist discipline to be accepted as a minimum standard. *Discipline for World Builders* by Dan West gives an excellent example of the areas of training that cannot be ignored.

Every person with whom we talk unconsciously knows whether we feel resentful, superior, inadequate, or loving. It is impossible to pretend. It is more important to control our thoughts to let people feel that no action should be attempted until this control over the human spirit is attained, lest as Gerald Heard says, we are as though "operating with unclean instruments." This control, or to use Brother Lawrence's phrase, "practice of the presence of

73

God," can sometimes be secured by going on with the tasks that call us. The discipline of the task is often more effective than an artificial discipline.

The pacifist group will need to seek special guidance in regard to the matter of labor discipline. Richard Gregg's recommendation that creative hand labor be a component of a universal pacifist discipline is worthy of serious consideration, but we would like to express the principle that labor discipline should be such as to balance the individual's daily life. A person doing routine labor all day should be doing creative work as a labor discipline. An executive who is accustomed to plan the use of his own time and that of others should learn the discipline of routine hand labor, or of working in a field new to himself under the direction of a skilled person. We can seek individually and as a group to discourage in ourselves idleness of mind and hand. In social pioneering, as in the early frontier pioneering, cooperative physical activity can be a form of recreation as well as a means of accomplishing a task. Waste of time and skill when confronting the needs of today is indirect murder.

Sometimes our severest discipline is in learning to say "no" to activities that are in themselves good, but not of primary importance. While it is important for the group not to become ingrown and isolated, it is also important to take a more significant stand in the community than to join, or even to lead, in every good but not complete program of action. Our primary function is to be the leaven in the loaf, and it is often the way of weakness and retreat to channel our energies through the good, respectable organizations in our community. Occasionally the group may divide its activities, appointing one individual to function actively in each of several struggling organizations on the right side of the ledger, to report back to the group for unified support whenever it is necessary for the total group to help at some strategic point. This policy does not need to make us insincere in our attitude toward other organizations, but it is often a great kindness to that organization to reserve our own place within it as a follower, promoting other persons to positions of leadership.

The small group will need to exercise self-renunciation in handing on the things which it starts to larger groups and other organizations. Often in order to get a great idea started it is necessary for a small group to make a beginning, mortgaging its very existence to the success of the project. If it sought, however, to keep the control of that project in its own hands it would hinder both its own usefulness, and the greater success of the project itself. As soon as possible, the group should forget that it was responsible for the beginning, and its member individuals should fit in as followers to more able persons who may be in a position to take over the direction of the task.

5. Building Beyond the Group

The spirit of unity realized within the peace fellowship through the mutual sharing of problems, experiences, and economic responsibility is but a miniature of what the group is striving to achieve in the larger society. There is no single point at which the development of the group ends and action begins. The challenge of the greater task brings into bold relief the weakness of the group; in trying to secure in other individuals and in laws and institutions the recognition of the equal value of human life and growth, we realize our own need for a further process of self-purification and discipline.

The most difficult choice for any group is in deciding upon which of the many types of social injustice it should concentrate. To spread our energies and resources on too many issues at one time keeps us always operating in the realm of superficial activities, some possibly harmful in effect.

The choice of our action should be based on the most immediate needs in our own community. As we become friends with our neighbors and with under-privileged groups and individuals in our own locality, the demands of friendship will show us their needs, and from a sincere attempt to meet these needs we shall inevitably be led to seek basic solutions for the difficulties. We should shrink neither from the discipline of helping individuals and families to make an adjustment to an overwhelmingly difficult environment, nor from the discipline of tracing the roots of the difficulties even to our own doorstep. A certain amount of ameliorative activity is necessary to help us bear the burden of knowing the facts and to give our efforts toward fundamental solutions a basis in reality. As we build a more complete picture of the problem within our own neighborhood, we find that we have gained also a knowledge of the factors in the international problem, and as we strive toward effective local solutions, we see the need and also the pattern to follow in building a new world order.

Aldous Huxley in *Ends and Means* cautions the pacifist to reserve his energy for those types of action which no one else will do. If we reserve for ourselves the right to concentrate on one type of action, we should be doubly careful not to judge others for tackling the problem in their own way, but seek to cooperate with their activities whenever it is consistent with our own direction. Although personally or as a group we are not able to do a significant thing toward all types of injustice, we should strive always to keep our sensitivity and our ability to suffer vicariously with the victims of all injustice. If we are really bearing the burden on our hearts, we are often able to recognize opportunities to help which we would otherwise pass by. This burden is often easier to bear if we keep a connection, through financial aid, with some other individual, group or organization working in those fields we are unable to touch. (For more complete suggestions regarding these fields see Chapters I and II on Some Areas for Positive Action Now.)

First we need to turn our attention to improving the quality of every-day living, by showing more neighborliness, by making our homes a place for others to find cheerfulness, refuge, sanity in a chaotic world, faith, and a sense of direction, or even by such a simple thing as inviting our less fortunate neighbors to use our washing machine or sewing machine. An intelligent and willing ear just to listen to accounts of failures, successes, psychological problems, or new strivings toward a more significant life is often a more important thing than we suppose. We should not feel that this always means that we are to give advice. More often we need to help our friend to realize that his problem is not unique, that it is a part of the great unsolved problems of the human race, that as he meets it either successfully or unsuccessfully he is contributing his attempt toward the final solution, and giving others the courage to go on.

Sometimes we forget that the greatest opportunity for action that we have is in the care of our own children. They are the ones who must develop enough courage and stability to be able to share it with the children of Europe and Asia, who will be psychologically, spiritually and physically deformed from their present war experiences. To find a balance between increasing their sensitivity through sharing our concerns with them and over-burdening them beyond their years, and a balance between caring for their essential needs, and teaching them to face squarely the difficulties in their environment, are problems to which there are no patent answers. Most of all we need to provide them opportunities to find their own "pathway to the realities of God."

Almost inexhaustible are the opportunities for interpretive or educational projects, such as forums, discussions, classes, lending libraries, making pamphlet material available by sale or lending, speaking before outside groups, or opportunities in every day conversation. In such activities we should show a respect for others' opinions, especially since many in these times will have undergone great sacrifice for their convictions. We should not thrust our ideas upon others, but yet make it clear that we feel we have a knowledge of facts and a sense of direction worth sharing. Maintaining a quiet but firm steadfastness in these bewildered times is of great value in itself when people are so confused. Well-founded convictions win respect even from those who may not accept them.

At no time should we neglect to take seriously the activities growing out of our duty as citizens. We should not allow ourselves to be lazy voters, or careless law-breakers. Though there are times when we conscientiously cannot serve both God and an unjust law, our objection should be set in a pattern of such scrupulous observance on lesser issues, that there can be no question of our intent nor any suggestion that we are chronic evaders of civic responsibility.

If, on occasions when a protest or statement of opinion to our congressmen or public officials is necessary, we are sure our words are grounded in fact and careful observation and analysis, our words will have more value and effectiveness. By having first-hand knowledge due to our own identification with under-privileged groups, and by speaking fearlessly regarding the things we know, we can perform a useful service in penetrating the veil of isolation which always surrounds persons in authority. In this modern world it is no longer possible for leaders and rulers to travel incognito as some of the more benevolent kings of old, but the need which that filled is still with us. By showing how laws work in action, as well as in theory, by commending our public officials as well as censuring them, by making channels whereby the victims of unjust laws can carry their own protests to the proper places, we can do much to create a more enlightened public and official opinion.

In planning direct action and protests we should take care that the moral force of that action reaches a person or persons who are in a position to rectify the difficulty, rather than merely creating embarrassment for someone who is himself a victim of the same situation. For instance, mass picketing or creating a scene in a restaurant which refuses to serve Negroes may be unjustly singling out one man for a reprisal whereas he is the victim of competition by other restaurants with the same policy, or of public prejudice.

At the present time there are many groups projecting themselves into useful community service. A number of farmers cut several acres of corn for a bed-ridden neighbor. Others in a city helped some Negro families go house hunting; this was not only a very interesting experience, but it created a desire to help establish a Negro credit union. Several college students are collecting clothing for war sufferers and books for German prisoners in Canada. A more advanced group formed a committee of reconciliation which helped secure justice in several labor conflicts by bringing to light certain facts. There is no end to things that wide-awake peacemakers can do. This unscheduled activity may well lead into regular evening work or to a Saturday project. An extensive task may warrant, for example, a week-end work camp.

In Philadelphia a small group is undertaking a week-end work project. They come together Friday night in a Negro settlement house, staying until Monday morning. Each person, where possible, pays a nominal fee to cover living expenses. The well-rounded program includes work, worship, study and recreation. The center is located in a slum area where the group is now helping a number of Negro families to rebuild their furniture. The campers, members of the community, and representatives from the Catholic Worker House go together to cut fire-wood on a New Jersey farm. A sense of universality is developed when the group mends clothing for war sufferers in Europe. Perspective is gained in the evening discussions when they study the relationship of their tasks to the world-wide problem of poverty, race antipathy, exploitation, etc.

Before embarking on such a project, however, a group should carefully count the cost. Here are a number of questions that might well be considered before proceeding.

1. Is there a definite physical need in your community? Here are some things being done now:
    a. Improving housing conditions.
    b. Promoting a cooperative grocery store.
    c. Providing recreational facilities and direction.
    d. Improving roads or other public areas.
    e. Helping develop a "boys' town," or self-governing groups of younger boys.
2. Is there a better way of meeting this problem than the week-end camp?
3. Can you get permission and necessary cooperation from public officials?
4. Has your group sufficient time, energy, and experience to underwrite morally the project?

5. Is your group able to finance the project, or will it be necessary to rely on local churches, service clubs, or individuals?
6. Are adequate living quarters available?
7. Is there a nucleous of six or eight that can participate each week in order to maintain a continuing fellowship?
8. Are there others from various churches or from the community itself who are willing to work with you?
9. Do you have qualified leadership to direct the project?

As the group develops in unity and self-control, the time may come when it is ready to engage in a project of more scope than a week-end work camp. Without necessity of outside subsidy, and by keeping our present jobs in the neighborhood, can we place the whole group community in a low-income area, rural enough to be effective, or in an area not hampered by segregation rules? In this way the group may have opportunity to rebuild an entire community pattern. Instead of using its funds for larger houses or common rooms for its own use, it may plan and largely support or initiate a community center for the whole community. Or the group might within its community build an extra two or three houses, on the same plan and standard as its own, however low that might be, and offer them, on the same pattern, as a refugee hostel. The building of the houses might be done with small expense by making the actual work a part of our labor discipline. The group itself in its time away from regular jobs, by the very process of everyday living could function as a refugee staff by helping to understand, teach, and find jobs for refugees within its own city.

Concluding Word

None of the suggestions made above are given as a rigid program of group development. It is hoped that those who read this will build a program based on the opportunities within their own communities. No sociological analysis can ever be transferred in its entirety to a new situation, but by keeping in touch with national peace organizations, our imaginations can be stimulated to discover plans for meeting similar situations with our own resources and abilities.

In dealing with any underprivileged group, our actions should be guided by a mutual choice of activities worked out by them and us thinking together in a group. We should not assume a problem for someone else, but act jointly with them toward the solution of a problem which is as much ours as theirs. Stimulating courage, self-respect, and a feeling of identification with the larger community is as important as meeting physical needs. Some of the most useless individuals in the world are the tired pacifists who say "I think

79

I have done my share of work on that problem," or "I did so much for these people, and they did not appreciate it." These attitudes grow from standing aloof from our fellow men. Once we have determined to live as citizens in the kingdom of heaven upon earth, we are no longer able to make the choice to do or not to do. When we have really achieved that singleness of purpose and become lost in the process of creative social evolution, then many of the matters of petty detail treated in these pages will have become irrelevant.

For Further Reading:
"The Peace Team," Douglas Steere, Fellowship Reconciliation, 1939, 5 cents.
"Training for Peace," Richard B. Gregg, Lippincott, 1937, 25 cents.
A. J. Muste, "Non-Violence in an Aggressive World," Harpers, 1940, $2.00.
Joanna C. Colcord, "Your Community," Russell Sage Foundation, 1939, 85 cents.
"Discipline for Non-Violence," Richard B. Gregg, Pendle Hill Pamphlet, 1941, 15 cents.
Richard B. Gregg, "The Power of Non-Violence," Lippincott, 1934, $2.50.
Gerald Heard, "Pain, Sex, and Time," Harpers, 1939, $3.00.
Aldous Huxley, "Ends and Means," Harpers, 1937, $3.50.
Rufus Jones, "The Faith and Practice of the Quakers," Methuen, London, 1930, $1.65.
Muriel Lester, "It Occurred to Me," Harpers, 1937, $2.00.
"Total War, Total Pacifism," A. J. Muste, Fellowship of Reconciliation, 1940, 5 cents.
"Reconstructing Our World," Philadelphia Yearly Meeting of Friends, 1940, 10 cents.
"Discipline for World Builders," Dan West, Brethren Service Committee, Elgin, Ill., 1940, 5 cents.
"Functional Poverty," Mildred Young, Pendle Hill Pamphlet, 1939, 15 cents.

For Individual and Group Worship:
Howard Brinton, "Creative Worship," Swarthmore Press, London, 1931, (paper) 50 cents, (cloth) 75 cents. (Sold by Friends Book Store, Philadelphia.)
Khalil Gibran, "The Prophet," Knopf, 1923 (Price depends upon edition).
Gerald Heard, "The Creed of Christ," Harpers, 1940, $2.00.
L. Violet Hodgkin, "Silent Worship; the Way of Wonder," Swarthmore Press, London, 1919, (paper) 50 cents, (cloth) 75 cents. (Sold by Friends Book Store, Philadelphia.)
"The Blessed Community," by Thomas Kelly, Friends Book Committee, 1939, 5 cents.
"Holy Obedience," by Thomas Kelly, Friends Book Committee, 1939, 10 cents.
"The Practice of the Presence of God," Brother Lawrence, Judson Press, Philadelphia, 15 cents.
"Why Worship?" Muriel Lester, Cokesbury Press, 1937, 25 cents.
Kirby Page, "Living Prayerfully," Farrar and Rinehart, 1941, $2.00.
Kirby Page, "Religious Resources for Personal Living and Social Action," Farrar and Rinehart, 1939, $1.50.
Walter Rauschenbusch, "Prayers for the Social Awakening," Pilgrim Press, 1910, 50 cents.
E. Merrill Root, "The Way of All Spirit," Packard, 1940, $1.75.
"Community and Worship," Douglas Steere, Pendle Hill Pamphlet, 1940, 10 cents.

Books and pamphlets mentioned in this pamphlet can be ordered through the Peace Section of the American Friends Service Committee, 20 South 12th Street, Philadelphia, Pa.; the General Boards of the Church of the Brethren, 22 State Street, Elgin, Illinois; or the Philadelphia Office of the Fellowship of Reconciliation, 1924 Chestnut Street, Philadelphia, Pa. Please send remittance with your order.

Have You Read?

Pacifist Discipline by Richard B. Gregg, Pendle Hill Pamphlet, Number Eleven, 1941 .... 10 cents

Pacifist Program—In Time of War, Threatened War or Fascism by Richard B. Gregg, Pendle Hill Pamphlet, Number Five, 1939 .... 10 cents

Standards of Living by Mildred H. Young, Pendle Hill Pamphlet, Number Twelve, 1941 .... 10 cents

Rethinking Quaker Principles by Rufus M. Jones, Pendle Hill Pamphlet, Number Eight, 1940 .... 15 cents

Quaker Education in Theory and Practice by Howard H. Brinton, Pendle Hill Pamphlet, Number Nine, 1940, paper .... 50 cents

Community and Worship by Douglas V. Steere, Pendle Hill Pamphlet, Number Ten, 1940 .... 10 cents

Sources and Nature of Quaker Pacifism by Howard H. Brinton, Pendle Hill Historical Study, 1941 .... 15 cents

Order the above from

PENDLE HILL

Wallingford, Pennsylvania

Civilian Public Service—Work of National Importance. Published by the National Service Board for Religious Objectors, March, 1941 .... 5 cents

What About the Conscientious Objector? Revised edition, 1940 .... 15 cents

Help Wanted by Robert Leach and Arle Brooks, Pendle Hill and A. F. S. C., 1940 .... 10 cents
Experience of Quaker C. O.'s in 1917-18.

The London Tribunal Questions the C. O., 1940 .... 5 cents

United States of America vs. Arle Brooks, 1941 .... 5 cents

Order from

THE PEACE SECTION

AMERICAN FRIENDS SERVICE COMMITTEE

20 South 12th Street

Philadelphia, Pennsylvania

AFSC—No. 178—3-41—12M